AN EMPIRE'S N

A foreign correspondent for fo
has filed eyewitness account
moments in recent Russian hi
the protagonists. A fluent Rus speaker, he studied
philosophy, sociology and political science at Cambridge University and has a special interest in the history of the Orthodox Church. He has been a foreign correspondent for *The Times* and is now the Diplomatic Correspondent for the *Financial Times*.

This book is dedicated to the memory of all those who laboured to tell the tragic tale of Russia, and died before they could tell the full story – especially my brother Miles.

Bruce Clark

AN EMPIRE'S NEW CLOTHES

The End of Russia's Liberal Dream

Published by Vintage 1995

2 4 6 8 10 9 7 5 3 1

First published in Great Britain by
Vintage, 1995

Vintage
Random House, 20 Vauxhall Bridge Road,
London SW1V 2SA

Random House Australia (Pty) Limited
20 Alfred Street, Milsons Point, Sydney
New South Wales 2061, Australia

Random House New Zealand Limited
18 Poland Road, Glenfield
Auckland 10, New Zealand

Random House South Africa (Pty) Limited
PO Box 337, Bergvlei, South Africa

Random House UK Limited Reg. No. 954009

A CIP catalogue record for this book
is available from the British Library

ISBN 0 09 958891 9

Papers used by Random House UK Ltd are natural, recyclable products made from wood grown in sustainable forests. The manufacturing processes conform to the environmental regulations of the country of origin

Phototypeset by Intype, London
Printed and bound in Great Britain by
Cox & Wyman, Reading, Berkshire

A VINTAGE ORIGINAL

CONTENTS

INTRODUCTION

FOR THE LAST five years, the world has by turns been exhilarated, bewildered and revolted by events in Russia. The Western imagination has been stretched to the very limit by scenes which are either more inspiring, or else more sordid than anything in the daily experience of more settled and comfortable parts of the world. Russia has been the wild card of the international scene: a mighty superpower; a desperate supplicant; a fawning penitent; a tough and sophisticated player of geopolitical poker. Villains have metamorphosed into heroes, destitutes into multimillionaires, and reformers into arch-conservatives and back again.

The bewilderment of the television viewers and newspaper readers of the world is felt at an individual level by any outsider who sets out to study Russia at closer quarters, as a journalist, scholar or diplomat. Every hypothesis runs into a dozen counter-examples; every apparent glimmer of understanding is obscured by a new mass of impenetrable data. It has been said of Russia that the newly arrived Westerner feels convinced he can write a book; after a month he feels he should probably confine himself to a chapter; and after a year, he wonders whether he can stammer a single sentence. Russia's sheer incomprehensibility is one of the country's many hidden mechanisms of defence.

Having been professionally involved with Russia for the last five years, as a writer and journalist, I hope I am well chastened, as any student of that country needs to be; convinced that the best one can aim for is not the discovery of answers but the ability to ask better questions.

While all enquiry into Russia fails in one sense or another, there is a difference between the failure experienced by close observers and those who stand further back. As a reporter in Moscow, first for the *Sunday Correspondent* and then for *The Times*, I was conscious at times of relaying information to a world which was so confused and fearful of the pace of change in Russia that it resorted to various strategems to deny the almost undeniable.

By autumn 1990, for example, it seemed clear enough to anyone who was following public affairs in Moscow that the Soviet Union was destined either to break up altogether, or at best to stagger on as a much looser association of territories. But readers and editors were so frightened by this prospect that it was very difficult to convince anybody in the West that break-up was inevitable.

Mikhail Gorbachev had tantalised the world with the image of a Soviet Union that was at once benign yet strong enough to act on its benign intentions; a Union capable of working actively with the West to settle regional problems, averting ecological dangers and managing the process of disarmament. Only in retrospect is it clear that Gorbachev's benign proposal was little more than a fleeting stage in Soviet decline. Even as the proposal was made, the Union was rapidly becoming too weak to deliver its side of the bargain.

During the two or three years leading up to the August 1991 coup, the pace of economic and political disintegration in the Soviet Union was much faster than most people in the West realised: so fast that the communist system, and the Soviet Union itself, was little more than a hollowed-out shell when the *coup de grâce* was delivered at the end of 1991.

Once the Soviet flag came down, and the pictures of Moscow as a city of desperate food shortages and rusting, superannuated factories finally penetrated the Western consciousness, there was a corresponding reluctance to part with that perception; with the idea that Russia, having ceased to be a superpower, was now chronically, and perhaps terminally, weak.

For several years after the collapse, Western opinion has clung to the idea that the only possible problem Russia could pose is that of being excessively feeble, and therefore unable to manage the deadly ecological problems posed by its nuclear arsenal and rotting industries. The process by which Russia has reasserted influence in most of the former Soviet republics has gone largely unnoticed.

In the early years of Russia's post-communist existence, Western perceptions were distorted by the peculiar terms in which that country's internal debate was conducted.

On one hand, the Yeltsin administration advocated co-operation with the West, the adoption of Western economic techniques and political models, and disengagement from the republics. On the other hand, the self-described 'patriots' denounced these policies as a betrayal of the hard-won achievements of the Soviet Union and a sell-out to the dastardly enticements of foreigners.

This debate was a confusing one to follow. Despite all the use and misuse of words like patriotism, it was the Yeltsin camp, and economists like Yegor Gaidar, who had discerned most accurately where Russia's short-term interests really lay – at least in the dire circumstances which existed in 1992–3. The so-called patriots were advocating policies such as rearmament, renewed confrontation with the West and instant reassertion of control over the republics, whose application would have been disastrous for Russia's interests at that point in time.

However, this equation started to change as Russia began to feel the benefits of 'treacherous' but highly sophisticated policies pursued by reformist governments in the first two years of Russian independence. From late 1993 onwards, Russia could afford to do many of the things the patriots advocated – stand up to the West, reassert control over the republics, increase the military budget – precisely because the policies of Gaidar and other 'traitors' had worked so well. These paradoxes provide one of the main themes of this book: the way in which pro-Western, enlightened governments paved the way for the pursuit of tough and self-assertive policies.

For most Westerners, the two most striking images presented by Russia over the last five years are the defence of the White House, the Russian Parliament, by Yeltsin and his supporters in August 1991, and the bombardment of the same building in October 1993.

The first of these dramas had all the appearance of a morality play acted out between the forces of good and evil. On the morning of 19 August, Muscovites were jolted out of the torpor of summer by a column of tanks moving down Kutuzovsky Prospekt, the avenue running west out of the city, and the announcement that President Gorbachev – who was holidaying in Crimea at the time – had been suspended from office because of ill health and replaced by his deputy, Gennady Yanayev. An eight-man junta, all of them hardliners within the Gorbachev team, proclaimed themselves in charge of administering the 'state of emergency' which had just come into force.

It became clear that the two most powerful figures in the junta were Vladimir Kryuchkov, the chairman of the KGB, and interior minister Boris Pugo, who also held the rank of general in the KGB. Anatoly Lukyanov, the chairman of the Soviet legislature, abetted the conspirators in the suppression of all the country's elected assemblies by announcing that there would be no session of the USSR Parliament for at least a week – by which time the junta hoped to have consolidated its power.

Later that day, the world was treated to the extraordinary spectacle of Boris Yeltsin, the newly-elected President of the Russian Federation, making a speech from one of the tanks which had converged on the White House. With little evidence to back him up, he asserted that the coup was doomed to failure and that workers all over Russia were heeding his call for protest strikes. A counterpoint to this image was provided by the lamentable press conference conducted by Yanayev, who stammered the junta's incoherent message with the trembling hands of a heavy drinker, and offered no answer at all to a 24-year-old woman journalist who put to him the bluntest of questions: 'Do you realise this is a *coup d'état*?'

The following day, supporters of Yeltsin gathered at the White House in even greater numbers – including many young people, who had previously shown little interest in politics – and in effect challenged the junta to storm the building. Would the conspirators dare to shed that much blood before the television cameras of the world? Flimsy defences, which would not have lasted for more than a few minutes in the event of an all-out attack, were erected under the instructions of Vice-President Aleksandr Rutskoy, a former bomber pilot and hero of the Afghan war. The defenders also included a contingent of Chechens, members of a formidable race of Sunni Muslim warriors from the northern Caucasus mountains.

Cynics suggested afterwards that there was never any real danger of the White House being stormed. That is an unanswerable, hypothetical question: the important point is that the Yeltsin supporters who holed up in the building had every reason to think that they might have to pay with their lives.

The Alpha unit, which comprised the KGB's top commandos, carved itself a place in history by refusing to seize the building. Afterwards, however, it began to look as though the unit's objections had been less moral than procedural: it would not take responsibility for the consequences of a storming unless it received written orders. In any case, it is not romanticising to say that the fate of Russia's democratic experiment hung in the balance on the rainy night of 20/21 August, when three people were killed in skirmishes with tanks on the central ring-road, not far from the White House.

As the third day of the coup dawned, it became clear that the conspirators had lost their nerve. The KGB chairman, Kryuchkov, and the other ringleaders made a desperate attempt to save themselves by flying down to see Gorbachev in his holiday home in Crimea. This move raised the suspicion that Gorbachev's initial attitude to the coup had been something less than total discouragement. In any case, by the time Gorbachev returned from Crimea in the early hours of Thursday, 22 August, it was clear that Yeltsin was the absolute master of the situation. Kryuchkov, Yanayev and the other conspirators were arrested, while Pugo was one of several figures in the hardline leadership who committed suicide. The funeral on 24 August of the coup's three victims turned into a celebration of the birth of a new, non-communist state called the Russian Federation.

Most of this book is concerned with events in Russia in the aftermath of the August 1991 drama. I begin, however, by looking at some of the intellectual developments of the late 1980s in the city of Leningrad, which I believe to have been a kind of laboratory which produced and refined many of the ideas – liberal and highly illiberal – that were put into practice during the early years of Russian independence.

It provides a personal, and somewhat quirky, view of Russia as it declined under one set of slogans and rose again under another.

I would like to thank my family and all those close to me for putting up with my neglectfulness and distraction while this book was being written, especially my parents who found me a home in Donegal and my grandmother who provided me with another home; also my colleagues at the *Financial Times* – especially Quentin Peel, John Lloyd, Leyla Boulton, Chrystia Freeland and John Thornhill – for their goodwill and co-operation. Among colleagues at *The Times*, Mary Dejevsky taught me an enormous amount – perhaps more than any other individual – about Russia, and how to approach that country with a proper spirit of scepticism and rigour; from Anne McElvoy, I gleaned a good deal about the presentation of arcane subjects in ways that are attractive and comprehensible to the general reader.

Warmest thanks for making this project possible are due to my literary agent and friend, Anne McDermid of Curtis Brown, and her successor Peter Robinson; to my editor at Random House, Neil Belton, who has been a tower of strength and encouragement in circumstances where many others might have lost faith; and to Kirsty Dunseath, also of Random House, who has filleted my manuscript, and put up with my vagaries, with intelligence, sympathy and patience.

By way of elaboration on the dedication, I can only say the following. Like many journalists who covered the worsening conflicts in Transcaucasia, I was deeply grieved by the death from a shrapnel wound in June 1992 of a brave, ebullient and talented Azerbaijani television journalist called Chingiz Mustafayev. He was one of many natives of Transcaucasia – others include Eduard Sakhinov in Armenia and Besik Urigashvili, Zurab Kodalashvili and Mikhail Tavkhelidze from Georgia – who shared with me their expertise on the tragedy unfolding in their native lands.

For much of my stay in Russia, I was sustained by the hospitality, generosity and infectious good humour of a person I had known since childhood: an exceptionally gifted war cameraman called Rory Peck. He was killed during the gun-battle outside the Moscow television headquarters on 3 October 1993. His courage and integrity have been an inspiration to me as I completed this book.

I

LENINGRAD: THE LABORATORY OF IDEAS

WHEN THE WAVE of anti-communism rolled eastwards over Europe, the first place in Russia that it seemed to engulf was Leningrad. Like every spring in that sub-Arctic latitude, it was a time of miracles, made all the sweeter by the hard fact that so many people knew instinctively that it would not last for long.

During the twilight years of the Soviet era, the city at the mouth of the Neva river had come to epitomise, like no other place, the ineptitude and complacency of the Marxist regime. In the cradle of the Bolshevik revolution, the communist ideal was dead, and pestilence was spreading from its carcass.

The most palpable sign of this was the decay which had overtaken the city's historic centre, that superb jumble of churches and palaces in which one Western style after another had been fused with a melancholy and an extravagance that is entirely Russian. Every day, the grime that encrusted the walls of the Belosels'ky-Belozersky Palace, on Nevsky Prospekt, seemed to grow thicker, hiding the lovely crimson underneath. The communist local authority which occupied the building, and might once have taken pride in maintaining appearances, was now past caring.

The Smolny convent, a riot of blue and white where Russian Baroque soars to its apogee, still seemed to float in mid-air above the long, ramrod-straight avenue named after General Suvorov. But there was nothing inspiring about the tawdry industrial exhibition which filled its interior, or the cynical stratagems for survival which the red city fathers were cooking up in the neo-classical Smolny Institute next door.

Grigory Romanov, the communist boss who ruled the city from that building in the early eighties, was a particularly boorish figure, even by the standards of Soviet *apparatchiks*. In a famous insult to his royal namesakes, he once borrowed Catherine the Great's dinner service from the Hermitage museum and smashed it at a drunken wedding party. His successor, Yuri Solovyov, was slightly more refined but equally unpopular. The communist bosses' legacy to Leningrad was an enormous, half-built flood barrier across the Gulf of Finland: a last gasp of Soviet industrial gigantism that served some powerful bureaucratic interests, and, by blocking the natural circulation of the sea, threatened to deal the *coup de grâce* to the city's ecosystem, which was battered enough anyway. Already, the tap-water had a tinge of pinkish-brown, and it was so riddled with bacteria that a teaspoonful could put the unwary visitor in bed for a week.

Under different governors, the city would have ended the twentieth century as a superior sort of museum; a centre of high culture and up-market tourism with shades of Amsterdam or Venice. Instead of that, whole streets looked ready to slide, in a cloud of dust, into the weed-infested waterways. This was not the genteel dilapidation of a Venetian palazzo or an Irish country house; it was the sort of decay that evoked bitterness and melancholy.

In the midst of all this despair, and perhaps in some perverse way because of it, glimmers of hope started to appear – tentatively in 1987, unmistakably in 1988, brighter still in 1989. The people who felt this hope first were the city's long-suffering intelligentsia: not only professors with grand titles, but also school-teachers, doctors, museum curators, tour guides – people who had struggled hard to keep the flames of independent thought flickering. Political repression was particularly harsh in communist Leningrad. Stalin had correctly sensed that the city's strong civic pride, and its traditional role as a filter and generator of ideas, would make it a tough source of resistance to his efforts to make everywhere, from Mongolia to the Gulf of Finland, think the same thoughts and worship the same idols.

That was why, in the birthplace of Gogol and Pushkin, not a single publishing house was allowed to function, and a professor could hardly exchange so much as a three-line letter with a foreign colleague without the say-so of a thought policeman from Moscow.

But within a year or two of Mikhail Gorbachev's arrival in the Kremlin in March 1985, extraordinary things started to happen. In a place where a discussion group attended by half a dozen people could lead to sackings and arrests, it became possible to demonstrate in public for the most outrageous of causes: to mourn Stalin's repression, to deplore the state of the city, and even to suggest that communism itself – and not some temporary aberration – might be to blame for both.

Warmer breezes also began blowing through the city's counter-culture – a semi-clandestine world of experimental poets, avant-garde painters and musicians which in the late Soviet years had provided one of the city's few outlets for dissent. The secret police who were once so ubiquitous – infiltrating, harrassing and playing dirty tricks – seemed to melt away. By 1990, desperate economic pressures and the temptation to prostitute oneself, metaphorically or even literally, to the West would cast a fresh shadow over life in the artistic underworld. But there was a year or two when the whole city seemed to belong to the dreamy souls who crooned ballads or produced *outré* paintings in the style of Hockney or Warhol.

At Leningrad University – still a repository of excellence after seventy years of war, privation and repression – the tradition of original thought re-emerged from the darkness. The survival of this heritage had been a close-run thing, and only by dint of an earlier miracle had a handful of teachers and writers emerged from Stalin's prison camps during the Khrushchev era and entrusted the torch of scholarship to a new generation. Now the flames were burning brighter again and the scholars of Leningrad were free once more to discuss out loud their arcane and intricate theories about what Russia was, and where it had come from: were its roots Byzantine or Scandinavian, was it of the West, the East, or a unique synthesis of both? In the Russian context, these are not hypothetical matters. The answers carried profound implications for the country's future, and they were felt to be as sensitive, in their way, as nuclear secrets. Only a massive failure of will and confidence among the followers of the communist cult had created an atmosphere in which fundamental questions about the country's identity could be debated freely.

One beneficiary of this period of freedom was Dmitry Likhachov, the gentle, octagenarian scholar of medieval Russia, who was finally given the public acclaim he merited. The state-sponsored hoodlums who had beaten him up in 1975 when he defended Andrei Sakharov, his fellow academician, now left him alone and as far as he could tell, the authorities had stopped bugging his wonderful old study in the scholarly institute known as Pushkin House. He was free to recount in full the unspeakable horrors of the Solovetsky Islands, the Arctic prison camp where the Bolsheviks had incarcerated him as a young man – including the terrible night of 28 October 1929, when he heard the sound of 300 inmates being shot and realised that he was one of the intended victims. (Ever afterwards, Likhachov used to confide in his whispery voice that he felt he was living not only for himself, but for the man who was mistakenly killed in his place.) As well as reminiscing about his past, the professor was able to expound his own mild sort of Russian patriotism; one which rejoiced in the nation's idiosyncrasy but did not look for enemies.

Likhachov staked out a moderate but original position in the bitterly politicised debate about the origins of Kievan Rus, the kingdom from which the three Slavic republics of the Soviet Union – Russia, Ukraine and Byelorussia – trace their roots. Most Western historians, and one faction of Russian scholars, accepted the evidence that the princes of Kiev were by origin Scandinavians, who had imposed themselves, either by conquest or invitation, on the fragmented eastern Slavic tribes in the ninth century. Without rejecting the Nordic origins of the early Russian princes, Likhachov believed profoundly in the originality, brilliance and distinctly Slavic character of Kievan civilisation, and its importance as a bastion of Eastern Christendom. In the words of one Western admirer, Likhachov showed that 'Russia did not have to be drawn into the European mainstream by Norsemen, because it was already part of that mainstream through its involvement with Orthodox Christianity'. As a chronicler of Kiev's glory, Likhachov could only view the conquest of that city by the Mongol armies in 1240 as an unmitigated tragedy.

Almost the opposite view was taken by another learned, elderly and long-suffering hero of the Leningrad intelligentsia who raised his voice during the late eighties – Lev Gumilyov, the historian son of poets Nikolai Gumilyov and Anna Akhmatova. His own travail and his family background placed him high in the pantheon of intellectual martyrs. It was Lev Gumilyov's arrest in the late thirties that inspired Akhmatova to write her *Requiem* for the suffering of the Soviet people, and when he was taken away again, in 1948, she was driven to the desperate expedient of penning a poem in praise of Stalin.

Gumilyov's biography was characteristic of Soviet intellectuals of his generation – in other words, it was a story of suffering and endurance that is almost beyond the comprehension of a well-fed Westerner. By 1956, when he returned from labour camp in Kazakhstan to his native Leningrad, with a box of dog-eared manuscripts under his arm, he had spent thirteen of the previous twenty years in jail or exile. None the less he had managed to take part in the capture of Berlin as a private soldier, shortly after his release from a term of hard labour in a Siberian nickel mine which, after considerable study of penal systems in world history, he cautiously judged to have been one of the harshest forms of correction ever imposed.

Likhachov thought highly enough of his fellow historian

to write a preface for one of Gumilyov's books but their views were very different. Whilst Likhachov stressed the openness and European character of Russian civilisation, Gumilyov believed strongly that the eastern Slavs and their Mongol 'oppressors' formed a single nation which differed sharply from the Teutonic and Latin cultures of Western Europe. To the claim, sometimes made by Russians to Westerners, that their country had 'saved' Europe and Christendom from the brutality of the Asiatic hordes, Gumilyov retorted that the Mongols' organisational and military genius had saved the eastern Slavs from the greedy sophisticates of the West.

In a project no less ambitious than that of Marx, Hegel or Nietzsche, Gumilyov had conceived a theory of nationhood which described the rise and fall of civilisation as a sort of biological phenomenon. He describes the unit of human development as the *ethnos*, or nation. Two or more such nations might occasionally fuse to form a 'super-ethnos'; one such super-ethnos was formed by the eastern Slavs, Mongols and Tatars, another by the Latins and Teutons. The great Russian super-ethnos was still relatively young – only about 500 years old – compared with the West European one, which was nearing the end of its 1,500-year span. Gumilyov used the word *passionarnost* to describe the collective drive or passion which fuels the development of nations, and one of his weirdest ideas was the suggestion that the source of this energy was somewhere in outer space.

While the ethnos in Gumilyov's world-view was not defined in narrowly racial terms, his teaching did have a disturbing side. Having stressed the links between an ethnos and its ancestral lands, he introduced the concept of the 'parasite ethnos' which had lost its own territory and preyed on the energy of other nations – for which read the Jews; and also the 'parasite state' which fed off the resources and cultural heritage of others – for which read the United States.

Strangely enough, these bizarre and easily abused ideas scarcely diminished the respect in which Gumilyov was held by fellow members of the Leningrad intelligentsia: what mattered to them was that Gumilyov, an heroic scion of an heroic family, was now free to publish his books, while formerly his ideas could only be aired, with difficulty, in specialist journals. In the final years of the Brezhnev era, party officials had tried to sponsor 'discussion groups' at the university, at which Gumilyov's ideas could be denounced for failing to taking proper account of the class struggle. However, other historians, including those who profoundly disagreed with the theory of the super-ethnos, resisted this pressure on the grounds that Gumilyov was first and foremost a colleague and fellow victim of ideological repression.

In stressing the difference between Russia and Western Europe, Gumilyov seemed, in the late 1980s, to be swimming against the intellectual tide. Just as the regime was losing its ability to keep the academic world in thrall, it also seemed to be losing its will to isolate Russian citizens from Western influences. This sense was reinforced when trips abroad – so long confined to the state's most obedient servants – became possible for almost anyone.

Changing times were written on the furious expressions of the clerks at Ovir, the state emigration service, as they handed over newly printed passports, documents which for so long had been tokens of their own power and the helplessness of ordinary citizens. By opening the border, the regime seemed inadvertently to have hastened its own demise. It was now possible for hundreds of thousands of people to see for themselves the neon-lit prosperity of Finland, only a few hours' drive away, and compare it bitterly with their own deepening poverty. By no means everything about the sated, bourgeois existence of Scandinavia or West Germany appealed to every Russian visitor; Westerners made a great mistake in vainly assuming that their own societies represented everything to which Russians would now aspire. But it only took one glimpse of the Western world to destroy for ever any lingering faith in the communists' claim to have discovered a unique formula for universal welfare; if anyone had found that formula, it was the capitalist world they had been taught to despise.

The spirit of the times was evoked by a bitter-sweet joke, often heard in Leningrad around 1989, 'Russia should declare war on Finland, and then surrender immediately. With a bit of luck, we should be annexed.' A few years later, as Russia regained its self-esteem, that sort of witticism would go right out of fashion.

A tendency to idealise certain aspects of the West was a touchstone for the broad political movement whose first incarnation was Memorial, a group founded by Andrei Sakharov to expose and draw attention to the crimes of Stalin, and for most but not all of the dozen or so political parties-in-embryo which later emerged from the loins of the human rights movement. Many of the new 'Westernisers' would have been hard-pressed to say which aspect of life on the other side of the looking-glass they admired most: prosperity, rational and humane administration, economic freedom or freedom of speech. Since the West appeared to have every one of these benefits in far greater measure than the Soviet Union, it was tempting to assume some strict connection between them; good countries had all of them, bad countries none of them. Moreover, such diverse thinkers as Vladimir Lenin and Milton Friedman had argued convincingly that liberal, multi-party democracy and capitalism went hand in hand.

In practice, of course, the connection between economic success and freedom was by no means as rigid as the Westernisers assumed; plenty of countries had one without the other, and there was no reason to expect that Russia would acquire both simultaneously. Yet this tendency to confuse and idealise aspects of life in the capitalist world was an understandable one, and it was particularly strong among the eager pro-democracy campaigners of Russia's second city, who liked to think that by virtue of their proximity to the Baltic states, Poland and points west, they were running far ahead of Moscow in the race to bury the old creed.

Russians have always reconciled themselves to the harshness of their present surroundings with vivid images of paradise. For many disillusioned Leninists, the dashed hope of a

Marxist nirvana was channelled into a simple, awe-struck reverence for the West and an expectation that the blessings of a Western existence could, and shortly would, be transferred to Russia. This helps to explain the recurring paradox of Russia's Westernisers, both this century and last: they bring to their struggle a purist idealism, an uncompromising passion, a spirit of self-sacrifice, and sometimes an otherworldly mysticism which is far more Russian than Western.

Without those qualities – qualities forced into existence by the authoritarian regime – no Russian protestor would ever have found the strength to speak out, but the dissident's embrace of moral absolutes is a world away from the rational, measured calculation and compromise which is the stuff of real life in the West. In the words of Nikolai Berdyaev, one of this century's greatest philosophers on the nature of Russia, 'Pro-Westernism is more of an Oriental phenomenon than an Occidental one.'

In the Leningrad branch of the Democratic Union (DU), a movement of intellectuals which called itself the Soviet Union's first anti-communist party, there was a moral absolutism which vividly recalled the radicals and revolutionaries of a century earlier. At meetings in upper storeys of gimcrack tower blocks, the activists insisted that there would be no compromise with the regime, no watering down of the demand for immediate political and economic freedom.

In May 1989, a few dozen members of that tiny movement brought about the city's first political miracle. Mikhail Gorbachev, in a bold move to turn popular discontentment into an instrument of his own power, had decreed the holding of semi-democratic elections to a new national legislature. Yuri Solovyov, the Communist Party boss of Leningrad, decided he would take no chances and fixed things so that he was the only candidate in his constituency. But he still failed: egged on by the DU and other anti-communist campaigners, a clear majority of voters went to the polling station and crossed out their ruler's name, rendering the election invalid. It looked as though the old regime was beyond saving.

The indefatigable pamphlet-writers, envelope-lickers and election campaigners of the pro-democracy movement sincerely believed that they were the driving force in the movement to abolish communism. But right from the start, the devotees of liberal democracy were only one part of the anti-communist movement. There were factory bosses who had grown tired of taking daily instructions from Party *apparatchiks*, and sensed that they could retain and even improve their own status under another system; there were also the brighter members of the KGB, an institution which overlapped heavily with the Party but was always distinct.

The would-be 'slayers' of communism were also a diverse bunch ideologically: while united about the sort of regime they did not want, their ideas about what to put in its place ranged from social democracy to monarchism. As long as the existing system remained in place, nobody examined the ideological credentials of its enemies too closely. The anti-communist camp welcomed all comers, and most people still saw public life in Manichaean terms: the communists versus almost everybody else.

The most dashing figure in the camp of 'everybody else' appeared to be a handsome, thirty-year-old television reporter called Aleksandr Nevzorov, who had made himself the most popular personality in Leningrad, and a nationwide celebrity, with an extraordinary daily news show called *600 Seconds*. For viewers reared on dull propaganda bulletins and sternly patriotic films, Nevzorov was quite unlike anything they had ever seen. He was glamorous, street-smart, and iconoclastic: a brave and sharp-tongued warrior who apparently sided with the ordinary man against the smug and powerful. Apart from knocking the foibles of the mighty and exposing their corruption, his nightly news show specialised in crime reporting, including snatched interviews with handcuffed killers and grisly footage of their victims. People found this disturbing but not inaccurate; instead of the usual platitudes and lies, he was showing them life in the raw. His police sources were very good indeed. Foreign journalists were fascinated by him. He flattered their own self-image by appearing to prove that investigative reporting in the Western tradition was transferable to the stony soil of the Soviet Union. If that were true, then there was nothing in the world that a good, tough newshound could not do: even the masters of a tottering superpower could be brought down.

Like so many first impressions in Russia, the perception of Nevzorov as an anti-establishment gadfly later proved to be about as wrong as it was possible to be. Back in spring 1989, however, it seemed to most people in his city that he was on the side of the angels. He was, after all, one of the twenty-nine would-be candidates whom the communist boss Solovyov had prevented from standing in his constituency. A year later, it was Nevzorov who finally put an end to Solovyov's political career by revealing that he had used party connections to buy himself a cheap Mercedes.

People were correct enough in thinking Nevzorov was no communist. He once described his programme as a kind of running war against the Bolsheviks, but that did not mean that he was liberal or pro-Western. Nor was his professional persona a clone of anything Western. He was a peculiar, arresting figure of very Russian pedigree, a master manipulator of high technology who was haunted, no less than the university professors, by his country's past. He was a former choirboy who had lost his religious faith, an aficionado of historical costumes and butch leather jackets. Old friends said he was intrigued by three characters in the Russian pantheon, all somehow evocative of tarnished sanctity: False Dmitry, a pretender to the throne in the seventeenth-century; Nikolai Stavrogin, the character from Dostoevsky who tells his confessor that he has committed rape; and Alexis, the beautiful, haemophiliac Tsarevich. But these darker recesses of the Nevzorov psyche took some time to emerge. In spring 1990, when Leningrad's second political miracle occurred, he was still viewed as a kind of folk hero, a valiant warrior in the anti-communist army. He called himself a monarchist, not a democrat, but for many people this was just an amusing variation on the anti-communist theme.

This new 'miracle' was the first ever multi-party election in the Russian Federation, a political entity of which hardly anyone in the world had heard, even though it occupied two-thirds of the territory of the Soviet Union. This was the election which restored Boris Yeltsin, an outcast from the Communist Party Politburo, to high office, and set in motion the transformation of Russia from sleeping partner in the Soviet Union to full-blooded state.

In Russia's second city, the results were sensational. After another desperate burst of hectic, amateur electioneering, a pro-democracy coalition swept the ruling party out of the city council. It claimed to have won 355 of the 400 seats. Instead of dull communists in dark, ill-fitting suits, an unlikely collection of dishevelled, excitable radicals and reformers shambled through the hallowed doors of the municipal debating chamber at the Marinsky Palace, where Aleksandr Kerensky had overseen Russia's last, short-lived experiment in liberal government.

They were idealistic, noisy and verbose. At times, it seemed to them that almost anything they did could only be an improvement on the city's previous masters. In darker moments, however, the shrewder among them wondered if they had walked into a trap. The real levers of power – power over buildings, shops, railway cars, factories and policemen – were still vested in the municipal executive, a bastion of the old guard which had every interest in letting the democrats take the blame for problems which in the short term could only get worse.

The councillors made some magnificent gestures. They held a minute's silence for the victims of communism. They unfurled the red, white and blue flag of pre-revolutionary Russia, eschewing the Soviet hammer and sickle. They talked eagerly of restoring the city to its historic name of St Petersburg. One of the most popular of the reforming councillors was Alexei Kovalyov, a former student activist and archaeologist who found himself in charge of a committee for the preservation of monuments. In a statement that was typical of the glib, breezy spirit of the time, he declared that the name of Leningrad should be retained as long as the city continued declining: once its revival began, then everybody would agree on reverting to St Petersburg.

Kovalyov realised better than most of his fellow councillors, however, that making emotional gestures was one thing, administering a city on the brink of collapse was another. 'Our greatest failing is that we can't organise anything', he admitted bluntly. He soon realised that it was far beyond the council's own means to save the ruined palaces; they would have to be transferred to private hands, and that was a bigger question than his committee could tackle.

The councillors desperately needed a leader, and after two months' squabbling they found one in a law professor named Anatoly Sobchak, whose credentials as a standard-bearer of reform seemed impeccable.

He was an adopted member of the Leningrad intelligentsia, a poor railwayman's son from Siberia who had learned refinement from his Czech grandmother. He had a fine legal brain and a well-honed talent for marshalling arguments and exposing hypocrisy. To those citizens who had spent a lifetime cringing over the crude provincial accents and grammatical slips of their rulers, Sobchak's rounded sentences were a joy to the ears. He had risen to prominence during that brief period in 1989 when high performance in televised debate seemed to take over from backroom skulduggery as the key to power. He cut through the blustering of Yegor Ligachev, the old war-horse of the Politburo, and exposed the old guard's responsibility for a massacre of Georgian demonstrators in April 1989. Once, he had reduced Nikolai Ryzhkov, the Prime Minister, to tears by questioning him over an arms export scandal. He had, in short, done some good work for Mikhail Gorbachev by cutting the conservatives in the Soviet leadership down to size.

For a month or two, the city councillors were very proud indeed of their chairman. Their approval only increased when he joined Boris Yeltsin and his Moscow counterpart, Gavriil Popov, in walking out of the Communist Party's last lamentable congress in July 1990. The walk-out meant that the three most important assemblies in Russia – the Russian Parliament and the municipal councils of Moscow and Leningrad – had non-communist chairmen, and broadly democratic majorities. In Leningrad, before anywhere else in Russia and perhaps a little prematurely, people drew the breathtaking conclusion: communism was dead, the Soviet era in Russian history had finished and the barbarians were in retreat.

Many residents of Leningrad believed, because of their city's location, that they had absorbed the message of the democratic revolutions in Eastern Europe sooner and more deeply than anyone in Moscow. Warsaw, Prague and Vilnius had shown the way; now Leningrad would follow. They clung to the belief that in their city, no less than in Hungary or Poland, communism had been an alien, Asiatic form of cruelty, whose mere abolition would enable a rich and diverse civil society to blossom quite rapidly. The argument was harder to sustain in the birthplace of Bolshevism than it was in Budapest or Tallinn, where bourgeois institutions had flourished within living memory; but the Leningrad intelligentsia could still maintain that Soviet communism was a Muscovite form of despotism, which had suppressed the humane, outward-looking spirit of north-western Russia.

The ideologue of democratic Leningrad was a small, wiry, garrulous and engaging historian called Professor Gleb Lebedev. He was bursting with enthusiasm and *bonhomie*, a fount of interesting ideas, not always tempered by intellectual discipline. He was one of the first public figures to proclaim the extraordinary news that the Soviet period was over. 'We shared the fate of all capitals of empire, to be sacked by barbarians . . . But the Huns are tired now, and the tragedy is over', he joyfully told a British reporter in April 1990. But what kind of new state would emerge from the ashes of the old? Lebedev had an intriguing idea about the model democratic Leningrad should follow. In his opinion, it was not the Imperial capital that was coming back to life, but the extrovert, mercantile and democratic tradition of the medieval principality of Novgorod.

This was an attractive, ingenious notion. Novgorod is indispensable to anyone anxious to prove that Russia does, after all, have a democratic tradition. It was the oldest Russian city of all, older than Kiev, and was situated approximately 100 miles east of the present site of Leningrad. It controlled the fur trade across a vast stretch of northern Russia and was linked by river to Byzantium, the Baltic and hence to western Europe. By a happy fluke of meteorology (an early spring flood in 1238), it was the only important Russian town to avoid being laid waste by the Mongol-Tatar invaders. In contrast with the other Russian cities, where warrior princes held absolute sway, Novgorod's political organisation was half-way to the modern bourgeois state: real power lay with the merchants, who elected princes with a carefully limited range of responsibilities. Unlike its deadly rival Muscovy, Novgorod aspired to prosperity through trade rather than territorial aggrandisement. It had a unique organ of self-government, a public assembly called a *Veche*, which was reproduced in each of the city's five districts. Throughout the thirteenth and fourteenth centuries, Novgorod was locked in rivalry with Muscovy, a power that was gaining strength by dint of privileged relations with the Tatars. In 1570, Novgorod's inhabitants were massacred or dispersed with indescribable brutality by Ivan the Terrible.

In the twentieth century, Lebedev reasoned, the locus of Russian power had again shifted to the Oriental despots of Moscow, with dreadful consequences for the civilised folk on the banks of the Neva and other parts of north-western Russia. There was some force in this argument: there were remote settlements in the far north which had only twice felt the murderous power of Muscovy – once under Ivan, and then under Stalin. But the next stage in Lebedev's enthusiastic discourse was more far-fetched; just as Novgorod had traded vigorously with the Germans and Scandinavians, Russia's second city would find a new identity as part of a flourishing, prosperous and liberal-minded Baltic community. Yet this was more than just a precocious intellectual conceit; it dovetailed with a very popular idea at the time that Leningrad could divorce its economic fortunes from the rest of the country, and free itself from the dead hand of bureaucrats in Moscow, by establishing itself as a free economic zone which, like the Baltic states, would reorient itself strongly to trade with Scandinavia.

Where Likhachov saw Russia as a sister state of Byzantium, and Gumilyov identified with the Mongols, Lebedev rejoiced in the Nordic origins of Novgorod, and hence of urban Russia generally. On the origins of the word Rus, one of the most emotionally charged issues in Russian scholarship, Lebedev was as unpatriotic as could be. He was perfectly sure it was Scandinavian and reckoned he had traced its origin to a Norse word referring to the troop of warriors who were closest to the Viking chief and sailed alongside him. As late as 1981, colleagues of Lebedev were being sent to labour camps for propounding such un-Russian ideas and if, by the late 1980s, he was simply bursting with excitement over the intellectual freedom that Gorbachev had brought, that was understandable enough.

Although he did not have the towering academic reputation of Likhachov or Gumilyov, Lebedev was a better exponent of the spirit of that particular time: a moment of devil-may-care optimism, impatience with established taboos, and eagerness to sing forth all the truths about the past, both recent and distant, which had so long been distorted by a giant ideological prism.

Lebedev still remembers his bewildered delight when an official of the party's ideological department gave him the green light for a demonstration by Memorial. He knew, of course, that the very same official was not only authorising, but helping to organise demonstrations by extremists of the ultra-right. The old élite was so desperate to stay in power and to fend off the menace of liberalism that it was prepared to use any stratagem, including the cultivation of ideologies from the other end of the political spectrum. But that was no disaster, for if there really was going to be a level ideological playing field, then the advocates of change could surely argue their opponents into the ground. He remembers, like every prominent liberal of that period, the inspiring experience of working with Andrei Sakharov: how from the same platform, he and the courageous physicist had proclaimed the lofty principles of repentance by the oppressor, and forgiveness by the oppressed. The Party must repent, collectively and individually, for the practice of state terror, and purge itself of the worst offenders; only then could the victims be expected to pardon their tormentors.

For archaeologists like Lebedev, the distortion of early Russian history to fit the changing demands of ideology was simply one more application of the totalitarian principle that truth must be subordinated to the demands of political expediency.

These demands had fluctuated wildly during the seventy years of communist rule, but the political climate had always been reflected in changing visions of the past as well as slogans about the future. For the first decade of Bolshevik rule, it was an article of faith that Tsarist Russia had no redeeming features, either in its internal organisation or its external behaviour. In their wilder flights of messianism, the Bolsheviks saw themselves not as the new government of Russia but as a phenomenon beyond time and space, responsible only to the workers of the planet and no one else. It was seen as an accident, and not a particularly happy one, that the world proletarian revolution had begun in Russia – if the location of the revolution in Russia reflected anything, it was the singular cruelty of its rulers, and not the virtues of its oppressed.

There was virtually nothing in the nation's pre-revolutionary achievements in which early Soviet citizens were allowed to take pride. Mikhail Pokrovsky, the doyen of Bolshevik historians, proclaimed that 'we Russians are the greatest robbers imaginable'. After describing the rapacious manner in which medieval Muscovy absorbed the surrounding Finnish tribes, he wrote: 'Great Russia was built on the bones of non-Russians, and the latter could hardly take comfort in the fact that 80 per cent of the blood in the Great Russians is theirs.' The influence of Pokrovsky's pure Marxist school of history surged to a crescendo in the winter of 1930–31, when scores of non-Marxist or semi-Marxist historians were arrested. Pokrovsky died at the height of his glory in 1932, but within two years, the wind was blowing in an entirely different direction.

Under the guidance of Stalin, Peter the Great was transformed from the debauched tyrant depicted by Pokrovsky, to a forceful visionary who waged 'an unflagging battle with Russia's backwardness'. The Crimean War and the campaign against Napoleon were again viewed as valiant feats, and the generals who fought them – especially General Kutuzov, the earthy, elemental figure who beat the French by luring them into the heart of Russia – regained their status as national heroes. Russian imperialism in Asia was justified as a 'lesser evil' than the primitive forms of despotism it was supplanting.

There were limits to how far this revisionism could go without shaking the foundations of communism, and therefore all the nineteenth-century Tsars and all the generals after the Crimea were still viewed as villains. But earlier periods of Russian history were a bountiful source of material for patriotic propaganda, of exactly the sort Stalin needed as he girded the country for war against Nazi Germany.

In the arts, the most spectacular product of this need was the film by the brilliant cinematographer, Sergei Eisenstein, about Aleksandr Nevsky, the Orthodox warrior-saint who defended Novgorod against the Catholic Teutons. In a carefully crafted propaganda message, the Russians were portrayed as simple, plucky, resourceful sons of the soil, ranged against the scheming, over-civilised Germans who were bent on seizing the country's natural wealth. In the opening scenes, Aleksandr parleys amicably with a Mongol envoy and pays him tribute. In the final moments – some of the most remarkable in the history of cinema – the Teutonic knights, weighed down by their sinister iron helmets and clanking armour, sink below the ice of Lake Peipus. The film struck some deep chords in the national psyche: it was a story of the bounty, immensity and cruelty of Russian nature which feeds the nation and also protects it from Westerners who do not understand its power. Eisenstein also foreshadowed the teaching of Gumilyov, by contrasting the close relationship between Russia and her neighbours to the east, with the hostility Russia can expect to encounter from ideologically and culturally alien powers to her west.

Stalin took his nationalist reading of history to its ultimate conclusion when he rehabilitated Ivan the Terrible. He instructed Eisenstein to portray the sixteenth-century tyrant as a 'great and wise ruler' who fought valiantly against domestic dissent and foreign aggression; evils which Ivan had quite correctly viewed as almost inseparable.

Eisenstein eventually fell from grace because he was too talented for his own good. His portrayal of Ivan the Terrible as a haunted, Macbeth-like figure, wading through an ocean of blood, was too close to the bone, so the second of his films about that Tsar was suppressed. But Stalin's admiration for Ivan the Terrible continued to be felt in university life. In the middle of the war, an elderly historian called Robert Wippers, who was Latvian and staunchly anti-communist, was dramatically readmitted to full academic honours because, twenty years earlier, he had found merit in the cruel Tsar. Until 1956, when the effects of the Khrushchev thaw were felt in the history faculty, it was compulsory to believe that Ivan the Terrible had been a great builder of the Muscovite state.

Few Westerners remember, if they ever knew, the extent to which Stalin was a theoretician as well as a practitioner of despotism. In between his own sweeping purges of Leningrad's political and cultural world, Stalin had found time to celebrate the achievements of a previous lord of the Kremlin who had also built up a secretive private army, and used it to ravage the cities of north-western Russia.

When, in spring 1990, the pro-Western democrats swept Stalin's party out of the Leningrad city hall, it was tempting fate to proclaim that the spirit of Novgorod was finally getting its revenge over the tyrants from the east. But

Professor Lebedev and his friends could not help saying it, and it is hard to blame them.

2

St Petersburg And The Uses Of History

WITHIN A FEW weeks of Sobchak's election as chairman of Leningrad's unruly council, the study of history seemed once again to be passing out of the academic world and into the realm of high politics. In a project that thrilled some townspeople and filled others with dismay, the new city fathers began proclaiming – as much through symbols and ceremonies as through words – their message that the Soviet parenthesis in the nation's life was over and Russian history could now progress to new glory.

Arguably, however, the official rediscovery of the Russian past was as much a denial of history as an embrace of it. By resurrecting one or other version of the pre-revolutionary heritage, it was almost possible to pretend that the Soviet period had never happened, and thus avoid the agonising task of assessing what went so tragically wrong, and who was responsible. Behind the smoke-screen of Imperial nostalgia, all manner of things could carry on in a very Soviet way.

Within days of Sobchak's election as city council chairman, Aleksandr Nevsky was drawn into modern politics for the second time in the twentieth century, to the bewilderment of those few citizens who were old enough to remember both exercises. In 1940, Stalin's regime commemorated the 700th anniversary of Aleksandr's defeat of the Swedes. Half a century later, Sobchak and his reformers brought their own style and mood to the 750th anniversary. With the nimble-footed Professor Lebedev acting as choreographer, the municipality treated its citizens to several days of pomp and ceremony. On 14 July, the newly elected chairman of the Russian Parliament, Boris Yeltsin, joined the regional commanders of the Soviet army for a solemn commemoration at the site of the battlefield, where the Izhora River flows into the Neva. The next day, it was Sobchak's turn to be master of ceremonies, along with Alexy II, the long-standing Bishop of Leningrad who had just been elevated a few days earlier to the Patriarchate of Moscow. By helping to organise the strange, ambiguous ceremonies which were held in 1988 to mark the 1000th anniversary of the conversion to christianity of Rus, the patriarch had already provided both Mikhail Gorbachev and Boris Yeltsin with invaluable help in endowing Russia with a new set of symbols and a new way of looking at itself. Now he obliged again by officiating at a service under the soaring dome of the Lavra Trinity Cathedral.

While the fortunes of the Church had ebbed and flowed under the Soviet regime – from virtual annihilation to carefully controlled revival – it was the first public occasion since the proclamation of the atheist state when senior representatives of political, military and ecclesiastical authority had stood side by side at a religious ceremony. It was a happy, colourful, summer's day pageant: along with the grandees, there were history buffs, veterans (including some aged holders of Stalin's Order of Aleksandr Nevsky), soldiers, and also sailors from the Kronstadt naval base, which to Professor Lebedev's gushing delight was busily readopting the blue-and-white cross of St Andrew and other Tsarist regalia.

There were also thousands of ordinary townspeople, the same people who had gone wild with delirium in 1961 when Yuri Gagarin had flown into the heavens and discovered – or so the radio announced – that there was no God. This time, the crowd was waving the blue, red and white tricolour of pre-revolutionary Russia. Only a few years earlier, the display of this banner would have incurred a spell in labour camp; now it had been adopted by the Russian democratic movement as part of their ingenious effort to fuse the symbols of old nationalism with modern Westernising reform.

Not all traditionally-minded Russian patriots fell for this trick; because the red, white and blue banner had been appropriated by the reformers, they revived the black, white and gold standard of the Tsarist army as the symbol of die-hard nationalism. On that summer's day celebration, just a few people, at the back of the crowd, were holding up the hardliners' standard. For that fleeting moment, at least, the liberals seemed to hold the Russian past, as well as the Russian future, in their hands.

Where Stalin's Aleksandr Nevsky was a symbol of uncompromising struggle against the Western invader, the Leningrad reformers reinvented him, even more fantastically, as a symbol of woolly, benign internationalism.

Part of the democrats' project was to establish a modern and sanitised version of the nation's history, one that was long on colourful pageant and short on blood and gore, just as England, for example, has turned the 'gunpowder, treason and plot' of Guy Fawkes into an innocent children's festival. In contrast to the bellicose message of Eisenstein, Lebedev's good-natured pronouncements on the subject of Aleksandr Nevsky sounded like an enlightened teacher of religious education struggling to give his pupils an anodyne, reassuring exegesis of some of the gorier moments in the Church calendar. The saint, he declared, should not be seen as a symbol of violence, but rather of the 'concentration of spiritual forces that were needed in the thirteenth century to preserve national unity'.

In a gallant effort to be relevant, the professor suggested that the holy warrior had something in common with Vladimir Visotsky, the gravel-voiced ballad singer of the late Soviet Union, whose 'pain and suffering for Russian land had led him to an early grave'. This was rather like comparing Richard the Lion-Heart with Jim Morrison, and was about as illuminating. The professor was adamant that the saint's anniversary, which was also a municipal holiday, was not an occasion to indulge in xenophobia. 'This is a Russian city which was built by Italians, Dutchmen, Swedes and Frenchmen. We have the biggest mosque in Eastern Europe, a world-famous synagogue, and churches of all Christian denominations along Nevsky Prospekt', he insisted. As part of the celebrations, a Lutheran pastor had come from Latvia, and a Buddhist cleric from near the Soviet-Mongolian border. What could be more ecumenical than that?

It was a worthy effort, but not quite so gripping as Stalin's portrayal of the medieval saint as an uncompromising opponent of all things Western. As Lebedev admitted afterwards with his usual disarming frankness, 'we had no Eisenstein'.

There was, of course, one person in the city who did have a remarkable talent for image-making and the conquest of hearts and minds through skilful use of historical references, and that was the TV star Nevzorov. But he had no patience with Lebedev's anodyne internationalism, or with the democratic majority on the city council, who quickly replaced the communists as the main target of abuse from his nightly news show. Nevzorov's true colours finally emerged in January 1991, when Soviet troops began their crackdown on the Baltic states by seizing the television tower in Vilnius, killing fourteen people and injuring hundreds of others. In a film entitled *Nashi*, or 'our boys', he heaped praise on the motherland's defenders, and questioned whether a single Lithuanian provocateur had really died. With Wagner playing in the background, viewers saw the familiar, stubbly figure of Nevzorov driving round the infamous tower with a rifle slung over his shoulder, boldly defying the nationalist 'fanatics' to do their worst.

It was a transformation which ought to have cured anyone of the illusion that the Russian political world could be divided simply into communists and anti-communists. Nevzorov had played his part in bringing down the communists (or at least the worst of them), but he regarded them as a lesser evil than the woolly-minded pro-Westerners who were in the process of dismantling the empire. It was reasonable to assume that many of his friends in the police, army and KGB (connections which he no longer bothered to hide), felt roughly the same way. They certainly did not mourn the communists, but viewed the democrats, at best, as useful tools in the business of replacing one model of authoritarianism, which had plainly failed, with a more effective one.

The Soviet Parliament, urged on by its chairman Anatoly Lukyanov, ordered national television to show Nevzorov's propaganda film not once but three times. Where Gorbachev, his old friend and contemporary at law school, dithered and changed tack, Lukyanov was coldly determined to keep the Soviet empire intact, at almost any cost, and he was always on the look-out for young, intelligent hardliners – an unusual commodity in those days – who might help the cause. Lukyanov greatly admired Nevzorov and they had something else in common – both happened to be passionate devotees of Gumilyov and his theory of Greater Russia as a Eurasian super-ethnos. Nevzorov used his television show to publicise Gumilyov, and he once managed to coax out of the old sage a frank admission that in the Baltic states, his sympathies lay with the Soviet army. Colleagues of Gumilyov concluded sadly that he was being used.

In November 1991, Sobchak treated Leningrad to another history lesson – an even more spectacular effort to wipe the slate of history clean and restore continuity with an idealised version of the Russian past. This time the protagonist was not a medieval saint but a living person, a shy, distinguished and craggy septuagenarian who spent most of his time in Paris, Madrid and a Breton fishing village. His Royal Highness the Grand Duke Vladimir Kirillovich, head of the house of Romanov and principal claimant to the throne of all the Russias, was invited to the city of his ancestors.

By this time, a great deal had happened which, on the face of things, underpinned the claim that the final curtain had been rung down on the Soviet era. On 12 June, the townspeople had voted, by a small majority, to revert to the historic name of St Petersburg.

The ballot was organised as a test of public opinion and carried no legal force. However, the rejection of Lenin's name in the birthplace of the revolution was an awesome vindication of the sonorous words which had been pronounced a few months earlier by Aleksandr Solzhenitsyn: 'the clock of communism has struck its last hour.' The result flew in the face of the opinion polls, which showed a slight majority in favour of retaining the name of Leningrad, but St Petersburg was the favourite among those who were politically conscious enough to vote. Supporters of the old name were thrilled, and slightly bemused, by their victory. On the same day, the triumvirate seen as the fathers of Russian reform – Sobchak, Gavriil Popov and Boris Yeltsin – secured election to three powerful new posts which they had designed themselves: as executive mayor of Leningrad and Moscow respectively, and executive President of Russia. Working closely together, the trio and their liberal advisers had concluded that chairmanship of legislatures and city councils – the soviets which gave the country its name – was not the key to real authority. What they needed was control of the levers of executive government.

In the case of the Russian Federation, this authority hardly existed as yet, and Yeltsin would have to build it from scratch. On the other hand, the machinery of municipal government in the two big cities was already formidable and had a breadth of responsibility for the housing, livelihood and security of every resident which was hard for a Westerner to imagine. As long as communism persisted, the city hall was one of those agencies which could make or break the lives of millions of people. In the event of privatisation, the municipality would be responsible for the fate of tens of billions of dollars' worth of property.

By the time he was elevated to the post of *maire* – the French word was borrowed to suggest firm, pragmatic administration – Sobchak was already unpopular with the liberal councillors who had propelled him into office. They accused him of being a crypto-conservative whose chosen assistants included a disproportionate number of arms industry bosses and intelligence officers. He retorted that at least his new associates had a modicum of administrative competence, while the councillors could hardly have organised a street bazaar, much less a whole city. Both sides had a point. But in August, Sobchak and the radical councillors appeared to be on the same side of the fence when the forces of authoritarian conservatism made their last, desperate attempt to hold the Soviet Union together.

The world was transfixed by the awesome drama that was unfolding in Moscow, as Boris Yeltsin and thousands of his supporters holed up in the White House, and defied the junta which proclaimed to the world that they had removed Mikhail Gorbachev from office. The public theatre in Russia's second city was no less impressive. Sobchak was in Moscow, at Boris Yeltsin's *dacha*, when the conspirators struck on the morning of 19 August.

After watching Yeltsin don his flak jacket and head for the White House, the mayor flew home, just in time to avoid a blood-bath by dissuading the local military commanders from bringing troops into the city centre. The following day, Sobchak led the workers of the city's best-known factory, the Kirov works, into the city centre, and addressed a vast public meeting in support of the city's legally elected institutions. Tens of thousands of citizens, sworn to defend democracy, poured into Palace Square and waved their red, white and blue flags in the soft northern sunshine. When the coup collapsed, and the Communist Party was suspended, its headquarters in the Smolny Institute was taken over by Sobchak's municipal authority. Despite the *apparatchiks*' frantic efforts to remove or destroy their files, the building turned out to be full of ultra-rightist propaganda sheets, thus confirming the suspicions of those who said the communists would try anything to remain in power.

There was an idyllic feel about the city during the unusually warm September that followed. A US news magazine devoted a gushing cover story to Mayor Sobchak and the revival of Russia's 'window on the West' as a centre of culture and enterprise. On 1 October, thanks to the downfall of communism, the city formally reverted to its historic name.

It was the change of appellation that gave Sobchak the

opportunity to bring the Grand Duke back. The mayor announced that the city would celebrate the rediscovery of its roots with a musical, theatrical and religious festival which, in a pompous throwback to the chant heard at Tsarist coronations, would carry the Latin name of 'Vivat, Sankt-Peterburg.' The Grand Duke and his wife, Leonida Georgievna, would fly in from Paris as guests of honour.

It is the nature of Russian public events – from the botched execution of the Decembrist rebels in 1826 to the funerals of Brezhnev or Stalin – that bathos, absurdity and searing emotion combine in wholly unexpected ways. The visit of the Grand Duke to the newly renamed city was no exception. Far from inaugurating a new era, the Grand Duke found himself walking into a thinly disguised version of the festivities which had been held every 7 November for the past seventy years to mark the overthrow of his ancestors.

Granted, the new festival would not include military parades or senile waves of acknowledgement from communist dignitaries in fur hats. But the celebrations' lighter side – brass bands, balloons, parachute drops, and appearances by famous actors in historic dress – turned out to be an exact reproduction of the Soviet public holiday, intended to keep the masses happy and loyal.

The paradox was not lost on the city's newspapers, which joyfully carried headlines like: 'His Imperial Highness celebrates Revolution Day'. The master of ceremonies for the Sobchak festival was a bureaucrat called Vladimir Voznenko who had spent half a lifetime stage-managing festivities for the communist regime and knew most of the tricks. He, for one, did not see any insuperable paradox in welcoming the Romanovs back and reliving the celebrations that traditionally marked their overthrow: 'Half the population recognises the 1917 revolution, half does not. But we are all inhabitants of one city, so we need our festivals to be as unifying and apolitical as possible.' His only regret was that this year, the city would not have the funds to send up special aircraft that would scatter silver iodide crystals on the clouds.

This was traditionally done to make it rain elsewhere, thus ensuring good weather for the festivities.

Others were not so sanguine. The city council, by now in open opposition to its erstwhile chairman, was quick to spot the absurdity of celebrating the name change on, and in much the same manner as, Revolution Day. It told people to stay at home. Democratic Russia, the liberal movement which had pioneered the idea of changing the name, insisted that only one sort of public event was appropriate for 7 November – an act of mourning for the millions of victims of the Soviet regime. Old-guard communists, meanwhile, protested bitterly at the replacement of their beloved holiday by what looked like public gloating over the revolution's reversal. 'What can defeated Leningraders, opponents of the historic name, feel except another insult? The process of changing their minds about the world is painful as it is, and now they get another slap in the face', was the plaintive cry of one newspaper.

As Vladimir Kirillovich arrived, there seemed to be a real risk of street clashes between rival groups. The authorities' nervousness was apparent from the moment the royal plane touched down on the scarred, icy runway of an airport where every notice still welcomed visitors to the proletarian metropolis of Leningrad. A few dozen of his most devoted supporters – zealous monarchists who wrote him adoring letters, treasured cheap prints of his countenance and thanklessly marked his birthday every 23 September – made their way to the airport, and rushed forward to greet him as he alighted on Russian soil. But they were brutally shoved aside by Sobchak's riot police, and the royal party was hastily bundled into a municipal limousine.

Every moment of the Grand Duke's visit was studded with tragi-comic reminders that no magic wand would dispel the Marxist legacy overnight. The first sights to meet the Grand Duke's eye as he raced northwards up the broad bumpy, thoroughfare that leads to the city centre were as Soviet as could be, beginning with the monument to Leningrad's defenders, marking one of the city's outer bastions during the Nazi siege. This stark, granite obelisk, towering over a stylised group of fighters, must rank, if only because of its subject, as one of the finer examples of Soviet triumphalist art, while the House of Soviets, a little further north, is a specimen of that genre at its most grotesque. Its unfinished façade, which depicts the economic achievements of the 1930s, is a reminder of just how Stalin, no less than Hitler, was determined to reduce the city's historic centre to ruin and irrelevance.

The royal visitor puzzled over the little pieces of red bunting with which some districts of the city were decked. This might have been an ideological gesture by district councils that were still loyal to communism, but it was more likely that the decorations were simply put up out of habit, because things were always done that way on 7 November.

If the Grand Duke's aim was to maintain his quiet dignity and stave off bathos, the building in which he made his first public appearance did not help. It was not one of the city's decaying palaces, or even the Hotel Angleterre, which had just been restored to the point where businessmen could plausibly be charged hundreds of dollars for its tiny rooms. Vladimir Kirillovich met the press, and any admirers who could talk their way past the doormen, in a concrete shell called the Leningrad Hotel, an eyesore alongside the River Neva where working-class Finns went whoring and drinking, and sightseers on low budgets submitted meekly to the barked commands of harridan guides from Intourist.

The assembled reporters and cameramen, glad of a 'soft' story after all the tumult of the previous two months, were left to fidget and gossip for about an hour in a cheaply furnished assembly hall, with the theme from *Doctor Zhivago* playing in the background. The Grand Duke contrived to bring a note of dignity to these banal surroundings. He began proceedings, in his careful, old-fashioned Russian, by asking for a minute's silence in memory of the Imperial family. This was a well-judged gesture. Over the past few years, the exhumation of the Imperial family's remains and a spate of books and films about the Romanovs had stirred something deep in the nation's collective conscience. Even when communism was at its zenith, the sordid end of Russia's anointed sovereign had never entirely ceased to trouble the nation. Recently publicised documents seemed to confirm that the royal family was killed on the orders of Lenin himself, and not, as the communist version of events had asserted, under a purely local initiative by the Bolsheviks of Yekaterinburg. This strengthened the feeling among traditionalist Russians that the communist era would only be finally closed when the Imperial family received a proper Christian burial, and when their chief executioner was removed from the mausoleum where he lay embalmed.

Having won over his audience, the Grand Duke went on, in a short prepared statement and through careful responses to the questions asked, to lay out his ideas about Russia, its place in the world and his possible restoration.

Whether Sobchak anticipated this or not, the remarks of his royal visitor provided yet another illustration of a point which in those days was still obscure: being anti-communist and anti-Soviet was not the same as being pro-Western, in either ideology, culture or geopolitics.

Despite his British manners and Parisian residence, the Grand Duke seemed almost obsessed with the dictum of his cousin, Tsar Aleksandr III, that 'Russia has no friends'. He described the humanitarian aid that was beginning to pour into Russia from abroad as no better than a necessary evil, and one that left him very uneasy. 'It is humiliating for Russian people, but at this critical moment there is no other possibility. We must be very careful about using the help given to us by foreign powers, so as to avoid falling into dependence on foreigners.'

On that question, and also on the future of the Soviet Union, the Grand Duke was, like most White Russians, closer in tone to the communists than he was to the 'democrats' who had overthrown the Soviet regime. Urging the ex-Soviet states to stay together in some sort of federation, he described the accelerating process of disintegration as 'something that will bring no happiness to those who are struggling to secede'.

It was a sensitive matter he was touching on, and one whose importance was becoming clear as the real implications of the coup of August 1991 emerged. When the junta collapsed, so did the coercive power of the agencies which held the Soviet Union together: the Communist Party, the army and, at least temporarily, the KGB. All those republics which had not already done so proclaimed full independence, even those like Turkmenistan or Azerbaijan whose rulers had warmly welcomed the hardline putsch.

When the Soviet Parliament, in a state of bewilderment, virtually dissolved itself and granted freedom to the Baltic states, the West immediately established diplomatic relations with those three countries, and with Russia. But that still left eleven more ex-Soviet republics, which spent the autumn of 1991 floating in a legal and diplomatic vacuum. Their leaders, and those of Russia, pointedly referred to the 'former Soviet Union' in all their pronouncements, yet Western governments were reluctant to sign the death certificate of their cold war adversary. The West continued to view Mikhail Gorbachev as head of the Soviet state and only the minor diplomats and visiting rock stars who called on him at the Kremlin realised that he was a president without a country.

Nor could that country be recreated. Ukraine, preparing for a 1 December referendum that would ensure world recognition of its statehood, had firmly ruled out any form of federation that compromised its own independence. As Boris Yeltsin realised more quickly than Mikhail Gorbachev, that meant no post-Soviet federation at all.

For traditionalist Russians, this meant reconciling themselves to the idea that historic cities which they had viewed as bastions of 'their' country – Kiev, Minsk, Riga, Odessa, Sevastopol – were now under the authority of new governments. This was as disturbing to the exiled Whites as it was to most Soviet communists. The Grand Duke was therefore speaking for almost every variety of patriotically-minded *émigré* when he protested.

The White community which the Grand Duke represented saw itself as the guardian of an authentic Russian tradition which had been snuffed out in Bolshevik-controlled territory. With varying success, they struggled to hold on to manners, customs, forms of speech and recipes which had been forgotten in Russia itself, and above all they preserved the religion which they regarded as indissoluble from Russian nationhood. A state in which the Orthodox Church was either ruthlessly suppressed or barely tolerated could hardly be Russian at all, they believed.

It was natural, therefore, for the Grand Duke to lay great stress on religion, affirming his own devotion to the cause of Orthodoxy and his fervent wish for the Church to flourish again on Russian soil. For those who saw the communist period as a deviation from Russian history, and the downfall of Marxism as a return to the track of 'normal' evolution, religion was generally the most important issue. Yet on ecclesiastical issues as well as political ones, the Grand Duke had to tread carefully. He was a communicant of the deeply conservative Synod of the Russian Church-in-Exile, which had canonised Tsar Nicholas II and yearned for the monarchy's restoration. The Synod was sharply at odds with the Patriarchate of Moscow, which had survived the communist era by dint of making huge compromises with the Marxist regime.

By travelling to Russia and attending services conducted by the Patriarch, the Grand Duke was in effect recognising a religious organisation which many White Russians viewed as uncanonical or worse. His mentors in the Synod found themselves quite literally *plus royaliste que le roi*, and the Grand Duke's personal confessor, Bishop Anton of California, accused him of betrayal.

There was something poignant about the sight of the royal visitor, standing bare-headed and rather lonely in the gloomy vastness of St Isaac's Cathedral, as Sobchak and the other dignitaries of the new Russian state looked on. On 7 November itself, the Grand Duke kept out of public view, but other versions of historical nostalgia were much in evidence. A thousand or so die-hard activists of the reform movement marched down Nevsky Prospekt behind a brass band, mourning the '100 million lives' claimed by communism. A similar number of loyal communists, mostly old women with tightly pursed lips, gathered to chant their beloved slogans at the battleship *Aurora*, which as every Soviet schoolboy knew, had given the signal for the Bolsheviks to storm the Winter Palace.

In this city of history buffs and ambiguous symbols, the slogans were characteristically pedantic. The reformist protesters demanded the recall of the Constituent Assembly, old Russia's last freely elected body which was closed by the Bolsheviks in January 1918. The communists wanted to switch the clock back a little earlier, calling for the reconstitution of 1917-style workers' councils to fend off the bourgeois counter-attack. Neither side seemed to have worked out how these extraordinary feats of exhumation or time travel would be achieved.

There was one thing they did agree on. Both sides attacked the new phenomenon of *nomenklatura* capitalism – the process by which members of the communist bureaucracy were converting themselves into successful private businessmen. The reformers objected because these cynical folk did not conform to their vision of scrupulously fair, competitive capitalism, while the communists demurred because their masters were departing from the altruistic ideals to which they supposedly subscribed.

In a sense, however, it was the nomenklatura capitalists who won the day. Sobchak's absurd municipal beanfeast in Palace Square – a mishmash of pompous speeches, poetry readings, aerial stunts and rock music – attracted tens of thousands of people, far more than any of the ideologically inspired demonstrations. Perhaps it was because there were plenty of cheap sandwiches for sale, and as people prepared for a winter of hardship and queuing, they knew, so to speak, what side their bread was buttered on. In any case, the sponsors of this curious event, which celebrated the revolution and counter-revolution simultaneously, were none other than the nomenklatura capitalists: communist functionaries who were demonstrating the principle that power can be wielded in more than one way.

The following April, Vladimir Kirillovich died suddenly in Miami. Friends said he was bitterly disappointed by the negative reaction of the Church-in-Exile to his journey to Russia, and by the failure of his appeals for 'Red' and 'White' churchmen to settle their differences. His family asked for permission to bury him at St Petersburg, and Sobchak readily agreed. With uniformed Cossacks in attendance, Patriarch Alexy conducted a four-hour funeral service in St Isaac's Cathedral, and delivered a eulogy that was fulsome but very careful not to recognise the dead man's claim to the throne. Vladimir Kirillovich was then interred in the Grand Dukes' vault at the fortress of Peter and Paul, a hauntingly beautiful church whose golden spire seems to pierce the sky like a needle. His strong-willed, bustling daughter, the Grand Duchess Maria Vladimirovna, proclaimed herself Empress-in-waiting, and her eleven-year-old son, Georgy, heir apparent. Their visits to Russia became more frequent and she was courted by all the new state's leading politicians, including President Boris Yeltsin and his turbulent deputy, Aleksandr Rutskoy. The most fitting tribute that anyone could pay her father is that he contributed his own share of pain to Russia's agonising search for a future and a past.

By the time of the Grand Duke's death, Sobchak was already a *bête noire* among the city's dwindling band of reformers, while many former communists said they had come to admire him, despite his role in abolishing the name of Leningrad. This reflected the conservative tack the mayor had adopted. He had come to the conclusion that underneath all the froth created by the liberal intelligentsia, there were millions of pensioners and arms factory workers who could not survive, physically or psychologically, the sort of economic shock therapy that was being decreed by the new rulers in Moscow. Sobchak's critics were probably right when they accused him of moving too slowly to dismantle the state planning system, but he had his political reasons for acting as he did.

As the contours of non-communist Russia emerged, it became clear that the change which had occurred was nothing quite so dramatic as the 'retreat of the barbarians' which the noisy city councillors had rushed to celebrate. It was more like a shift in the balance of power between different parts of the ruling élite. Sobchak's rise to power, examined more closely, was a case in point. His election as city council chairman in mid-1990 was made possible when his communist opponent, Admiral Vyacheslav Shcherbakov, withdrew his own bid and agreed to become Sobchak's deputy.

Shcherbakov let it be known that by withdrawing his candidacy, he was defying the instructions both of the Communist Party and the local garrison, but he would not have acted as he did if he had not been confident that some part of the military-industrial establishment would support his decision to shore up the reforming law professor. A submarine commander and expert on naval electronics, Shcherbakov represented a part of the Soviet élite which was badly disillusioned with both doctrinaire Marxism and the self-serving Party machine; he spoke for the high-technology sector of the defence industry.

At the height of the communist system, the Party had established asphyxiating control over industry. Bureaucrats from the Smolny Institute would tell factory directors exactly how many switchboards or gun-sights to produce and where to deliver them, while factories relied on help from the Party to procure raw materials. Industrial bosses, who regarded themselves as more knowledgeable than any Party official, came to resent this system more and more. In their own way, some were as anti-communist as any Westernising history professor or underground artist.

By accepting the communist Shcherbakov as his deputy, Sobchak had acquired a minimum of leverage over the old establishment – without which he could not have exercised any authority at all. However, in doing so, he had also merged with that establishment. This became clearer than ever in June 1991, when Sobchak became executive mayor and kept Shcherbakov as his deputy. The two men found themselves at the apex of a power structure which also included the heads of the city police (including riot police) and Leningrad KGB.

The local police and KGB chiefs were, of course, also subordinate to the Soviet interior ministry and KGB headquarters in Moscow, and there was nothing in the rule-book to say what should happen if they were forced to choose between the mayor's office and their masters in the capital. During the key moments of the August 1991 *putsch*, Sobchak and Shcherbakov were able to persuade the local garrison, police and KGB units to put their municipal loyalties first and avoid bloodshed in the city, but this was only possible because the two men were themselves part of the ruling élite. Shcherbakov could talk to the local army commanders, who had counted on him to support the coup, as one very senior officer to another. Sobchak acted not as spokesman for the city council, but as intermediary between the council and the military commanders. He promised the garrison there would be no disorder or strikes, and at one point threatened to prosecute anyone caught building barricades.

Whatever it was, the process unfolding in Russia was not quite the Manichaean struggle between light and dark – or between one era and another – which was sometimes portrayed.

It was, moreover, nonsensical to pretend that the Soviet era had not happened, or to suggest that its trials, cruelties and achievements were not part of Russian history. But in a curious way, half-pretending that the Soviet era had never happened at all was the best way to ensure that relatively little really changed when the hammer and sickle was replaced by new slogans. A real break with the Soviet past would require a very close and painful examination of that period, an honest attempt to identify the sources of Russian authoritarianism. For every idealist who understood the need for such an exercise, there were five ordinary, compromising citizens who could not bear very much reality and were happy enough to munch cheap sandwiches under any flag. Sobchak was, perhaps, a dishonest historian, and a faint-hearted reformer, but he was a good judge of popular psychology and an inveterate practitioner of expediency.

3
CHANGING DOGMAS

MAYOR SOBCHAK WAS a pragmatist who judged, in the end, that the cause of expediency was best served by caution and conservatism. That is why his early followers, whose guiding light was a purist and uncompromising form of idealism, were so bitterly disappointed.

In other Russian quarters, however, theory and practice came together in a more satisfactory way. The passionate belief of a few key individuals in the newly discovered doctrines of Adam Smith and John Stuart Mill was married to a pragmatic, skilful, even Leninist approach to the translation of these theories into practice, and as any Bolshevik will tell you, extraordinary things can happen when this combination of tactics and ideology is successfully achieved.

In January 1992, as the post-Soviet era began in earnest, many of the country's new theoreticians of democracy and the market emerged not from the margins, but from the heart of the old ideological apparatus. They were not just adherents but priests of the Marxist cult.

Sergei Yushenkov – a big, lolloping figure with a pleasant, moon-faced appearance – led the pro-Yeltsin faction in Parliament. He had devoted almost half his forty years to the thankless task of instructing army officers in Marxist philosophy. His knowledge of the communist writ was famously encyclopaedic; he could reel off chapter and verse, so to speak, of almost any pronouncement by Marx, Lenin or Engels. As his faith collapsed and he realised that the whole communist project was mistaken, he suffered a nervous breakdown. On his recovery, however, he quickly emerged as a forceful and articulate exponent of Western libertarianism, in the tradition of Abraham Lincoln and John Stuart Mill, and also as an artful communist-baiter who had the advantage of knowing the enemy very well. What made Yushenkov unusual was the frankness and vulnerability with which he would talk about his transformation, over grainy coffee and stale sandwiches in the Parliamentary cafeteria. Other pilgrims on the road to Damascus were as cold, dogmatic and single-minded in expounding their new beliefs as they had been in propagating their old ones.

Gennady Burbulis, the shrewd humourless character who laid the foundations of Yeltsin's new Russian administration, had for much of his life been a professor of Marxist philosophy in Sverdlovsk, the industrial city in the Ural mountains where Boris Yeltsin had been Communist Party boss. He had devoted his dissertation to the 'Marxist-Leninist guidance of the world-view of young scientists and technicians' and was deputy head of a social sciences faculty, at a time when only one sort of sociology was tolerated.

When Burbulis began dabbling in reformist politics in 1987, he seemed indistinguishable from the hundreds of thousands of Party officials all over the country who, under instructions from Moscow, were encouraging the formation of clubs and discussion groups which would provide a relatively harmless outlet for dissent, without threatening the communist system.

At some point, however, Burbulis passed over to the other side of the looking-glass, from communism to real anti-communism. Like many others who made that journey, he brought with him an ability to expound and manipulate grand theories: theories about the world, the human race and the destiny of classes and nations, which purport to be scientific but in fact draw heavily on mysticism and intuition.

It is an axiom among Russian intellectuals that their country must always have a mission, a lesson to teach the other nations of the world which cannot be learnt from anyone else. The stewardship of Orthodox Christianity, after the fall of Byzantium to the Turks in 1453, was one such mission; the ideological and political leadership of the communist bloc another. Amidst the dislocation and decay of Russia in 1991, it was hard to see what the country's new mission could be. A nation which had once set itself up as a teacher to the world now appeared to be in desperate, almost pathetic need of instruction from the West about how to husband and manage its resources and avoid total collapse.

Burbulis nevertheless came up with a truly ingenious piece of doctrine. The world, he said, owed a debt of gratitude to Russia because in an act of supreme self-sacrifice, it had injected itself with the bacillus of communism, enabling the rest of humanity to study the effects. By making itself the guinea-pig in a giant experiment, Russia had demonstrated (for the benefit of any other nations that might be tempted to try), which economic and social system to avoid. The rest of the world now had a duty to help Russia back on its feet as it recovered from the effects of this heroic stunt.

No Western philosopher or Jesuit could ever have come up with such a fantastic piece of casuistry. In the case of Burbulis, facility with ideas was combined with great skill in the more down-to-earth business of political manoeuvring – learned, perhaps, from a lifetime's study of the stratagems employed by Lenin.

Although he was a less glamorous figure than the charismatic young Turks who became the champions of reform in Moscow, Burbulis was the man chosen by Yeltsin to mastermind his presidential campaign in June 1991. In the autumn of that year, when the Yeltsin administration took up the reins of real power, Burbulis consolidated his own power in the ill-defined but enormously influential position of secretary of state.

Yeltsin did not always follow the advice he received from his lieutenant, but it was hardly ever wrong. In a back-handed compliment to his political skills, Burbulis became known as the 'Grey Cardinal' or even the 'Killer'. In autumn 1991, Burbulis was one of those who saw how rapidly the interests of Russia were diverging from the other Soviet republics. He concluded that instead of struggling to keep the old federation alive, Russia should concentrate on establishing its own position as the sole or principal heir to the rights and obligations of the Soviet Union: its foreign debts and assets, its seat on the UN Security Council, its stewardship of a vast nuclear arsenal, and its role as co-guarantor of the treaties and institutions that underpinned the international order.

Burbulis was the prime mover in the extraordinary decision to dismantle the Soviet Union that was taken on 8 December 1991, in a hunting lodge in the Belovezhsky Forest, near the Polish-Soviet border. Presidents Boris Yeltsin of Russia, Leonid Kravchuk of Ukraine and Stanislav Shushkevich of Byelorussia resolved that since their republics had been co-founders of the Soviet Union in 1922, they should now take the initiative in terminating the USSR's existence. In its place they agreed to set up a loosely-structured Commonwealth of Independent States which made no claim to be a sovereign government in its own right. To the spluttering protests of Mikhail Gorbachev, who was informed in a telephone call from Shushkevich that 'the state of which you are President has ceased to exist', Burbulis had a characteristically dry retort: the three republics were not so much killing the Soviet Union as making the 'medical diagnosis' that it was already dead.

The Belovezhsky wood is not far from Brest-Litovsk, where in March 1918 another newly established Russian regime, headed by Lenin and Trotsky, had bought itself some breathing space to concentrate on internal issues by surrendering all claims to the western provinces of the empire, including most of Ukraine and Byelorussia. Both the Brest-Litovsk accord, and the meeting in the forest seventy-three years later, would go down in the annals of Russian nationalism as acts of terrible treachery, gratuitous abandonment of territory that was no less Russian than Moscow or Yaroslavl.

However, Burbulis was a practitioner of a more sophisticated school of statecraft, which regarded both charges of betrayal as mistaken, even from a standpoint which viewed the interests of Russia as the only thing in the world that mattered. It might be true that at most times in Russian history, the acquisition and retention of territory has been the state's main method of gaining strength, but as Burbulis correctly sensed, there are also times when the Russian state is best served by a tactical surrender of territory. In any case, this surrender is likely to be a temporary one, because once Russia's internal conflicts have been settled and she has relearned the art of exploiting her own vast resources, the difference in objective strength between Russia and her neighbours will start to have its effect.

For millions of people who had spent a lifetime on the receiving end of Soviet propaganda, which urged them to rejoice in the size, strength and indissolubility of their country, this was not an easy argument to follow. But those who did follow the argument included some of the manufacturers of Soviet propaganda; ideologues like Burbulis who had learned from Marx and Hegel to think in vast, bold generalisations and to look for paradox and apparent contradiction instead of simple truth.

For anyone struggling to comprehend the morass that was Russia in 1991, the analytical tools, or at least the habits of thought, provided by Marxism were almost indispensable. The Soviet wreckage was at once a dreadful testimony to the failure of that doctrine, and a labyrinth that was far easier to negotiate with some help from a Marxist map.

Perhaps the most important thing which Russia's modern theoreticians had absorbed from their nineteenth-century mentors was the idea of dialectical progress: the idea that every phenomenon generates its opposite, or antithesis, until the resulting tension forces into existence a third phenomenon which amounts to a synthesis of the previous two. Soviet students regarded their compulsory instruction in dialectical materialism – *diamat* in campus slang – as pure tedium. Yet almost none of the features of Russia in its transitional phase could be understood without a very clear sense of the way in which one extreme can trigger an equally powerful movement in the opposite direction.

The concentration of power in the hands of the old, inflexible and incompetent was giving way to an even crueller tyranny of the young, clever and imaginative. The jaded inertia and conservatism of one generation was replaced by the boundless, ruthless energy of their children and grandchildren, who believed nothing their parents or teachers had told them and therefore had nothing to unlearn. The hamburger chain McDonald's (not usually associated with the ideas of Hegel or Marx), discovered this extraordinary contrast when it established its first Russian branch in 1990. It found almost any Russian above the age of thirty to be unteachable, while most of its Russian employees below the age of thirty were unstoppable, so long as they could be prevented from pilfering the frying-pans.

The colossal incompetence of the services provided by the Soviet state had created the conditions in which a slick, brassy new private sector could grow at astounding speed. The extreme self-isolation of the communist regime had created a desperate, exaggerated thirst for all things Western – ideas, clothes, products – and was therefore bound, sooner or later, to generate some synthesis of Western techniques and Russian style.

If Burbulis was the cold-fingered obstetrician who brought the new Russian state into the world, its infancy was overseen by a group of formidably talented friends who provided the world with even more spectacular evidence of what can be achieved when deeply held beliefs are combined with an intelligent, even cunning approach to their implementation. The head of this team was Yegor Gaidar, a brilliant, intense workaholic with a pudgy, schoolboy face who was virtually unknown to the world until Burbulis persuaded President Yeltsin to put him in charge of the Russian economy.

By comparison with the blue-blooded Bolshevik ancestry of Gaidar, Burbulis was an obscure provincial hack. Gaidar came from the very heart of the communist establishment. His grandfather, Arkady Gaidar, was a Red Army commander and the founder of Soviet childrens' literature, and his father, Timur, a distinguished admiral and advocate of military reform. During his childhood, these famous forebears were almost a burden to him. Whenever he turned in a less-than-perfect essay, his teacher would remonstrate: 'This cannot be the work of the grandson of Arkady Gaidar.'

Like many of the ministers who began reshaping the Russian economy in 1922, Yegor Gaidar was a pupil of Professor Stanislav Shatalin, a frail, wheezy and enormously respected figure who had diagnosed the ills of the dying Soviet economy but was never allowed to start treating them.

In 1987, Gaidar became economics editor of the theoretical journal *Kommunist*, which was steadily becoming a journal of anti-communism, and in 1990 he was given the same job at *Pravda*, which was still the Communist Party's official daily. It would be an exaggeration to say that either of these jobs required the holder to have any sincere belief in communism. What they did require was an ability to describe the real world, and Russia's place in it, in a realistic way while also paying a minimum of lip-service to the tenets of Marxism.

Gaidar and several members of his reforming team had worked together in highly technical branches of mathematical economics – so abstruse that nobody realised what amazing heresies they were dreaming up – and they had served briefly on a commission for economic reform established by Yuri Andropov. Another source of talent for the new Russian government was a semi-clandestine club of radical economists that was set up in 1984 by Anatoly Chubais, a young lecturer at the Leningrad Institute of Economics and Engineering. Gaidar was in discreet touch with this group, which included Pyotr Aven, the first foreign trade minister of independent Russia, and at least four other figures who would later hold high office.

What all these economists had in common was that at some point in their lives, they had encountered, absorbed and understood the economic theories of Adam Smith about the power of the market's invisible hand to allocate resources rationally and maximise the creation of wealth.

Later of course, they progressed to Smith's modern disciples, such as Milton Friedman and, in order to understand the link between economic and political freedom, Karl Hayek. However, as Gaidar would frankly admit to his foreign colleagues, his first, blazing revelation came from the primary source: the theories conceived in Edinburgh 200 years ago and laid out by Smith in *The Wealth of Nations*. Successful academics like Gaidar, who on the face of things were good communists, enjoyed an access to these forbidden texts which was denied to the ordinary man; it was necessary, after all, to know the enemy. Yet, as every Russian tyrant knows, unpredictable things can happen when highly intelligent people are exposed to powerful ideas.

Gaidar and his colleagues were thrilled by Adam Smith in the same way that Russian thinkers of the mid-nineteenth century were thrilled by the theories which trickled eastwards from France and Germany: the ideas of Comte, Saint-Simon, Hegel and Marx. Just like the nineteenth-century philosophers (one of whom postulated that Russia had a unique aptitude for the understanding of Hegel), the young economists of the 1990s were endowed with that very Russian ability to believe grand and subtle theories: to absorb every nuance of those theories, down to the very roots of their consciousness, and to take those theories to all their logical conclusions, and well beyond.

Any account of post-Soviet Russia which places too much stress on ideas, as opposed to cynical calculation, runs the risk of sounding naïve. It is certainly true that many of the leading figures in Russia's transition were successful in enriching themselves, and incidentally in advancing the cause of reform, for the very reason that they hardly believed in anything at all, except in pursuing power and seizing opportunities.

For example, one of the most prominent figures in the economic revival of 1992 was a man who was remembered by students at Moscow University in the mid-1980s as a particularly zealous officer in Komsomol, the communist youth movement, long after it had ceased to be fashionable. He kept tabs on the opinions and behaviour of his fellow students, and anyone who was heard to criticise him in public found that his academic career took a mysterious downturn. By the late 1980s, this character had secured for himself a prominent place in the pro-democracy movement, and was elected to represent a Moscow constituency on a reformist ticket. He next emerged as one of the prime movers in the commodity exchanges which were picking clean the bones of the planned economy: he was now a wealthy and respected businessman and strident advocate of further economic reform.

Observing a career like that, which was by no means unusual, one is tempted to write off the entire reform movement as a cynical move to translate power and privilege from one medium into another, and that is certainly an important part of the story. But Russia's transition to capitalism could not be accomplished by opportunists alone, any more than the transition to communism could have been. Both projects depended crucially on the willingness of a small group of highly intelligent people to work twenty hours a day because they passionately believed in an idea.

It was, in a perverse sort of way, very exciting to be a rigorous and tough-minded free marketeer in the dying days of the Soviet Union. The insights of Adam Smith helped to pin-point the staggering profligacy of the existing system, and they also gave a glimpse of a burst of energy and wealth-creation which could be triggered if the market were used to allocate resources and labour rationally. It was tempting to believe that if only capitalist techniques for rewarding efficiency, matching supply and demand, and mobilising wealth were systematically applied to the natural resources of Russia for a couple of decades, the country would become several times richer and more powerful than any other on earth. It was true that enormously powerful vested interests militated against the rational use of resources, in favour of their diversion to this or that special interest. But the advanced degree of ruin to which these vested interests had brought the economy was a small window of opportunity in that it had created a state of such despair that almost anything, even reason and logic, might be given a try.

Neither Gaidar nor any of his close associates were active in politics in the late 1980s; they never thought it certain or even probable that they would have the chance to put their ideas into practice. But from spring 1991 onwards, as director of a newly founded Economic Policy Institute, Gaidar raised his profile as an advocate of rapid change. He established contact with Jeffrey Sachs, the high-flying American expert on transforming communist economies, and Professor Richard Layard of the London School of Economics. In May, Gaidar attended a conference in Paris organised by Pyotr Aven, and the idea of hitching themselves to the Yeltsin bandwagon took shape.

In mid-1991, Moscow's best-known advocate of economic reform was still Grigory Yavlinsky, a great bruiser of a man whose rough, chain-smoking manners were in curious contrast to his intellectual reputation, which was first-class. He enjoyed some influence with Mikhail Gorbachev, whom he had twice guided to the brink of economic reform, but no further, because so many other voices kept muttering in the President's ear to stop.

After the August 1991 *putsch*, Yavlinsky and Gaidar found themselves at the head of rival camps, competing for Yeltsin's attention. They agreed on many things; they were, after all, fellow members of a tiny group of people, a few dozen at most, who had a sophisticated grasp of the dimensions of Russia's crisis and the options available to deal with it.

There was one particular point on which they concurred, although it was not something they stressed when they were dealing with their Western admirers. It would never be politically acceptable for Western investors to take control of a significant part of the Russian economy – the masses would endure indescribable hardship, but would not stand for foreign ownership of their oilfields and factories. If the country was to have capitalists, they would have to be

Russian capitalists and since no Russian capitalists existed, they would somehow have to be conjured out of thin air.

All the same, that was tomorrow's problem. There was a more immediate issue on which the opinions of Gaidar and Yavlinsky were diametrically opposed: whether it was worth struggling, in the immediate future, to rescue the Soviet Union from total disintegration.

Yavlinsky was heavily involved in efforts to maintain the Union as an economic space. He argued that it hardly mattered which political arrangement – confederation, commonwealth or whatever – replaced the USSR, as long as the coherence of its densely interlocking economy was maintained. Together with Professor Graham Allison of Harvard University, he had devised a plan under which the West would provide billions of dollars' worth of aid to preserve and reform the Soviet Union. That had happened before the August coup, but he still thought the principle could be revived.

Over vodka at a smoky Moscow dinner-table in mid-September 1991, Yavlinsky was taken to task by Vladimir Bukovsky, the dissident who had just returned to Moscow after many years of exile. 'Speaking as a British tax-payer, I don't see why my money should go towards propping up the Soviet Union,' the argumentative Bukovsky insisted. But Yavlinsky shook his head: 'It will be a disaster if Russia has to go it alone.'

Gaidar, like Burbulis, took a different view. He argued that the smaller republics were a drain on Russia's resources and must not be allowed to stand in the way of reforms that were desperately needed. If the republics were prepared to join a reform programme on terms dictated by Russia, well and good, but that was unlikely to happen, because the republics were at the height of their (pathetically misplaced) confidence in the prospects for real independence. So Russia should simply call the republics' nationalist bluff, and let them go their own way. In any case, not a single minute more should be wasted on a fruitless search for consensus.

From the point of view of Russia's selfish interests, there

was much to be said for Gaidar's position. One of the effects of Soviet political reform, and the conduct of separate parliamentary elections in each republic, had been to exacerbate the differences in political atmosphere across the Union.

In the Baltic states, which were rapidly spinning out of Moscow's orbit, there was an overwhelming consensus on the need to recreate a stable, bourgeois, property-owning society as rapidly as possible. Nothing like this existed in any other part of the former Soviet Union, and the astonishing pace at which Estonia, in particular, returned to the capitalist fold is powerful evidence that values are more important than resources or physical geography as a motor of economic development.

In Ukraine and Byelorussia, almost the opposite situation applied. Compared with the ravaged state of Russia, the old, planned economy appeared to be functioning fairly well. The great show-pieces of Soviet heavy industry were still turning out tractors and combine-harvesters, public services were still in operation, and the streets of Kiev and Minsk were relatively clean and orderly in comparison with the dirt and decay of Moscow. Underneath, of course, the apparent state of health was an illusion. The western republics depended on cheap raw materials and credit which could not be sustained for much longer, either by Kiev or Moscow. Nevertheless the illusion of a stable economy meant that there was no strong incentive to change quickly. President Leonid Kravchuk's campaign for Ukrainian independence owed its remarkable success to a peculiar coalition of interests: militant Ukrainian nationalists in the west of the republic, and complacent Russian-speaking factory directors in the eastern cities, who wanted to avoid the economic reforms which were being imposed on their neighbours in Russia.

In the Central Asian republics, there were other reasons why reform could not be introduced quickly. In places like Tashkent and Ashkhabad, communist ideology was a wafer-thin cover for an old-fashioned form of Oriental despotism, in which economic and political power was concentrated in the hands of a small élite. These regimes were not only harsh, but brittle. Whenever disorder did break out, it could spread with terrifying speed, as happened in the Fergana valley of Uzbekistan in 1989. This in turn reinforced the rulers' dependence on the security police. Under these conditions, the Central Asian élites were understandably more nervous than their Russian counterparts about raising the prices of basic goods, and about privatisation, which, even in its tamest form, would run the risk of diluting their own authority.

As for Russia, its political culture had no place for the rock-solid bourgeois traditions of the Baltic, or even the Ukrainian instinct for good husbandry. It had another, less obvious 'asset': a strong, atavistic sense among Russian people that any worthwhile enterprise should involve suffering on a gigantic scale; a feeling that desperate situations require desperate remedies; almost a yearning for apocalypse, combined with a bored indifference to anything short of apocalypse; and famously, an almost infinite capacity for endurance.

So many things about Russia made it seem one of the least promising environments for a capitalist revolution – its legacy of hopelessly outdated industry, its over-militarisation, its collectivist tradition, its alcoholism and its inertia. Against this, however, it was necessary to set the curious fact that Russia had always shown far greater aptitude for the impossible, or near-impossible, than it had for the simple tasks, such as road-building and plumbing, that most countries saw as routine.

The precondition for the accomplishment of these 'impossible' feats was a sense of real desperation, a sense that all the easier options had been tried, and that a giant leap into the unknown was the only alternative to annihilation. As the euphoria of the August coup dissolved and winter set in, the collapse of the old economy took on such frightening dimensions as to create in Moscow that very mood of desperation in which radical change was, for the first time, conceivable, even inevitable.

This mood had not existed any earlier, contrary to what many people claim. One of the commonest, and most mistaken, charges levelled against Mikhail Gorbachev is that he was wrong to put political reform before economic reform. In other words, he should have attempted some cautious experiments in market economics in 1985 or 1986 – when the apparatus of the communist state was still strong, and public finances were still healthy – and only after that embarked on the risky enterprise of democracy.

This argument sounds plausible enough, but it ignores the realities of power as they existed in 1985 or 1986. It would have been quite impossible to make any serious moves towards market economy at that time (even if Gorbachev had understood the meaning of the word), because power was firmly locked in the hands of a Party élite which viewed any sort of market as an intolerable threat to its interests. By instituting free speech and holding semi-democratic elections, Gorbachev used one of the very few tools available to dislodge the worst parts of that élite from power. But even this was not enough. In the end, the old élite, of which Gorbachev himself was part, would only loosen its grip on power when it had brought the country to the very brink of ruin, and simply exhausted the possibilities for draining off the country's resources. This tragedy had to be played out until very near the end, for only then could another drama begin.

By late 1991, the moment for radical change had finally come, because, in economic terms, it was only a few minutes to midnight. Most of the country's gold reserves had been sold off, and foreign exchange reserves had dwindled to less than $100 million, a negligible sum. Foreign debt was ballooning. In the course of 1991, Mikhail Gorbachev had traded on his international prestige to borrow $20 billion with no prospect of repaying the money on time. In another act of desperation, the state-owned foreign trade bank, Vneshekonombank, had plundered nearly $11 billion from its Soviet clients' hard-currency accounts, thus ensuring that many Western exporters to Russia would never be paid. Oil revenues, which had acted as a cushion for the Brezhnev regime and removed all incentive to modernise the economy, were tumbling – from $22 billion in 1986 to $7 billion in 1991 – thanks to lower world prices and some grossly incompetent investment decisions in the oil industry a decade earlier.

The mountain of debts alone was a compelling reason why the Union was virtually doomed to disintegrate. Yeltsin's Russian government was more and more reluctant to accept responsibility for reckless borrowing by the crumbling Gorbachev administration. By putting a formal end to the Soviet entity, the Russian Federation was able to make a distinction between the new state's borrowing – which would be cautious and repaid promptly – and the inherited mountain of Soviet debt, which would be cleared gradually as public finances permitted.

Gaidar and his team could read these economic signals only too clearly, and they confirmed Gaidar's view that Russia could not possibly afford to go on bankrolling the republics by supplying them with cheap oil, gas and credits to the tune of several billion dollars a year.

Yeltsin did not have such a detailed understanding of the economic crisis, but his famously keen intuition, his peasant instinct for judging people, situations and timing, told him that Gaidar and his brash young colleagues, with their peculiar jargon and workaholic zeal, had something the country needed. Presented with the choice between Yavlinsky's efforts to save the Union, and Gaidar's 'Russia-first' shock therapy, Yeltsin chose the latter.

On 28 October 1991, Yeltsin used the enormous prestige which he still enjoyed after the August putsch to persuade the Russian legislature to give him emergency powers over the economy for twelve months. He announced that most prices would be free of state control at the end of the year, as Gaidar had recommended. A few days later, Gaidar was made Deputy Prime Minister in charge of the economy, while Yeltsin himself – in a pledge that he would share responsibility for the cabinet's actions – became Prime Minister as well as President.

While Yeltsin was always careful to leave a minimum of space between himself and the reformers, so as to ensure some room for manoeuvre, he lent them a substantial piece of his personal charisma and prestige, without which they could not even have started work. Precisely because of their youth, intellectual gifts and cosmopolitan outlook, the Gaidar team was as alien to the Russian masses as the Bolshevik commissars who had driven them out their villages and wrecked their churches sixty years earlier.

Lectures from jumped-up schoolboys about remonetising the economy or altering the terms of trade meant nothing whatever to the hard-pressed factory-hand or *babushka*. On the other hand, when a man of sixty with a raddled face and a gravelly voice told them to tighten their belts for the sake of the country, at least some of them were prepared to do as they were instructed, without presuming to reason why.

In his autobiography, Yeltsin had told the country of his childhood in the staggering, brutalising poverty of an unheated Siberian peasant's hut in which the family snuggled up to a goat to keep warm. He was able to retort, when people complained about their living conditions, that he had been hungry for much of his youth. Gorbachev could have said the same about himself, but it would have been less convincing.

Whatever the blights left on his childhood by collectivisation and war, Gorbachev was a product of southern wheatfields where nature had been kind. Yeltsin evoked the remote, northern forest where only the hardy and vigilant could survive.

When historians come to assess Yeltsin, they will surely give him credit for his ability to spot and back young talent. Nothing in his record as a Party boss in Sverdlovsk would suggest that he ever thought much beyond the tired dogmas of communism in its late Soviet form. He probably did not have much active belief in the Leninist gobbledegook he was forced to spout in May Day speeches, but he does not seem to have felt any strong impulse to look for other answers to life's mysteries. He was happy enough, in those days, to trade in the only currency in which political power was then denominated. If he stood out at all from other Party bosses, it was in his populism – he was prepared to spend hours explaining his policies at public meetings – and in his long, unforgiving memory, which made him a terrifying man to work for.

After 1987, when Yeltsin was forced out of the ruling Politburo and his bitter power struggle with Mikhail Gorbachev began, another quality started to emerge. Although he was no intellectual, he could master almost any brief very quickly, when he put his mind to it. Sensing that Moscow's pro-Western liberals were on a rising political tide, he presented himself, with a mixture of shyness and arrogance, to the Moscow intelligentsia, and asked for lessons on liberal political philosophy.

Galina Starovoitova, an erudite, high-principled matron who coached Yeltsin on ethnic issues was fascinated by the earthy character who sat before her. She still remembers her first impressions:

> His vocabulary is poor, but he has a rich talent for mimicry, he's quite an actor. He uses non-linguistic methods to communicate; he can raise his eyebrows in a way that gives an extra meaning to his words. The words he uses can be quite primitive but you feel that something lies behind them.

Equally non-linguistic and intuitive, it seems, were the methods by which Yeltsin extracted information and formed impressions of people and places. Like many a Soviet communist, humble and mighty, he found that any doubts he had about the superiority of the Western economic system were settled by a single visit to a US supermarket in 1988. Ideology or no ideology, it was obvious that the West had mastered something which the Soviet Union had not. When it became clear that Gorbachev was taking lessons on the market economy, and had started regurgitating them in the form of insufferable, half-baked diatribes to the press, Yeltsin determined to outbid his rival. When Gorbachev commissioned Yavlinsky to write a 500-day plan to transform the economy, Yeltsin ordered a 400-day plan, and used an inspired phrase to proclaim the absolute incompatibility of one plan with the other: 'You cannot cross a hedgehog with a snake.' It is very unlikely that he gave either document more than a cursory glance, and perhaps he was right not to waste his time, for neither stood a chance of being implemented in autumn 1990 when they were issued.

A year later, however, the situation was different. Once the imminent freeing of prices had been announced, the mood in Moscow and the other major cities became apocalyptic.

All Russian winters carry intimations of disaster; with the darkness and violence of nature there comes a sense that no nightmare vision is too awful to come true. But these sentiments were particularly powerful in December 1991, as the Soviet Union lived out its dying days in a drama that left many people too stunned to react. The state shops, unwilling to sell anything at the old prices, became not merely ill-stocked but entirely empty.

Many Russians have already forgotten the nightmare of the last few winters under communism, as the planned economy and with it the entire wholesale and retail trading system, progressively collapsed. It is an understandable form of amnesia, and by no means the only one from which Russians collectively suffer.

Those winters, particularly the last one, were a grisly, frightening and humiliating time, when people who had taken a quiet pride in somehow managing to provide for their families were no longer sure of doing so. Every morsel of food that arrived in the warehouses of the big cities was siphoned off illegally. If it got as far as a shop, it would be sold by the back door; if it got as far as a works canteen, it would be pilfered by the staff there. Millions of city-dwellers depended for their next meal on knowing someone who worked in a shop or warehouse, and the worst thing was that even these forms of subterfuge were losing their efficacy, as the spectre of monetary collapse loomed.

Money had never played a very important role in the Soviet system – it was at best a reflection, not a determinant, of power. Factory managers and Party officials were issued by the state with money, as well as far more significant, non-monetary advantages, because they enjoyed political muscle;

they did not (except in the southern republics) gain power because they had accumulated money. Now, however, money was in danger of dying out altogether as an instrument of exchange. From individual craftsmen to the governments of cities and republics, more and more transactions were being conducted by means of barter. Anybody who could lay their hands on a consumer durable of any kind was desperate to do so. It was rational to spend one's life savings on two sofas or three television sets, if one was lucky enough to get the opportunity. Furniture and electronics – even Soviet television sets with an alarming tendency to explode – promised to be a better store of value than any banknote or savings account.

So the first and most urgent task facing the Gaidar team was to restore some meaning to the concept of money. Without money, it was impossible to have a monetary policy, to stimulate or protect this or that part of the economy, to transfer resources from one part of the country to another, or simply to pay the wages of policemen, customs officers and railwaymen.

If the monetary system imploded completely, the country would become ungovernable, and that spectre was already so close that the government had very little room to manoeuvre or even regulate the pace of change. Anybody who suggested rebuilding the planning system, or dismantling the old economy in carefully graduated steps over several years, had simply failed to realise the weakness of the state. This weakness was a quandary which left the country's new masters with very few options.

Arkady Murashev, a well-liked reformist politician with an infectious toothy grin, quickly discovered some of the limits of state power when he took up his unlikely appointment, made at the height of post-August euphoria, as commander of the Moscow police. On paper, he was in charge of a force as big as the British Army, at around 120,000, but King Canute had a better chance of reversing the tide than Murashev had of stamping out petty corruption. The only reason why anyone became a traffic policeman was to pocket 'fines' for imaginary driving offences (preferably from foreigners in dollars), and if Murashev had tried to stamp out this practice, he would have faced an uncontrollable flood of resignations. Nor was it remotely possible to stop his men moonlighting for private security firms, which paid far better wages, had far better weapons and were rapidly becoming a power in the land. Freedom to moonlight was one of the conditions on which his employees condescended to offer a little of their time to the semi-bankrupt government.

Most Western minds have difficulty imagining the might of the Stalinist state at its height, its ability to save or ruin millions of lives, and to regulate the smallest and largest of events from the Baltic to the Pacific Ocean. Now the Russian state presented the opposite problem – it was hard for people to believe that the government had become enfeebled to the point where its writ hardly presided in the capital, let alone beyond.

Stalin's crash programme of urbanisation and industrialisation was proving to be one more example of an extreme that generates its opposite. The whole enterprise had been akin to rolling an enormous boulder up a hill: it could not have been achieved at all without the concentration and application of tremendous force, but once that power began to falter, the stone would roll backwards at an alarming speed. At the beginning of 1992, there seemed to be a real possibility that the stone would run right back down to the very bottom of the hill again. Russia would de-industrialise, de-commercialise and de-urbanise, with millions of people abandoning their city apartments for a life of subsistence farming. A disturbing sign of what could happen if urban life collapsed had already come from the Eastern city of Khabarovsk, where the municipal heating system broke down and dozens of people froze to death in their homes before they could reach the soup-kitchens in the street.

All this provided Yeltsin, Gaidar and his team of surgeons with the necessary degree of desperation. Russia lay before them, like a patient etherised upon the operating table.

4

The Economy: The Experiment Begins

As they surveyed the wreckage, Gaidar and his fellow reformers were good enough ex-Marxists to see that the sheer madness of the existing situation contained nuggets of hope. Merely putting an end to the most glaring of the existing absurdities would be enough to generate quite substantial sums of money. For example, billions of dollars could be saved by simply stopping the flow of arms, machinery and other 'exports' to former Soviet clients in the Third World, because these were delivered on such soft terms as to be virtually free. Billions more would be saved by restricting the flow of credits and subsidised raw materials to the other ex-Soviet republics. Vast sums could be gained by selling a slightly higher proportion of Russia's oil, gas and other raw materials on the world market instead of insisting on their delivery, at negligible prices, to rickety old factories.

Even more money could be saved by closing the worst of the country's industry. Once their activities were costed by international standards of accountancy, an extraordinary fact became clear: most of Russia's factories subtracted far more value from the economy than they added to it. The energy and raw materials which these factories consumed were more 'valuable', at least in Western terms, than the produce which came off the assembly line. This would not have troubled the Soviet leadership when their self-confidence was at its height, as their whole purpose was to provide humanity with a new definition of what constituted value. Now Russia had abandoned that project, it had resolved to run in the Western economic race, and if it really wanted to do that, the thing it needed to do most urgently was shut about half its factories.

Soviet industry had not been built to create value in the Western sense of the word. It was designed to serve two ends: the manufacture of weapons, and increasingly, the vested interests of those who wielded power in the economy. These interests were deeply entrenched and, by now, ran almost directly counter to the interests of the country as a whole.

As long as the old, communist economy served its purpose of ensuring the flow of energy, metals and skilled manpower to the war industry, it had a certain logic. It guaranteed the country's power within the very narrow definition of power which the Soviet leadership used. Now the limits of that logic had been reached and even if one accepted that defence was the only thing that mattered, Russia's capitalist rivals were demonstrating that the Soviet model did not work. It was impossible to have a strong defence sector without a flourishing, innovative civilian economy, and a strong position in the international trading system.

Yet any attempt to deal with this problem in a piecemeal way ran into insurmountable opposition. Toom Pungas, an Estonian scientist, realised the intractability of the problem in the early 1980s when he was put in charge of a project to speed up the application of high-technology inventions in Soviet industry. Before he started work, the average time-lag between an invention and its use on the assembly line was an amazing seven years. At first, the team enjoyed considerable success – among its achievements was the pioneering of a new type of compact disc. Then, however, the inventor started to make powerful enemies within the industrial ministries, as they had been very well-served by a system that guaranteed them seven years' funding for every project, with few questions asked. Pungas was detained by the security police and given a stern warning: 'You are creating a deeply mistaken illusion about the so-called possibilities of efficient work.'

This was the kind of vested interest that Gaidar and his lieutenants would have to weave their way round. One of the striking features of Russian history is the speed with which stubborn pockets of conservatism, conspiracies of laziness or incompetence build up whenever they are given the chance. In the jargon of sociology, Russia has a recurring tendency to throw up élites which are 'dysfunctional' because they actively prevent the country from building up strength and competing effectively with its rivals. These dysfunctional élites ranged from the Muscovite gentry whose backwardness infuriated Peter the Great to the incompetent commanders of the Crimean War.

Only two things have served to break the power of these entrenched interests: the pressure of foreign competition, and the emergence of despots who are strong enough to break the élite's power and force the country to make whatever sacrifices are necessary to confront that competition.

As Russia entered its first full year of independence, the worst part of its industrial directorate was as dysfunctional, as inimical to the country's chances of further modernisation, as any élite in Russian history. The only lobby which inflicted even greater damage was the agricultural one, the collective farm chairmen, who worked the soil so inefficiently that it would probably have been better for Russian cities to procure all their main foodstuffs abroad. The collective farms not only failed to feed the cities, they leeched off the urban economy by demanding a continual supply of cheap farm machinery and fuel. On the other hand, they were among the best-organised lobbies in the land, and they were well practised in the art of holding urban politicians to ransom by threatening to stop deliveries.

The country's new regime was given a vital window of opportunity by the shock which the old élites suffered after the failure of the August 1991 coup, whose instigators included the arms industry, heavy industry and the farm lobby. Only by the following spring did the old guard fully recover.

Starting in January 1992, the Gaidar team had three historic months in which to implement its policies in more or less undiluted form. The weakness of the state machine forced them to rely more on deregulation, abolishing old rules, than on introducing new ones. This was not a matter of being fanatical or doctrinaire; it was pure recognition that every attempt at positive intervention in the economy would only create opportunities for policemen or bureaucrats to take even more bribes. In the frank words of Pyotr Aven, the foreign trade minister: 'Any obstacle to economic activity . . . will be circumvented in Russia, and therefore this country has to be more liberal than any other.'

Apart from freeing most prices, the government made it legal to sell almost anything, almost anywhere. It also abandoned the effort to manage trade, and removed all obstacles to imports, as long as they were paid for at a realistic exchange rate, determined by the market.

In the boldest step of all, the military budget and arms procurement were cut to a fraction of their previous level. Only the stunning psychological blow suffered by the army and the defence industry in August 1991 made this move possible. However, this apparent blow to the military's interests was a vital prerequisite to the rebuilding of Russia's strength, whether this was measured in military terms or in any other way. Simply put, Russia could not rebuild its army until it had a monetary system and it would not acquire a monetary system worth the name unless the exchequer was given some temporary relief from the burden of military spending. Both the arms factories and the army itself responded to the cut-off of state funding by launching themselves, with desperation, into the new commercial world: selling arms to all comers – from Mafia bosses to the warlords who were carving up the republics on Russia's borders – and, in the case of tank drivers or bomber pilots, offering their own services as mercenaries. This had some grotesque side-effects, notably that of stoking the brutal wars within and between the Transcaucasian republics of Georgia, Armenia and Azerbaijan. But the next result of this process was not unsatisfactory from Russia's point of view: it left Russians richer, and Transcaucasians dead.

There were some areas in which the Gaidar government had to make compromises. It lacked the courage, or perhaps the political muscle, to free the price of fuel and thus end the peculiar state of affairs in which oil was cheaper than distilled water, and caution over this issue dictated caution in others. As long as the world price for fuel and other raw materials was up to thirty times higher than the price paid by Russian industry, it was necessary to limit exports, otherwise not a single drop of oil would have been left in the country. Despite its *laissez-faire* instincts, the Gaidar cabinet found that it had no choice but to maintain some restrictions.

One reason for this was the fact that the captains of state industry, with no shareholders to watch over their actions, started selling off metals and other merchandise at a fraction of world prices in return for giant kickbacks from their Western customers. This kind of abuse made it easy for Yavlinsky and other jaundiced observers to point out the dangers of freeing prices while the economy was still in state hands.

Going by the textbook, it would of course have been desirable to privatise and deregulate at the same time, but finding the right terms for privatisation was a tricky exercise which would take another year to pull off, and the liberalisation of prices could not wait that long.

The immediate effect of abolishing state control on most prices was wildly miscalculated by many people, simple and sophisticated. Western ambassadors were sure there would be riots. The ordinary folk who put their savings into furniture or gold rings did so in the belief that the impending firestorm of inflation would be unquenchable, and the rouble would be reduced to a heap of ash.

Murashev, the young police chief, took a different view. He confidently told his friends that freeing prices would produce a feeling of calm and relief, an easing of social tension, as a heavy, artificial constraint was lifted from the economy. His friends wondered whether he had taken leave of his senses; surely this was taking faith in the market-place a step too far.

But Murashev was right and the Cassandras were wrong. By early February, the atmosphere in Moscow had palpably improved. Prices jumped by about 500 per cent of their old, state-controlled level (at which virtually no goods were available) and then more or less stabilised. At first nobody bought much, and food rotted on the shelves, but with every passing day, shoppers and shop managers learned the elementary skills of a consumer society.

Suppliers learned that it was sometimes necessary to cut prices in order to stimulate demand and buyers forgot their old habit of snapping up every piece of merchandise they were offered in case supplies ran out.

The deregulation of imports and street trading had some striking effects. Hundreds of thousands of ordinary people, finding that their wages in the state system had lost most of their value, crossed the border to Poland, China or Turkey to buy clothes and other consumer goods which they resold in Russia. The sale of a single leather jacket could bring them more than a year's normal wages.

Moscow and other cities turned into gigantic bazaars. Every inch of pavement was covered in makeshift stalls offering everything from old sewing machines to pornographic novels. The sellers ranged from sharp-witted teenagers to old women selling knick-knacks to keep themselves in food. The latter phenomenon seemed to confirm the critical observer's opinion that market reform in Russia was an unmitigated evil, a vicious assault by capitalism on a country which had once been synonymous with all-embracing social welfare.

Dreadful it might have been, but things would have been far more dreadful if the critics of reform had prevailed. At the onset of winter in 1991, the economy had deteriorated to the point where there was a real possibility of millions of people going short of food and fuel. The thing most likely to trigger that disaster was a breakdown in the monetary system, which was a real enough danger. By flooding the consumer market and allowing people to make money in any way they could, the authorities staved off the spectre of a monetary collapse, and it never returned. If there was one thing crueller than encouraging an old lady to sell her possessions, it was preventing her from doing so – or making it impossible for her to do so by debasing the currency.

It might have seemed absurd that able-bodied citizens were spending their time and energy travelling to Turkey to bring home a few track suits or training shoes to sell to other people; but it was less absurd than the old system, when Muscovites would travel for hundreds of miles to Lithuania to buy themselves a pound of cheese, and risked being punished for 'economic crimes' if they were caught trading on a larger scale.

In the new situation, a minimum of utility was being created as people – however amateurishly and haphazardly – earned money by bringing goods from countries where they were plentiful to places where they were in desperate demand. The old system gratuitously wasted people's efforts by placing artificial barriers to the procurement of daily necessities. The mere removal of this ridiculous situation would pave the way for an economic upturn.

Hundreds of thousands of young Russians were now making a living by the simple practice of arbitrage between one city and other; if anoraks were cheap in Ryazan, they would be bought up and resold in Tyumen. In the final days of the old system, the country was in danger of breaking down into medieval fiefdoms as local governments tried to prevent merchandise from leaving their regions. Now energetic youngsters were doing a far better job than any hardline politician of recreating Russia as a single economic and monetary space.

At long last, because there was something to buy with roubles, the value of Russian currency actually rose, which for many people was a miracle on a par with water flowing uphill. From a low point in December of about 140 per dollar, the rouble had almost doubled in value by mid-February.

This was the beginning of what could have been a virtuous circle. A rising rouble made it easier for small entrepreneurs to obtain the foreign inputs they needed to start businesses; it narrowed the difference between world and domestic prices for oil, bringing closer the prospect of deregulating fuel prices; and it also brought nearer the day when it would be politically feasible to allow some foreign investment in the economy.

For as long as the rouble was so weak that an American student could almost buy a Russian engineering factory with the proceeds from his holiday job, it was obvious that no Russian government would take the political risk of 'selling out the country' by opening the gates to foreign capital. The more the rouble strengthened, the more conceivable it became to allow some foreign equity in.

All this seemed far too good to last, and so it was. At least on paper, the initial effect of the Gaidar reforms was to push more of Russian industry into technical insolvency.

There was nothing wrong with that; it was precisely the sort of cold shower that industry needed. But the response of the old enterprises was typically stubborn. They simply jacked their prices way beyond the means of the customers, and folded their arms. A giant backlog of outstanding arrears, amounting at one point to about one-third of the value of the country's annual output, built up within the industrial sector. Industrial managers – who were used to claiming money from the state as soon as they made a delivery, but had no experience of claiming money from customers – calculated that the authorities would have no choice but to rescue them. If the Gaidar cabinet did not do so, then the central bank, which was under the authority of Parliament and had a free-spending agenda of its own, would surely oblige.

On one side, the government was confronted with the industrial lobby, which could only be faced down by a cunning strategy of dividing the relatively healthy from the chronically unviable. On the other, it was receiving a barrage of contradictory signals from the West. The International Monetary Fund was urging the Gaidar cabinet to head in a straight line for the Holy Grail of monetary stabilisation – low inflation, low deficits and a stable exchange rate – while Western governments could not quite make up their minds what they wanted. At times they echoed the IMF's demand and delivered condescending lectures on the need for fiscal rectitude, and at others they seemed to concur with Gaidar's critics and accuse him of being too draconian and hard-hearted.

The Western attitude was based on a series of misunderstandings. First of all, nobody at the IMF was more committed to sound money and financial stabilisation than Gaidar himself was. Like every Russian convert to a Western philosophy, he embraced the new creed with purist fervour and would sometimes find himself upbraiding Westerners who seemed to be backsliding. This was not because Gaidar felt any loyalty or love for the IMF or any other Western institution. It was because he held the firm – and very well-founded – conviction that sound money and financial stability were in Russia's interests: they had to be achieved if Russia was to rebuild its strength and reassert its place in the world.

On the other hand, Westerners failed to grasp the power, tenacity and cynicism of the lobbies with which Gaidar and the reformers had to contend. They were very poor judges of the tactics that would be required to deal with the lobbies; when to compromise, when to beat a tactical retreat, when to drive a wedge, and so on. This sort of judgement could only be made by a person within the Russian political game, who understood its peculiar rules.

Thirdly, some Westerners were too inclined to take the lobbies at face value when they claimed to speak on behalf of the suffering masses and warned darkly of a social explosion in this or that sector. In fact, the lobbies were more cynical than most people realised, and the masses more willing to bear hardship than most people could imagine.

When an industrialist or collective farmer stood up in public and said the Russian people could endure no more, this generally meant that he and his narrowly defined interests were being damaged. Concern for the Russian people was often only a cheap rhetorical device.

In March 1992, the government officially informed the IMF in an open letter that it intended to deregulate the price of fuel soon. This was very unfortunate, because it united all industrial managers – from the most progressive to the most reactionary – against the government. The following month, when the Congress of People's Deputies assembled, the industrial lobby went on to a blazing offensive, triggering the first of many stand-offs between Russia's administration and legislature. Gaidar and the cabinet walked out of the chamber after a majority of the 1,000-strong assembly passed a resolution binding the government to spend more money.

There seemed to be a real possibility that the legislature would force Yeltsin to appoint as Prime Minister someone like Arkady Volsky, the sleek servant of the Soviet Politburo who had set himself up as chief spokesman for industry, and was threatening, rather unusually for an industrial boss, to organise a general strike.

This first battle (which was relatively tame compared with the ones which followed), was resolved in part because Western governments hastily put together a $24 billion credit package which they presented as a gesture of support for Gaidar.

It was still, on balance, politically advantageous in those days for a Russian politician to be seen to enjoy Western backing, but this would not be the case for much longer. Gavriil Popov, the former mayor of Moscow who had won Western acclaim as the mastermind of the pro-democracy movement, was caustic in the extreme about the financial package. He sensed, quite correctly, that it would arouse false expectations about what the West could do, and would lead in the end to an anti-Western backlash. In fact, he argued, the so-called aid was just 'debt forgiveness' – the minimum needed to avoid a default on Soviet loans – and a contribution towards the cost of dismantling nuclear weapons, which was as much a Western concern as a Russian one.

Popov, a dishevelled but immensely shrewd economics professor of ethnic Greek origin, also made another controversial, prescient observation. There would be no substantial aid to Russia from the West as a bloc, because the Western nations were in competition with one another over the commercial opportunities in Russia; capital would only start flowing towards Moscow when it had been established which particular country or countries would be Russia's strategic partner.

In any case, even after the $24 billion financial package, the future of Gaidar's position, and his policies, looked precarious. As part of a compromise stitched together by Yeltsin, three new deputy Prime Ministers were brought into the cabinet: Georgy Khizha, an arms industry boss from St Petersburg and former associate of Sobchak; Vladimir Shumeiko, former head of an instrumentation factory in southern Russia; and Viktor Chernomyrdin, chief of Gazprom, the Russian gas conglomerate which was arguably the biggest energy concern in the world. None of these men subscribed to the purist economic theories of the old cabinet.

Chernomyrdin, as a captain of energy, might have been expected to favour the liberalisation of fuel prices, but in those days he was still locked into the old way of thinking which held that industry ought to be supplied with cheap power. The cabinet was now a coalition; it was no longer a closely knit group of old friends who knew each other's reactions and way of thinking. In an immediate reflection of this change, both the government printing presses and the central bank started to emit money at an alarming pace. By the end of the year, the central bank had issued credits amounting to 40 per cent of the GNP and a quarter of this money had simply been doled out to the republics and would never be repaid.

One of the oddest bits of asymmetry in the relationship between Russia and the newly independent republics in early 1992 was in monetary matters. Russia had the monopoly over the printing of roubles, so the republics had to plead with Moscow if they wanted banknotes, but at the same time the republics could write themselves unlimited lines of credits on the Russian central bank, and Moscow was powerless to stop them. Gradually these anomalies were cleared up; the republics issued currencies of their own, most of which plunged in value far more rapidly than the rouble, and their access to Russian credits was restricted. But on this matter, too, there was continual tension between Gaidar's 'sound-money' camp and the industrialists. The industrialists wanted their trading partners in other republics to be topped up with money, however artificially, so that Russian suppliers still had a chance of being paid.

Gaidar's monetarists saw things from almost the opposite perspective. Despite their best efforts, they had not succeeded in shutting down many of the country's ruinous factories by dint of financial discipline alone; after all they were only in the early stages of introducing that very concept to Russia. The fact that industrial production had fallen – by about 20 per cent since the previous year – was mainly because the break-up of the Soviet Union had made it difficult to trade across the borders of the new republics, and old supply lines had therefore been disrupted. This was not a bad thing.

Since most of these 'trading' relationships had been imposed by the Soviet planning system and would not be viable if transport were properly costed, there was no strong reason – at least from Russia's point of view – to mourn their passing.

Russia was in the bizarre situation where its most desperate need was to conserve wealth, and reduce the pointless subtraction of value by simply calling a halt to a high proportion of what passed for economic activity.

The slump in industrial production which was caused by the collapse of the Union and the termination of cross-border links was not, therefore, a disaster. To put things in the bluntest terms, reducing the territory of one's country by a third is not an ideal form of deflation, but it is probably better than no deflation at all.

By the end of 1992, many observers of the economy, including the IMF, felt that Russia had wasted its first year of post-Soviet existence. Inflation, which trailed the money supply by three months, had climbed back to 27 per cent a month after dipping into single figures in August. The longed-for prize of stabilisation seemed further away than ever.

However, despite, or even because of, all the compromises, the year had actually seen enormous progress. Russia had come back from the brink; it was now a functioning economy, albeit a badly functioning one, and the ghost of a complete monetary meltdown had vanished. A flourishing foreign exchange market had been established – monthly turnover was around $1 billion, compared with $18 million at the beginning of the year and the exchange rate determined in this market was used for exports and most imports. Russia was gradually starting to act like a normal participant in the world economy, trading by the laws of comparative advantage. Export revenues were rising, and above all the quality of exports had increased. More goods were going to promising markets like South Korea, whilst fewer were being shipped virtually free to old Soviet friends like Cuba and North Korea. The state's foreign exchange reserves had risen from less than $100 million to more than $1.5 billion; this was still low, but would treble in the next half-year.

In various legal and illegal ways such as commodity exportation, retail and distribution, and commercial banking, large amounts of capital were accumulating in private Russian hands for the first time in seventy years.

This meant that the government, having gone through the motions of inviting foreign bidders, could now give Russian-dominated consortia the contracts for the forthcoming round of multi-billion-dollar projects in drilling and mining. These included the Shtokman oil and gas field in the Arctic, awarded to a group of companies in which the defence sector was well represented; and the Udokan copper deposits in Siberia, whose exploitation was entrusted to a tycoon in his early thirties. A couple of years ago, the idea of a Russian-led consortium assembling the necessary capital and expertise would have been hard to imagine; now it seemed perfectly natural.

Gaidar and his colleagues had not simply sold out their principles to industry as a whole; they had done something much smarter. The fluctuating inflation rate over the past year had a salutary educational effect for all kinds of people in Russia, beginning with the industrialists. One group of industrialists had profited cynically from high inflation, using it as an argument to extract extra credits from the central bank which were promptly stashed away in hard-currency accounts.

Another group – particularly high-technology defence enterprises with hopes of a civilian spinoff – reckoned that they could do better under conditions of sound money, when it was possible to make investment decisions and take out loans for more than a few months a time. Gaidar sought out the most competent of Russia's manufacturers and made a deal with them. In October 1992, Gaidar went to Togliattigrad – the home of Lada cars – and formally sealed an alliance with sixty senior captains of industry, under which he would maintain the flow of relatively cheap credit to the more promising parts of the economy.

By compromising with one part of industry, the government had not merely broadened its own political base, it had also cleared the ground for one of the most astonishing economic transformations of modern history – the privatisation, starting in December 1992, of most of Russia's larger enterprises.

This exercise would give most of Russia's factory directors the chance to make themselves very rich, richer than they had ever dreamed of becoming; but in return for this they would gradually be forced to bring a minimum of commercial logic to the administration of their companies. Gaidar could see what the IMF could not: buying off the red directors was a small political price to pay for the fabulous prize of 'turning round' the industrial heritage of a superpower, so that it created wealth at the same formidable speed as it had formerly consumed wealth.

Yet from the point of view of Gaidar's Western well-wishers, who were nursing the infant of Russian capitalism as though it were the tenderest, most fragile and precious of creatures, some disturbing and unforeseen paradoxes were already arising. First of all, by encouraging Russia to embrace a system that favoured the competent over the incompetent, the best parts of industry over the worst, they were promoting that section of the Russian economy which was, in the medium term, the most threatening to Western commercial and strategic interests, in other words, high-technology defence manufacturing. Secondly, by encouraging the new Russian state to pursue sound financial policies, they were, in effect, telling Gaidar to turn the economic screws on the smaller republics by staunching the flow of cheap credits and subsidised raw materials. Those same Western governments which had reacted in horror to Moscow's military crackdown on Lithuania were now full of praise for an economic policy which, among other things, had the effect of vastly increasing Russia's ability to dictate terms to its smaller neighbours.

Western influence was not decisive. With or without Western prompting, Russia had little choice but to draw in her horns and think of her own economic needs first. But one of the main achievements of Yeltsin, Gaidar and the other politicians who nursed Russia through her first year of independence was to find a method of reconcentrating power, and reversing the disintegration process, which won plaudits rather than rebukes from the West.

5

THE NEW RUSSIA: WHAT SORT OF STATE?

WHOOPS OF JOY came resounding through the night air when they yanked 'Iron Feliks' from his pedestal. For a few moments, the crane operator kept him dangling in the air, creating an image that was self-consciously reminiscent of the Lenin statues coming down all over Eastern Europe; and then the old killer was dumped lengthwise in the back of a lorry and driven away.

It happened on the day after the August coup collapsed, as crowds of Yeltsin supporters were roaming through the centre of Moscow in a state of delicious euphoria. The destruction of the monument of Feliks Dzerzhinsky, the Polish landowner and priest *manqué* who founded the Soviet secret police, was the nearest Muscovites would ever come to the elation of demolishing the Berlin Wall.

The amazing week when communism fell was full of public drama, all of which seemed to be making the same point. In the twinkling of an eye, a vast country was passing from one side of the looking-glass to another. It was turning itself inside out, instantly refashioning itself into everything it had not been before. As the giant pendulum swung, nobody could believe the width of its arc.

Where there was arbitrary rule, which acknowledged no restraints on its freedom to detain, blackmail or simply bully, there would now be rigorous respect for the rule of law.

Where there was thought control, there would now be freedom of thought.

Where government had been opaque and mysterious, and relied on those qualities for its effectiveness, it would now become transparent and open to scrutiny by citizens and their elected representatives. A new, law-based state would scrupulously respect the integrity of property and an individual's rights. Where the old regime had monopolised economic and political power, the new one would promote diversity in economic and political life, and rely on that diversity as a source of vigour, and a guarantee against a relapse into tyranny.

The old system could bestow favours or inflict pain on particular citizens and groups, without having to account for itself or abide by any fixed code of behaviour. The new system would be based on formal equality before the law, regardless of class, ethnic origin or religious belief. The old regime had engaged in sophisticated sorts of discrimination – positive as well as negative – among the Soviet nations, even as it mouthed slogans about international brotherhood; the new system would for the first time establish a definition of Russian citizenship which made no distinction between Slavs and Tatars, Bashkirs and Jews.

If Soviet Russia was a byword for despotism, the new Russia would not merely match but outdo every government in the world with its commitment to human rights and freedom of speech. That is what Andrei Kozyrev, the diminutive, soft-spoken foreign minister told his counterparts from Western Europe and North America when they came to Moscow for a conference on human rights in September 1991. A year earlier, Moscow's suitability as a venue for this conference had been a thorny issue in East-West relations; some Western governments doubted whether the bad old days of framed trials and psychiatric abuse were really over. Now Kozyrev was lecturing his colleagues on the need for even tougher diplomatic machinery to ensure the observance of human rights; no regime could be too demanding, no standards too high.

At that time, few Western politicians would have dared to contradict Kozyrev, or raise awkward questions about the gap between theory and practice. The gentle-mannered foreign minister, along with the whole of the Yeltsin team, was still basking in the warm glow of the August events, the magnificent, televised *auto-da-fé* in which the Russian people appeared to take their country back and return it to the mainstream of history, whatever that was presumed to be.

The removal of the Dzerzhinsky statue, which had personified the god of terror, was one defining moment; there was another a few days later, when hundreds of thousands of people walked from the Kremlin walls to the Russian Parliament, behind the coffins of the coup's three victims. This was a happier funeral march than most, for it also heralded the birth-pangs of a new state.

The dead – an Afghan veteran in his thirties, a pale, scrawny youth in his early twenties and a Jewish architectural student – had all been killed on Moscow's central ring-road during the chaotic skirmishes between demonstrators and some frightened tank drivers on the second night of the coup. Although nobody would have put it quite that way, their deaths had served as a fitting, proportionate blood-sacrifice to usher in the new state; civil society was seen to have paid in blood, the proper, small amount of blood for its victory over tanks and manacles.

In a booming, brilliantly judged address to an electrified mass of people at the back of the White House, Yeltsin had begged the pardon of the dead and their families: 'Forgive me for the fact that as President I was unable to save these lives . . .' The subliminal message was clear: where Yeltsin had failed with the three martyrs, he would succeed with his remaining 150 million subjects.

Before the funeral march, there was a giant public meeting in Manezh Square. It was addressed by Mikhail Gorbachev, who sounded crestfallen and confused after his return from isolation in Crimea to a polity that was shifting under his feet at a pace he could not follow. He made the announcement (a slightly pathetic one), that the three martyrs would posthumously be made into 'Heroes' of a dying state called the Soviet Union. There were a few words in the rich, stentorian tones of Yelena Bonner, the widow of Andrei Sakharov who had inherited the great physicist's mantle as moral leader of the human rights movement. Patriarch Alexy II intoned some of the glorious obsequies that are laid down by the Russian Orthodox Church, and then came something which took the mourners by surprise: the Kaddish, or Hebrew Prayer for the Dead, in honour of Ilya Krichevsky, the Jewish coup victim.

A sort of shudder passed through the crowd when this awesome sound came over the loud-speakers: not reflecting prejudice (it was not that kind of crowd) so much as nervousness. Were the victors of the recent drama pushing their luck a little too far? Was this too audacious a gesture of the new state's commitment to respecting the beliefs and ethnic origins of all its citizens? Yeltsin had revived an old word, *Rossiane*, to describe any citizen of his emerging state, regardless of that person's ethnic origins. Yet when he spoke of reviving Russia, it was never quite clear which Russian heritage he was invoking. Was it the brief liberal experiment of 1917, which for a few months had offered equal rights to all the empire's nations, or was it the far older Imperial tradition, to which the very idea of rights was alien?

Still, the post-coup euphoria was so powerful that most people suppressed whatever doubts they had. The public pressure to believe that everything was turning out for the best was such that it seemed churlish and pedantic to raise objections or predict serious problems.

Most liberals and reformers still felt as though the world was full of pleasant surprises, and indeed one of them came the very day of the funeral march. The different religious traditions meant that it was not possible to have a joint committal ceremony for the three martyrs, but Aleksandr Rutskoy, a man whom the democratic camp had never quite trusted, volunteered to attend the Jewish ceremony. It turned out that beneath his bluff military exterior, he was intensely conscious of the half-Jewish origins of his mother. A more devious politician with Rutskoy's political profile would have hidden this family background, but he did not suffer from that sort of guile; this was both his strength and his weakness.

Yet one person who read the signs that August and did not suppress her doubts was Yelena Bonner. She had spent a lifetime drawing attention to awkward, unpleasant truths that most people would prefer to forget, and she would not allow the heady public atmosphere to change this habit. In a long and closely argued commentary in the daily *Izvestia*, she identified what she thought she had been defending when she and tens of thousands of other Yeltsin supporters had barricaded themselves into the White House and defied the eight-man junta: not Gorbachev, or any other leader, but the principle of law. This was the principle on which the new, post-Soviet confederation or commonwealth should be constructed. It should be a freely negotiated and transparent arrangement between sovereign republics which were democratic and law-bound in their internal affairs, and also respectful of legal constraints in their dealings with one another.

At the risk of puncturing the balloon of public optimism, she pointed out that the prospects for a strong legal culture in the new political environment were much poorer than most people imagined. She drew attention to the unpleasant fact that millions of people had welcomed the coup on the first day, hoping for a badly needed dose of order and discipline after several years of mounting dislocation and chaos. Her article concluded on a Cassandra-like message which was utterly out of tune with the giddy high spirits of the moment. If anyone was tempted to give order a higher priority than law, they should dig out an old photo album and think for a moment about the relatives and friends – every family had them – who had been incarcerated or killed by a regime that placed itself above all legal constraints.

To Westerners, it might seem peculiar that Bonner found it necessary to make such an admonition. Surely the political campaigns of the past five years, brought to a triumphant conclusion by the downfall of Dzerzhinsky and everything he stood for, had all been about the posthumous vindication of Stalin's victims: re-establishing the truth about what happened, and using the resulting torrent of moral indignation to establish iron safeguards against the tragedy being repeated? Was it conceivable that close relatives of the dead – the bereaved families in whose name the pro-democracy campaign was being waged – really needed reminding of that tragedy? Did they, of all people, need reminding of the dangers that it could happen again?

As anyone who has lived in Russia will confirm, this reminder was desperately needed, and its chances of being heeded were all too poor. Other members of the liberal intelligentsia might convince themselves that they were speaking for the whole nation when they denounced Stalin's terror, but the formidable queen of dissidents had no such illusions.

Over the past five years, as the Soviet regime lost confidence, declined and fell, its leading intellectuals had focused public attention on the staggering price in blood, terror and blighted lives which had been paid to shore up that regime. Would this onrush of self-doubt have occurred if Stalin's side of the deal had been respected, and the Soviet Union had continued to be powerful as well as cruel?

As Bonner and her generation knew only too well, millions of people had, outwardly and in many cases inwardly as well, accepted the Faustian pact offered by Stalin: allow me to tyrannise and decimate you, and I will make you – or at least those of you who are lucky enough to survive – into a mighty collective force.

The question of how 'freely' the bargain was accepted – to what extent people kept their own private counsel, even as they outwardly conformed – is an almost unanswerable one. People's own, self-justifying memories are not an accurate guide. But in practice Stalin was successful in securing control of a large part of his subjects' minds, as well their bodies. Only when his half of the bargain – the nation's greatness – began to falter, had people focused their minds properly on the diabolical deal they had made.

In any case, a new phase was beginning now; the dismantling of the Soviet state, ideology and ruling party was over and the construction of a new Russian polity was starting. However noble the initial intentions, there was little in Russia's history to suggest that the country's rebuilders would be squeamish about small matters like civil rights and law: hence the forlorn appeal for citizens to look closely at their family photo albums.

In a second *Izvestia* article – another of her tough-minded exercises in kill-joy journalism – Bonner expressed doubts about the religious ceremony, co-starring the Patriarch and the Rabbi, in which she had taken part. She was a good, strict civil libertarian in the tradition of Voltaire, an uncompromising supporter of the right of others to profess beliefs that seemed wrong or even repugnant. But her restless, rigorous mind was troubled by the idea of Orthodox Christianity as an official or semi-official religion. Surely the best way to guarantee religious freedom was to follow the American model, in which the government of a deeply religious nation was defined as a strictly secular entity?

The parents of Ilya Krichevsky had shyly requested the presence of a rabbi after it became clear that the two ethnic Russian martyrs would be lamented by the Patriarch; but as the boy's father admitted, they had never heard of the Kaddish or been inside a synagogue. Most of the ethnic Russian mourners were equally ignorant of their own religious traditions.

The presence on that podium in Manezh Square of the Patriarch and the Rabbi was on one hand an encouraging sign that the ideological shackles of the atheist state had finally been loosened, but it might also have been a disturbing harbinger of the reopening of old divisions. If the Patriarch was to be given a quasi-official position as the new Russia's spiritual leader, where would that leave those citizens whose religious heritage was Muslim or Jewish, Buddhist or non-existent? Would the renewed salience of those differences compromise the principle of equal rights, regardless of racial or religious background, for every citizen of the emerging state?

It was not popular to ask these questions in late 1991. In the final years of the Soviet state, all religious organisations – in the etiolated form to which the communist regime had reduced them – were suddenly back in fashion with officialdom. They benefited from an atmosphere of woolly-minded benevolence towards all traditional creeds that was cultivated by officialdom as it searched desperately for some substitute to the dying doctrine of Marxism. A striking feature of the half-democratic Parliaments of the Soviet Union and the Russian Federation was the presence of gorgeously robed prelates of all the ancient religions. There was Patriarch Alexy and several of his senior colleagues, as well as the Muslim Mufti of Tashkent and dignitaries of the Tibetan Buddhist faith from near the Mongolian border, even a Siberian woman who practised Shamanism.

It seemed reasonable to expect, therefore, that Orthodoxy would metamorphose into a kind of *primus inter pares* among Russian faiths; a semi-official religion in a tolerant, pluralist state. Just as the Archbishop of Canterbury takes part, along with the hierarchy of other faiths, in British public events such as Remembrance Day.

The cautious public pronouncements of Patriarch Alexy – keeping up with the reformist wisdom of the moment, never running too far ahead or behind – suggested that he would settle happily into this role. His willingness to preside over the spiritual life of a liberal state was strengthened by the remarkable speech he made to an audience of rabbis in New York in November 1991.

The Patriarch scoured Russian history (and this was not an easy exercise), for examples of the happier moments in Christian-Jewish relations. After greeting the rabbis with the words 'Shalom to you in the name of the God of love and peace, the God of our fathers who appeared to righteous Moses in the flowers of the burning bush . . .' he went on to describe the Old Testament and the New Testament as 'two landmarks in a single theanthropic process'.

The trial in 1913 of Mendel Beilis – a Kievan Jew who was accused of the 'ritual murder' of a Ukrainian youth, and was eventually acquitted – is usually seen as one of the blacker pages in Jewish-Russian relations. But the Patriarch drew attention to the testimony in Beilis' defence that was offered by several leading churchmen. He also quoted Vladimir Solovyov, the religious philosopher, as saying the Jewish question was 'not a matter of whether Jews are good or bad, but whether we Christians are good or bad'.

This astonishing homily appeared to be opening a new chapter in relations between Russian Christianity and Judaism; in fact it turned out to be more of an end than a beginning. So furious was the reaction of ecclesiastical conservatives that the Patriarch never again felt emboldened to strike that note of tolerance in a public statement. In church politics, Alexy found himself subjected to the conflicting pressures of a Western-oriented minority, led by the former political prisoner and pro-Yeltsin politician father Gleb Yakunin; and an ultra-nationalist movement led by Bishop Ioann of St Petersburg, who rapidly emerged as one of the brightest stars in the firmament of Russia's far right. Ioann was a frequent and impassioned contributor to such hardline publications as *Sovyetskaya Rossiya*, the former official daily of the Russian Communist Party. He quoted with approval from *The Protocols of the Elders of Zion*, the classic work of 'anti-Zionist' propaganda, and made it plain that he entirely agreed with its conclusion: both socialism and liberal democracy were the products of a gigantic malicious conspiracy. He was a devout believer not only in monarchy, but in absolute monarchy. He regarded constitutionalism, and the existence of separate political parties, as a violation of the ancient Russian tradition of collectivism.

The most active organisation of Orthodox laymen, known as the Union of Orthodox Brotherhoods, was led by an energetic and politically astute young monk called Kirill Sakharov, whose opinions were as different as could be from the benign tolerance of his namesake, the Nobel Prize winning physicist. From his base in a small church in central Moscow, Brother Kirill was a tireless propagator of Orthodoxy with an anti-Western gloss. He regarded both Roman Catholicism and what he called Talmudic Judaism as forces chronically hostile to Russia; and yet he described himself as a moderate in the world of the Brotherhoods because some of his fellow activists regarded resistance to these alien religious phenomena as the main task they faced, whereas he thought many other issues – from strict liturgical observance to the re-establishment of ecclesiastical courts – were also important.

Politically, Brother Kirill was very much on a wavelength with the hardline opposition to Yeltsin. Like the traditionalists who excoriated the foreign advisers of Peter the Great, he believed that the country would only be saved when it had a genuinely Russian government.

Yakunin and a group of lay activists urged the Patriarch to call to order the ultra-rightist forces within the Church. But as these liberals themselves acknowledged, it was very hard to imagine how Alexy or anybody else could assert real authority within an organisation whose structure and personnel had to such a large extent been determined by the political police.

For better or worse, it was largely on the whim of the KGB and its predecessors that the outward existence of the Church had been preserved during seventy years of atheist rule. Of the two pillars on which the Soviet regime rested – the Communist Party and the political police – it was plain that the former would always be radically opposed to the church, in accordance with the teaching of Marx and Lenin. On the other hand, the latter agency, whose only immutable commitment was the preservation of the Greater Russian state, was prepared to pursue that goal by any instrument available, including the Church, if it could be made sufficiently malleable.

It was in this spirit that Stalin, at the height of the Second World War, entrusted a security police general, G. G. Karpov, with the task of reviving the Church in its most 'useful' form. After the war, the Orthodox Church served Stalin as an instrument of Russification in Ukraine, particularly in the newly annexed western provinces of the republic where the Uniates – Christians who used the Eastern rite but were loyal to Rome – had deep local roots. Under Nikita Khrushchev, when the power of the Party reasserted itself and that of the security police waned, the closure of churches resumed with a new fury, and it seemed very possible that every single place of worship in the country would be shut down. Only in the nick of time was a desperate deal made between the senior clergy and the security police; the Church could stagger onwards, but on condition that it convert itself into a virtual propaganda arm and investigative agency of the KGB, with a brief to infiltrate and manipulate the World Council of Churches.

The Orthodox tradition of rendering loyal service unto Caesar, in return for a degree of protection from the state, was thus given a new twist. Patriarch Alexy himself was an outstanding representative of this strange concordat; the entry of the Russian Church into the WCC in 1961 coincided with his own elevation to the senior ranks of the Church, and he became one of the best-known faces of the Soviet clergy among the worthy but naïve do-gooders of the West. The interaction between the Protestant churchmen of the West and the Russian hierarchy became a kind of outrageous caricature of all interaction between Russians and Westerners. The Western clergy doggedly believed that their Russian interlocutors were at least partially free agents, speaking in good faith, and in this belief they were absurdly mistaken. The Westerners simply could not think themselves into a world where all public pronouncements were being secretly manipulated by forces whose purpose was anything but religious. The whole idea of a dialogue between Churches on essentially secular matters – disarmament, development or Third World politics – reflected a very Western idea of what religious organisations were about; while it was an Eastern form of subtlety and deceit which made it thinkable to use this half-baked dialogue as a front behind which the mysteries of religion could be sheltered from the full force of the atheist state.

On the face of things, the advent of a new post-communist regime which smiled on the Church, and gave its blessing to the reopening of thousands of parishes, should have been a time of rejoicing and reconciliation. Yet a Church which had been moulded under communism found it very difficult to adapt to life under liberal democracy.

Like many Soviet institutions, the Church was neither willing nor able to tout for souls in a competitive market, where fast-talking American evangelists were buying airtime on newly established television channels and renting football stadiums for open-air meetings in a furious drive to capture Russian souls. For both religious and non-religious Russians, the onrush of Western preachers – along with the Moonies, the Hare Krishna movement, and cults which had acquired a dubious reputation in the West – triggered a profound sense of antipathy; a sense that Russia's helplessness and vulnerability were being cynically exploited. It seemed to many people that the foreign preachers were little different from Western marketing managers who regarded Russia as nothing more than a promising, untapped market for the sale of soap powder or training shoes; except that Western ideas were somehow more threatening to Russia than Western products.

Hence the rather disturbing fact that from mid-1992 onwards, the leadership of the Russian Church was devoting much of its energy to lobbying for the reimposition of some restrictions on religious freedom. These efforts bore fruit in mid-1993, when Parliament passed an amendment that would force religious organisations based outside the country to apply for registration with the state before they could start operating on Russian soil.

Depending on who did the registering, it seemed possible that this measure might lead to a huge clamp-down on the activity of mainstream as well as fringe religion. There was an outcry in the West, particularly among US legislators whose voters adhered to the religious right, and President Yeltsin vetoed the amendment, but members of Yeltsin's staff said they fully agreed with the principle that the Western model of a religious free-for-all simply could not be applied to Russia. From the state's point of view, people had to be guided away from the temptations of fringe religion, to which Russians seemed particularly vulnerable, towards some ideology which was not harmful to social order or the public purpose.

As the Soviet experience demonstrated, Orthodoxy knew how to be a *religio illicita*, an underground faith in whose name the believer was prepared to undergo unbearable suffering; it knew how to be a state religion, at once underpinning and mitigating the authority of an emperor; but it could not easily adapt to the Western model of a level playing field, in which the prize of converts went to the richest and most energetic.

From early 1992 onwards, it became clear that whatever role the Patriarchate was to play in the new Russian state, it would not simply be that of benign, decorative chaplain to a Westernising liberal democracy. This was despite the fact that Orthodox prelates were by instinct loyal to all their earthly governors, and looked for ways to make themselves useful to the state – in keeping with their tradition that almost any political compromise is worth while in order to preserve theological integrity.

To the Western mind, this uncritical loyalty to the State sounds like an advanced form of cynicism, but Eastern Christendom profoundly believes that coexistence with earthly powers – so long as they do not interfere in theological matters – is less spiritually damaging than actually becoming an earthly power, complete with an army, treasury, and diplomatic service, which was the path followed by Rome.

In Byzantium, Orthodox philosophers had seen an image, however tarnished in practice, of a Christian empire in which the power of the state was used to ward off heresy and defend pure doctrine, while Christian ideals suffused and sanctified the workings of the state. In its Russian manifestation, Orthodoxy took on a slightly different role: it acted as a kind of balm to heal the wounds of a nation as one Tsar after another whipped it onwards towards modernity. The Eastern Church owns up unhesitatingly to the charge laid by Marx that religion is the 'opium of the people', but with the defiant rider that this 'opium' is vastly more precious than anything that any worldly project can offer: it is not an escape from reality but entry into a higher form of reality. The Western Churches, by contrast, have gone a long way towards accepting the Marxist critique of 'other-worldly' religion: the view which insists that the overwhelming, if not the sole, purpose of all human enterprise is the improvement of life in this world, as opposed to preparation for the after-life.

As the price of survival under the Soviet regime, the Russian Orthodox Church had been prepared to parrot modernist platitudes about peace, disarmament and the Third World at meetings of the World Council of Churches, but in its heart of hearts, when it was being true to its own traditions, Eastern Christendom looked down on both socialism and liberal democracy as worldly projects which are bound by the shortcomings of all worldly projects.

Far more than the West, the Eastern Church was conscious of the limits of human reason, and it regarded the claim of the Renaissance that 'man is the measure of all things' as a step backwards, not forward, in the history of ideas. It would never idealise the 'people's will' as expressed through the ballot-box as an infallible source of wisdom; the people's will was as likely to be misguided, or led astray by some scurrilous orator, as it was to be inspired. All this helps to explain the paradox that the Russian Patriarchate had in some ways coexisted more comfortably with the atheist regime than it did with the caricature of bourgeois democracy that took hold in post-Soviet Russia.

The reasons for the Patriarchate's discomfiture were not, of course, purely ideological. It was very hard indeed for Moscow's religious hierarchy to forgive Yeltsin for agreeing to the break-up of the Soviet Union. One of the main reasons for this was that Ukraine had been the most heavily churched area of the communist state, and its political independence isolated the Patriarchate from more than half its parishes and revenue. Ukraine's President Leonid Kravchuk, a lifelong communist and avowed atheist, insisted that an independent state should have an independent Church. He encouraged Bishop Filaret, a colleague and rival of Patriarch Alexy, to establish himself in Kiev at the head of the new Ukrainian Church, in defiance of Moscow.

In a sordid and bitter dispute, Russia's bishops formally defrocked Filaret on grounds of disobedience and improper behaviour in his personal life. Another bishop, Vladimir, remained loyal to Moscow and won the loyalty of most of the parishes in the Russian-speaking areas of eastern Ukraine. In other words, Russian unhappiness over the independence of Ukraine surfaced in ecclesiastical affairs sooner than it did in worldly affairs, and the Russian regime which was judged guilty of 'letting Ukraine go' was bound to be resented by those clerics who had never set much store by democracy anyway.

If the result of democracy was the break-up of empires, then it seemed to many Church people that the country was better off without it. Having suffered so badly itself from the dissolution of the Union, the hierarchy was poorly placed to serve Yeltsin as an active apologist for the new democratic order. The independence of Ukraine was one blow, and the adaptation to the new economic system, where cash counted for everything, was also an uphill struggle for the Church.

Gradually, however, the clergy did come to terms with the new world of 'sponsorship' in which wealthy businessmen could sometimes be persuaded to fund the reconstruction of churches. But the 'natural constituency' of the Church was among the first victims of the new order. Patriarch Alexy had to struggle hard to keep the clergy apolitical because he realised that if they were politically engaged at all, it would be on the side of Yeltsin's most uncompromising opponents.

Both sympathisers and adversaries of Russian nationalism have often laid stress on the organic links between Orthodoxy and the cause of Russian statehood. Sympathisers, like Bishop Ioann of St Petersburg, see a link between the religious doctrine of *sobornost* or fellowship – the principle that nobody can find salvation alone – and the communal or collectivist character of Russian models of political and social organisation, which leave little room for individual dissent. Adversaries have pointed out the usefulness to Russian rulers from medieval times onward of Orthodox traditions of passive endurance and reverence for authority.

However, the coincidence of purpose between Church and state was by no means total. Many of the greatest periods in Russian spirituality – from the catacomb churches of the 1930s to the Optina monks who defied Peter the Great's effort to restrict monasticism – have been in spite of, and not because of, the state.

For the clergy, Yeltsin's liberal democratic experiment was yet another modernising project, to be endured rather than celebrated or promoted. The Church had other business, which was not of this world.

6

The Revival Of The Political Police

LIKE MANY DEFINING moments in history, the details of what happened to the Dzerzhinsky statue have been distorted in the national memory. It is not quite true to say that crowds of indignant citizens pulled the monument down; the whole incident was not as spontaneous as it seemed.

The anger of the crowd had been genuine enough, but Moscow's altar to state terror did not lend itself to amateur demolition efforts as easily as the Berlin Wall had done. The demonstrators did what they could with hammers and pickaxes, and there were peals of delighted laughter when a couple of wags climbed onto the secret policeman's shoulders and slipped a rope round his neck, but still he would not budge. Then somebody tipped off the city hall that things were getting out of control, and people might get hurt unless the authorities took matters into their own hands. So Sergei Stankevich, the deputy mayor whose cherubic features and perfect English endeared him to Western television interviewers, sent along a proper municipal demolition unit, complete with truck, chains and blowtorches, to take the statue away.

For several days afterwards, demonstrators milled happily around the empty pedestal and chanted their defiance at the Lubyanka, the huge sandstone headquarters of the KGB which loomed above them. They daubed a couple of slogans, and planted the new Russian tricolour, on the forbidding exterior of a building that epitomised, like no other in the world, the pure essence of power.

For Western correspondents, this was an extraordinary and moving spectacle. 'The people are taking their country back', exclaimed one journalist to his colleagues, but this was an over-simplification, because Russia's people were as much inside that building as outside. They were the authors of the Lubyanka's 10 million files, as well the subjects; perpetrators as well as victims in a system that managed to make almost every citizen into an accomplice.

This bitter truth was quickly discovered by the politician who was given the assignment of reforming Russia's political police. Vadim Bakatin was as sincere a 'liberal communist' as it was possible to be, and the frustrations of his career are a good illustration of the limits of that political doctrine. He was a conscientious lieutenant of Mikhail Gorbachev, one of the few members of the presidential entourage who remained loyal to his master. Ironically, he had just the kind of rugged good looks that would have fitted him perfectly for a role in one of the spy films that were made to give the KGB a more glamorous image: a strong, clean-cut jaw, with just enough jowl to add distinction, and a steady, clear-eyed gaze that recalled his upbringing in the open spaces of Siberia.

Yet he had few illusions about the Lubyanka's glamour. As he recalls in his memoirs – optimistically entitled *Getting Rid of the KGB* – one of the first files he dug out was one which described the arrest on 27 July 1937 of his grandfather, an accountant with no political affiliations, by the West Siberian branch of the security police. The arrest warrant claimed he had confessed to participation in a monarchist conspiracy; but the case had been reopened in 1966, and it was ascertained that the alleged monarchist movement never existed. The elder Bakatin had been shot to fulfil a 'quota' of killings demanded by Stalin. His grandson's reaction was characteristically mild: 'Strangely enough, I feel no hatred . . . probably because it is impossible to hate the history of one's own motherland. One simply has to know it, however it might have been.'

Even this principle, the belief that past sins should be

known and then quietly forgiven, could not be carried very far. Barely five days after arriving at the Lubyanka, he was explaining to the press the reasons why he could not allow a general opening of the KGB files, of the kind which happened after the fall of communism in East Germany.

His main argument was that public revelation of who had informed on whom – in recent times as well as under Stalin – would have torn Russia apart, making it virtually ungovernable. There could have been an uncontrollable spate of recrimination, reprisals, kangaroo courts – and in wilder places like the northern Caucasus, blood feuds lasting for decades. There was another argument which was probably more decisive, even though Bakatin was shy about using it: nobody would ever act as an informer again if the precedent was set that covers could be blown.

On 29 August, Bakatin gave a firm retort to newspapers that were urging him to reveal all:

> I am convinced that opening the files would not only be inexpedient, but highly dangerous. It is not people who are to blame, but the system, which brought citizens up in such a spirit that they often turned, willingly or unwillingly, into informers. The great majority of them are honest people, who have not besmirched themselves in any other way . . .

From the start, Bakatin's mandate was ambiguous. He was informed of his appointment on 23 August, the day after the Dzerzhinsky statue came down. He walked into Gorbachev's office in the Kremlin to find him flanked by the leaders of all the republics, including Russia's Yeltsin. 'We have decided to offer you the chairmanship of the KGB,' Gorbachev announced. 'But you are sending me to an organisation which I think ought to be dissolved', Bakatin recalls blustering, after unsuccessfully counter-proposing another candidate. 'Then we order you to do precisely that', growled Yeltsin, who suggested that wording to that effect be added to the official announcement of Bakatin's new job. Gorbachev scribbled an amendment to a statement whose basic, four-line text had already been printed; Bakatin was made KGB chief with a mandate to 'present proposals for the radical reorganisation' of the agency. Nobody was impolite enough to point out that dissolution and radical reorganisation are not quite the same thing.

The combination of technology, secret knowledge, fire-power and manpower that Bakatin reluctantly inherited was unique in the history of the world. Nearly half a million people were on its full-time payroll, and many times more were part-time informers.

In the social and political disintegration of the previous few years, the KGB had suffered much less damage than the other components of the Soviet state. The Communist Party's membership and prestige had plummeted; the new Soviet Parliament had failed to fulfil its promise; the regular army was in disarray after its humiliating withdrawal from Eastern Europe; the KGB, meanwhile, had quietly taken control of several of the army's crack divisions.

Bakatin sincerely believed that citizens of the new Russia had the right to know as much as could reasonably be disclosed about the security apparatus which their taxes sustained. This belief – indeed the very idea that holders of power should be accountable to anyone at all – was utterly foreign to his country's political tradition. But Bakatin held it all the same, and in that spirit his memoirs provide at least a cursory account of the vast machine which he tried to bring under control.

About half the personnel who fell under Bakatin's authority were border troops, responsible for guarding the longest land and sea frontier in the world. This meant keeping intruders out – from Afghan mujahedin raiding Tajikistan, to Greenpeace vessels protesting over nuclear waste in the Arctic – and keeping Soviet citizens in, unless they had been through the burdensome procedure of acquiring an 'external passport' which involved vetting by another branch of the KGB.

About a quarter of the KGB's budget went on telecommunications, which are always one of the keys to power in a totalitarian state. This meant using earth stations, satellites and all kinds of gadgetry to provide politicians, generals and spy-masters with instant, high-quality connections across the vastness of the Union, and above all denying these facilities to everybody else. It also involved eavesdropping on the conversations of others, from the banal family quarrels of obscure politicians to the secret deliberations of foreign powers.

The tapping of telephone conversations was one of the many weapons at the disposal of the KGB's Fifth Administration which acted as the regime's guardian over hearts and minds. Its task was the surveillance, infiltration, guidance and, where necessary, suppression of social, religious, and political movements of every kind. This was the section which kept tabs on dissidents – in the early 1980s, it had refined the technique of using psychiatric treatment as a more effective substitute for show trials. Its various subdivisions dealt with intellectuals, students, nationalists, Jews; the fourth division oversaw religious organisations and required them to report regularly on the propaganda efforts they were waging on behalf of the atheist state.

While the Fifth Administration was the most bitterly resented part of the KGB, easily the most glamorous was the First Chief Directorate, which engaged in foreign intelligence and was located at lavish premises of Finnish design on the southern edge of Moscow. This was where talented young men (never women, apparently) were groomed in the finer nuances of Western politics and society, before being sent out, under the guise of diplomats, trade representatives or journalists, to spy for the motherland.

Another valuable asset that Bakatin inherited was the Ninth Administration, known as the *devyatka*, which was responsible for guarding the country's leadership, the buildings in which they lived and the Kremlin. This gave the devyatka *de facto* control of scores of luxurious apartments, hunting-lodges, pre-revolutionary mansions, and seaside homes. Also highly prestigious was the Seventh Administration, responsible for the 'external surveillance' of important buildings. Its ranks included the 'Alpha' anti-terrorist squad, trained to storm hijacked planes, and carry out *coups d'état*. Alpha had been used to storm the presidential palace in Kabul in 1979, killing President Hafizullah Amin and paving the way for the Soviet invasion of Afghanistan.

Border security, telecommunications, the monitoring of culture and religion, espionage, high-level military operations: to Westerners, this seems a peculiar mixture of functions to be concentrated in a single agency. Only on reflection does it become clear what they have in common – they are all crucial to the establishment, consolidation and maintenance of totalitarian power in a state which regards itself as perpetually under threat from external penetration by missiles, saboteurs or simply by ideas.

The Western and Soviet worlds differed so fundamentally in the way power was conceived and organised that products of one system had perpetual difficulty in understanding the other.

Soviet observers of the the West found it hard to believe that a capitalist country could function without some powerful, secret centre which directed its political and economic life. They could not understand what exactly it was that made industrialists defer to bankers, bureaucrats to politicians, politicians to pressure groups, newspaper editors and voters.

This difficulty was understandable: it reflects the fact that in advanced capitalist societies, power is diffused in such a broad and subtle way that its origin is very hard to track down. Protest is not repressed, but channelled and blunted by political parties, unions and pressure groups. The property rights over giant estates enjoyed by dukes and property tycoons are underpinned by millions of mortgage agreements on suburban houses; and the power of industrialists is at once defined, restricted, and shored up by the way in which their interests interlock with those of countless small investors.

Small wonder that many a Soviet analyst found the entire thing so difficult to grasp. Equally puzzling was the way that a capitalist regime seemed to demand so little from its subjects: all they were required to do was conform outwardly to a limited number of laws, and consume the products which were spread before them. Within broad limits, people were free to believe what they liked, and to do as they pleased in their private lives. To the Soviet mind, this looked like dangerous laxity on the part of the ruler – unless of course, some secret centre was really taking care of things behind the scenes.

In fact, Western societies do have all sorts of visible and not-so-visible means of ensuring that most citizens conform outwardly to certain minimum standards of behaviour, from the values projected in the media and advertising to the teaching of civic values in schools. But the rulers of traditional societies – such as Imperial Russia or indeed Soviet Russia – lacked these subtle devices; they had to rely on more deliberate and self-conscious stratagems for inculcating fear and faith.

That was the factor which Western observers, in turn, had repeatedly underestimated. Unless presented with clear evidence to the contrary, their instinct was to assume that parties, peace movements, trade unions and religious organisations were 'spontaneous' phenomena. This mistaken assumption had been played upon by successive Russian regimes to great effect.

The combination of border security with ideological surveillance, superior electronics with battle-ready presidential guards, was actually common enough in authoritarian states. What made Russia unique was the vastness and diversity of the geographical and social space that these instruments were called on to protect. Another decisive feature was the fact that Russia was locked in perpetual competition with countries whose strength rested on far more elaborate and sophisticated forms of social, political and ideological organisation than her own. The stronger Russia's Western rivals grew on the back of liberal capitalism, the more ruthlessly Russia's rulers resorted to their own, very different methods of husbanding strength.

By suggesting that Russia could dispense altogether with

secretive forms of thought control, Bakatin was flying in the face of his country's history. The protection of Russian frontiers and the insulation of Russian minds had been viewed as closely-related projects since medieval times, when the German and Polish Catholics – with their dangerous, Western idea of mitigating autocracy with social justice – were perceived as a source of territorial ambition and ideological contamination. After the Reformation, the Protestant vision of the individual treating directly with God was viewed as no less threatening to Russia than Scandinavian guns; and the idea of equality before the law, which had always existed among Jewish communities on the western fringes of the Russian empire, was the most threatening of all.

In the light of this tradition, any demand for a more liberal form of governance in Russia was liable to be equated with conspiring treacherously with those countries where these principles already applied. A version of this idea was used by the Soviet KGB to demonise all forms of dissent, by systematically blurring any distinction between legitimate protest and treason. Even in the declining years of communism, conservative sections of the establishment had repeatedly tried to tar the pro-democracy movement with the charge of sedition: was it not from the West that these noisy agitators received their fax machines, laptop computers and draft constitutions?

Bakatin took office at a time of widespread acknowledgement, even among Soviet conservatives, that thought control as an instrument of state power had been taken to absurd, self-defeating lengths: instead of strengthening the state, it had served to prop up the power of the incompetent and stifle the creative energy of the talented.

Yet was it *really* conceivable, in autumn 1991, that the state would divest itself altogether of the instruments of ideological repression, or disband the agency which orchestrated that control? Bakatin longed to believe that it was conceivable, and yet his own musings on the subject are a touching illustration of the eternal dilemma of the moderate Russian reformer.

Bakatin could not quite decide whether he agreed with the liberal critique of the Soviet experiment, which maintained that the Bolsheviks' slide into vicious totalitarianism began within days of the revolution, on 20 December 1917, with the secret resolution that established the 'All-Russian Extraordinary Committee for Struggle against Counter-Revolution and Sabotage', which soon became known as thc Cheka.

The Cheka inherited and reproduced on a vastly increased scale the traditions, methods and even some of the personnel of the Okhrana, the secret police of the Tsars. It masterminded the terror which began in mid-1918 after the assassination attempt on Lenin by Dora Kaplan, a supporter of the Social Revolutionaries who were rivals of the Bolsheviks. It was the instrument used by Stalin to visit terror on the countryside, and then on his own Party, then on the new Soviet dominions of Eastern Europe. The power of the Cheka dipped under Khrushchev but rebounded after the downfall of that Soviet leader, which it helped to bring about. Bakatin knew all this, and yet he longed to believe in the good chekist: the brave, clear-sighted secret agent whose sharp wits and conspiratorial talent were deployed for no other purpose than the good of the motherland. His musings on the subject are all the more human, even a little touching, for not being entirely consistent. At one point in his memoirs, he describes Dzerzhinsky's Cheka as a 'sword that was assigned to the legitimate defence of the revolution against its real enemies, but was wielded instead against the whole of society'. Did he then consider the revolution itself to have been legitimate? He is not sure: several pages on, without seeing the contradiction with his earlier thoughts, he concedes: 'It is probably naïve to think that the "provisional" committee [ie the Cheka] was ever intended to be provisional. Marxist-Leninist theory speaks of the dictatorship of the proletariat – and any dictatorship needs punitive instruments, not legal ones.'

As Bakatin was rapidly concluding, however, post-Communist Russia could not possibly follow the East German or Czechoslovak example and simply disband the security police. The KGB was in one sense a danger to the security of the state – virtually every division of the KGB was involved in some way in planning the disastrous 1991 coup – but it was also the very key to that security: its borders, nuclear power-stations, satellites and rockets. It was both lethal and indispensable – as Bakatin put it, 'it was a bad KGB, but it was the only KGB we had'.

Given that he could not abolish the agency, the best he could hope to do was purge the leadership and separate the organisation's component parts. In the immediate aftermath of the August coup, some fourteen senior officials, including the heads of most of the Administrations, or main divisions, lost their jobs; just three of them were prosecuted. A further nine senior KGB men, plus ten regional bosses, were dismissed in late September when the Lubyanka's internal investigation into the coup completed its preliminary findings, while thirteen, including some whose role in the coup had been more than peripheral, were let off with reprimands.

As Bakatin acknowledges, he showed his 'well-known liberalism' in the lightness of the purge, and as he soon discovered, the Soviet political police were not in the habit of responding graciously to lenient treatment.

At least for the first few months after the coup, nobody could question the principle that too much power had been concentrated in the Lubyanka, and its functions ought to be divided up. The crack divisions which had recently been placed under its authority were returned to the defence ministry; the Alpha 'anti-terrorist' unit and the Kremlin guard were placed under the direct control of the head of state. All government communications and electronic intelligence were combined in a single, powerful agency known as Fapsi which also reported directly to the President. The border guards were detached from the KGB, cutting the agency's numerical strength by half, and foreign espionage was also spun off into a separate agency, the Central (later the External) Intelligence Agency.

A trickier problem for Bakatin was how to divide up the KGB's resources between the fifteen republics as central Soviet authority – of which he was one of the few remaining representatives – faded into oblivion. Like the heads of all other agencies of central power, he found himself fighting a losing battle with the rising influence of the biggest republic, Yeltsin's Russia. He struggled to maintain cordial relations with Vladimir Ivanenko, head of the Russian Federation KGB, but Ivanenko's rapidly growing agency quickly became a focus of opposition to Bakatin's reformist approach.

When a security policeman was murdered by a mob of Chechen nationalists in the northern Caucasus, the Russian Federation KGB used its influence over the press to ensure that Bakatin was personally blamed. An anonymous group of Russian KGB officers also signed a letter denouncing the reluctant secret police chief for giving away too many of the organisation's inner workings in press interviews.

Bakatin's gravest sin in the eyes of the Russian old-timers emerged in December: it became clear that he had given the US government details of the eavesdropping system in the American Embassy building in Moscow. This gaunt redbrick structure had lain unused for a decade because the CIA knew it was bugged, although it could not ascertain precisely how. The hapless Bakatin pointed out that the bugging system had been deactivated since 1982, when the Americans first became suspicious; providing Washington with the details, he argued, would not deprive Russia of any intelligence capacity, it would merely save the Americans the $300m that it would cost to build a new building from scratch. Moreover, he insisted, the decision to inform the Americans had been approved by both Gorbachev and Yeltsin. However, none of this prevented Bakatin from being made the scapegoat in a storm of denunciation.

Leonid Shebarshin, the foreign intelligence chief who had resigned after a few weeks of unhappy coexistence with Bakatin, said his rival's behaviour proved that 'there are two kinds of madness – paranoia and rose-tinted euphoria'. The latter, he snorted, was the most charitable explanation he could imagine for Bakatin's gift to the Americans.

When the Soviet Union ceased to exist, the few remaining security functions which Bakatin retained were of course transformed from 'Soviet' to 'Russian Federation' control. If Bakatin had been prepared to woo the Lubyanka, he might have stood a chance of becoming security chief in Yeltsin's republic. But in fact the Lubyanka had relegated him to virtual political oblivion.

There was something very revealing about the fact that, for the few months in which they coexisted, the Russian Federation KGB had become a far tougher organisation than the dwindling remains of the Soviet KGB.

In making himself the top politician in the Russian Republic, Boris Yeltsin had, at first, pulled off the extraordinary trick of creating a semi-mythical state which overlapped in time and space with the Soviet Union but seemed to have a different atmosphere. Where the Soviet Parliament passed bad, old-fashioned, reactionary laws, the Russian Federation legislature adopted relatively progressive ones. Where the Soviet Parliament mulled over economic plans that were unworkable, unwieldy and reflected the old way of thinking, the Russian legislature debated and even adopted economic ideas that were fresh and original. Neither side's plans or laws were implemented in practice, but this scarcely seemed to matter: it was to defend this half-imaginary 'Russian' world that Yeltsin's supporters had flocked to the White House during the August coup.

Now that process was going into reverse: as they acquired flesh and blood, Russian institutions were becoming a repository of hardline thinking, while the vestiges of the Soviet government, under worthy souls like Bakatin, were a fading bastion of moderation.

The come-back of the KGB was discernible from the moment the new Russian state began to establish itself. One of Yeltsin's first acts after signing the death-warrant of the Soviet Union was to order the creation of a super-ministry which brought under a single roof the ordinary police (in other words, the ministry of the interior) and what was left of the KGB. This meant the creation of an enlarged agency of social control which at least on paper would resemble Stalin's commissariat of internal affairs, the NKVD.

The apparent purpose of this move was to dilute the power of the Lubyanka, which Yeltsin did not fully trust, by subordinating the security apparatus to its bitter rival, the regular police. The latter was a more corrupt institution than the Lubyanka, so it promised to be easier for the President to manipulate. To judge by press leaks that clearly emanated from disgusted KGB men, the upper echelons of the interior ministry had been told that they would be spared from the KGB's corruption probes if they would help the President to bring the Lubyanka to heel.

In part because of Yeltsin's towering international reputation as a democrat, the move attracted very little criticism. But it did, of course, trigger some alarm bells in Russia amongst civil libertarians who feared the creation of a vast new organ of repression, and of course within the KGB itself – which as Bakatin had discovered, was still a formidable political lobby.

The super-ministry's creation was unanimously vetoed on 14 January 1992, by a recently created body, the constitutional court. The decision seemed to be a powerful vindication of the hopes which reformers had vested in this new tribunal, whose thirteen members had been nominated by various factions in the Russian Parliament. At long last, it appeared that law courts were acting as a constraint on the power of government, instead of being an instrument of state power. Another interpretation is possible: the super-ministry may have been barred as a result of quiet pressure from the Lubyanka. To hail the decision as a victory for reform could be an expression of the 'rose-tinted euphoria' which Shebarshin found so deplorable.

In late January 1992, the vital function of military counter-intelligence – monitoring the political loyalties of the army – was switched back to the Lubyanka. At a time when the military was seething with discontent over living conditions and the 'loss' of the western republics, it would have been very risky for Yeltsin to leave the defence establishment free from monitoring by a third party. The former KGB network, which had penetrated the armed forces at every level, was of course the only third party which was qualified for the job. In June 1992, the border guards were restored to the Lubyanka's authority; this turned out to be a temporary move, but it was a telling sign that the authorities were now looking for ways to reconcentrate power, not dissipate it.

Despite his setback in the courts, Yeltsin continued his efforts to tame the Lubyanka by putting a regular policeman and personal friend, Viktor Barannikov, in charge of the security ministry. But Barannikov quickly showed signs of going native in his new environment, where he was hailed as a vast improvement on his predecessor Bakatin.

Within a few weeks of taking office, Barannikov was actually defending the KGB's record during the Soviet era, saying that it was not as black as it had been painted. In testimony to Parliament, he gave the total number of arrests during the Soviet period as a mere 3.8 million; this was a figure first used by the disgraced former KGB head, Vladimir Kryuchkov, and had been discounted by other sources as absurdly low. 'One could scarcely talk about total surveillance or an all-embracing police state,' the minister said, dismissing at a stroke the righteous indignation of the demonstrators who had cheered the removal of Iron Feliks less than six months previously. This indignation seemed, in any case, to be fading in the public consciousness.

The pace at which the Lubyanka re-examined the files of the victims of Stalinist repression slackened considerably – in part because the public, or at any rate newspaper editors who claimed to follow the public mood, seemed much less interested. A spokesman for the security ministry made the forlorn complaint, in September 1992, that material on this subject had become almost impossible to place in the press.

Once the flurry of real or feigned self-reproach over the KGB's role in the August coup had died down, it emerged that there was only one activity for which the Lubyanka was unequivocally prepared to apologise.

That was the infiltration and in some cases virtual takeover of all the major religious organisations which were allowed to maintain some precarious existence under the atheist regime. The fourth section of the KGB's Fifth Administration – in other words, the department which guided the churches – was closed, and it was solemnly promised that the security police would never interfere in religious affairs again.

Even here, however, the spirit of contrition was quite short-lived. In early 1992, some astonishing material came out into the open about the way in which the Moscow Patriarchate had been guided in its wordly activities by the KGB. The source of these leaks was the two liberal deputies – Lev Ponomaryov and the ex-prisoner of conscience Father Gleb Yakunin – who had been allowed into the KGB headquarters as part of a parliamentary investigation into the origins of the August putsch. Yakunin had a particular interest in the KGB's control of religious affairs because of his own travails. He was suspended from the priesthood in 1965 for speaking out against the repression of the Church, and in 1979 he was sentenced to labour camp, where he served seven years for his activities as leader of a group of campaigners for believers' rights. He regarded the Church hierarchy as an accomplice, whether willing or unwilling, in the repression of outspoken believers like himself, and he was dismayed by their apparent reluctance to acknowledge their past role.

The documents which Yakunin and Ponomaryov leaked were enough to confirm beyond all doubt what most people had suspected. The bishops who made up the Holy Synod were almost all regarded by the KGB as useful agents who reported loyally on the successes they were chalking up for secular Soviet diplomacy by participating in the WCC. The two parliamentarians were quite sparing in that they released to the press: for example, they disclosed the KGB code-names of three members of the Holy Synod, but they held back from making public the Lubyanka's name for the Patriarch. Also made public were reports from senior clergy to their KGB controllers about the politics of the WCC, how quiet lobbying had 'led to the adoption of positions favourable to the USSR' and this or that meeting had 'made a favourable impression' on some gullible visitor or led to a personnel appointment in the WCC which suited Moscow's book.

In most other ex-communist countries, these revelations would have led to a purge in the senior ranks of the Church, and that was probably what Father Gleb hoped to stimulate. He regarded the Patriarch Alexy as a somewhat more enlightened figure than most of his colleagues on the Holy Synod, a thirteen-member body which was irreverently known as the Metropolitburo. It looked possible that selective leaks would help the Patriarch's ability to prevail over his rivals, if that was what he wanted.

In fact, nothing of the kind happened. Details of the bishops' KGB involvement were greeted by the liberal intelligentsia with wry amusement, but their flock did not seem unbearably shocked. Often, they were sympathetic to the defences that were constructed by apologists for the hierarchy; almost everyone who lived under Soviet power had made his or her own compromises, for the sake of family, security and a quiet life. Father Vyacheslav Polosin, another priest-politician who had begun his career as an ally of Yakunin, argued that by doing their civic duty the bishops had not been compromising their spiritual integrity.

Far from picking political fights, the Orthodox prelate instinctively looks for political institutions which can provide a source of support for the Church; establishments to which the Church can attach itself, like ivy round a tree, without ever fearing that the ivy will become the tree, because to a good Orthodox theologian, the Church and the institutions of the world are engaged in fundamentally different purposes. If Orthodoxy feels able to co-operate with the organisations of the world, that is partly because it believes that ultimately the world does not matter; the chance to hear confession or serve communion is more important in the light of eternity than a hundred fawning reports to a KGB controller.

Those were some of the theological arguments in defence of the hierarchy's behaviour. Among those who had least reason to be satisfied by those arguments were former prisoners of conscience like Yakunin or Zoya Krakhmalnikova, another Christian intellectual who was sentenced to labour camp for her beliefs. Part of the Holy Synod's concordat with the State required it to co-operate actively in the persecution of Christians who insisted on speaking their mind in public. Parroting Soviet foreign policy before an audience of Protestants at the WCC headquarters in Geneva might be a reasonable concession to expediency, but actively repressing those brave souls who refused to make such a compromise was harder to justify.

Yakunin, for one, was not inclined to forgive his persecutors; he felt it was incumbent on them at least to apologise. Nevertheless the efforts made by himself and his parliamentary colleague, Lev Ponomaryov, to draw attention to the bishops' record brought few dividends, political or ecclesiastical. On the contrary, it provided the former KGB with an opportunity to tell the world that by mid-1992, it had already recovered a great deal of its former self-confidence and institutional muscle.

With the full support of Barannikov, senior officials at the security ministry asked the public prosecutor to start criminal proceedings against Yakunin and Ponomaryov for leaking state secrets. This was despite the fact that the secrets in question related to an activity – the monitoring of religious life – which was officially admitted to have been scurrilous and unjustifiable. The two politicians were defiant, saying in a joint statement that they 'believed that it was impossible to reform the KGB as the mechanism of a totalitarian system without creating such a precedent'.

Precedent, of course, was precisely what concerned the Lubyanka. The security empire would find it impossible to go on functioning if informers felt they were in danger of being exposed because of some change in the political climate. On the other hand, as long as the names of informers and the tips they had provided stayed firmly under lock and key, the KGB's power to blackmail and compromise would remain undiminished.

The public prosecutor, Valentin Stepankov, declined to act on the KGB's request and lay charges against the two deputies. But the Lubyanka had made its point; the brief period when its cupboard opened, and a few small skeletons tumbled out, was now over.

Just to make sure of this, the Lubyanka's bosses inserted some tough wording in a law on state security that was passed by the Russian Parliament in August 1992. Deputies involved in 'parliamentary scrutiny' of the intelligence services were no less liable to prosecution than any other citizen if they divulged state secrets; there could be no question of claiming parliamentary immunity.

The plethora of legislation relating to the former KGB's activity pointed to another irony. The standard liberal critique of the communist system would cite the KGB as the biggest single reason why Soviet Russia could never be regarded as a law-based state. The overwhelming concentration in a single agency of secretive and non-accountable power was the absolute antithesis of the Western ideal, in which individuals and institutions were allowed to interact freely under an agreed set of rules that did not predetermine the outcome.

Yet the plain fact was that few agencies were better placed to take advantage of the new Russian slogan of a 'law-based state' than the KGB. The Lubyanka had always been able to attract some of the country's best legal brains and at least since the 1930s, had regarded the trappings of legal correctness – the ability to formulate a case, extract confessions, and construct a legal argument – as one of the main weapons in its arsenal.

So the former KGB responded with alacrity to the challenge of formulating new Russian laws which would supposedly circumscribe its activity. In the spring and summer of 1992, the Russian Parliament passed three wide-ranging laws on intelligence and security which notionally restricted the actions of the former KGB but in fact lent them legitimacy.

In a graphic illustration of the Russian ability to mimic Western institutions while bending them to entirely different purposes, the law provided for wide-ranging 'scrutiny' by Parliament of security and intelligence work. In theory, this was supposed to prevent the security empire from stepping outside the limits of its competence; in practice, it simply consolidated the security empire's channels of communication with all parts of the Russian political spectrum. Since the security ministry made no apology for the fact that it continued to monitor and infiltrate the 'independent' political world, it was a fair assumption that many of the parliamentarians who were supposedly scrutinising the security system were themselves under the influence of that system, more controlled than controlling.

As a power struggle between the Yeltsin administration and the Russian Parliament intensified, each side competed for control over the security ministry and hence for access to the enormous power that it could still wield. This enabled the ministry to follow its own agenda without fear that anyone would try to abolish it.

The former KGB was not only an accomplished practitioner of legal formalism; it was uniquely placed to serve as both referee and player in another new game – that of market economics. The skills and infrastructure required to run a successful private business were to be found in the KGB: sophisticated internal communications systems, networks of people who could trust one another, personnel practised in dealing with foreigners, skilled in procuring information, including information about rivals, and in protecting commercial secrets.

Businesses which did not have those assets would have to buy them off the shelf from the only quarter where they were available. Leonid Shebarshin, the newly retired foreign espionage chief, set up a private consultancy called the National Economic Security Agency in which the skills of his *alma mater* were put out to hire.

Interviewed in his comfortable Moscow apartment in mid-1992, he explained the basic principles of his business with the affable ease of an American putting an idea to a friend at the golf club.

> Suppose you are a businessman in Russia, what do you require for your enterprise, bank or factory? First of all

you require that it is properly guarded, and we can give advice on how this should be done, or even find people to do it for you.

If you want to protect your commercial secrets, see to it that nobody listens to what you say, we can suggest measures which would preclude that possibility . . .

Security, like every other commodity in post-Soviet Russia, from burial plots to sex, was being commercialised; but that did not mean Shebarshin had forgotten about all other values besides lucre. He and his associates were also committed to reviving the Russian economy, and they believed that they were well placed to do so.

One of the greatest gifts to the security empire was the rediscovery of the hard reality that no Russian government, however liberal in its economic philosophy, could avoid regulating the export trade quite heavily. Here was another task that only the former KGB was qualified to perform, and by early autumn 1992, it was preening itself with delight over its new-found indispensability.

In late August, it was triumphantly announced that the 'security services had prevented the shipping out of the country of about 9 million tonnes of metal, including rare-earth and non-ferrous metals, and thirty-one tonnes of super-rare-earth metals that formed the basis of a number of strategic domestic industries.' All this was the happy result of a recent law 'freeing the state security bodies from everything that immobilised them until recently and giving them a free hand to work for the preservation of our national wealth.'

The Baltic states were identified as the main channel through which wild-cat exports were passing, and it was perfectly true that Estonia, which has few metal reserves of its own, had suddenly jumped to the top of the international league table as a metal exporter. By drawing attention to this phenomenon, the security ministry was able to blacken the image of the Baltic republics, which were already the object of Moscow's ire because of their treatment of Slav minorities. (In fact, beneficiaries of the metals trade through the Baltic ports included the Russian garrison and ethnic Russian businessmen.)

Shebarshin, a sophisticated veteran of postings in Iran and India who was in his mid-fifties but looked younger, epitomised the undiminished *esprit de corps* of the Russian political police as he explained his feelings about the later Soviet and post-Soviet worlds. He did not appear to have any dogmatic belief in communism, but he did believe in something else. Despite his ease of manner, which only betrayed the occasional hint of steel, he exuded a profound commitment to a Russian Imperial tradition which long predated the Soviet era and would long survive it. For all his chagrin over the demise of the Soviet Union, he took considerable comfort from the fact that he now lived in a state called Russia:

> I am Russian, and there is some consolation in the fact that I can say so openly. I feel perfectly alright as a citizen of Russia . . . Before it was not fashionable to say 'I am Russian'.

Shebarshin felt sure that 'the patriotic feeling of Russians is going to play a greater role in developments, a greater positive role'. Despite the appearance of disorder and social tension, the KGB officer had 'some inner feeling that things will be all right' for Russia. This patriotic hope was in contrast with the disdain he felt for the gushing internationalism of the Gorbachev years. He and his colleagues had tried to tell Gorbachev some home truths:

> You talk about all-human values, but everybody else thinks of his national interests. That ought to be the foundation of any sound policy, not all-human values. You are not Jesus Christ, so remember that charity begins at home.

That, curiously enough, was Yeltsin's slogan too – Russia first.

7
BUILDING POLITICAL EMPIRES

AS GAIDAR AND his friends were discovering, the reconstruction of the Russian state after a period of weakness has always required great ingenuity. The ruler is continuously obliged to tack, gybe and manoeuvre; buying off some opponents, goading others into unequal battles, avoiding direct clashes until the time and circumstances are exactly right.

A similar amount of flexibility and calculation is needed by any leader or faction that is bent on seizing the Kremlin from its incumbents. Would-be destroyers have to assemble their coalitions from the most unlikely mixture of sources, without ever forgetting that once their destructive purpose has been achieved, the coalition's constituent parts will almost certainly turn their destructive power on one another.

Boris Yeltsin displayed extraordinary coalition-building skill during the three years when he was preparing to wrest power from Mikhail Gorbachev and the Soviet Communist Party. From the very moment in late 1991 when he attained supreme authority, an even more diverse and opportunistic coalition started forming with the sole aim of ousting or neutralising him.

The ranks of the anti-Yeltsin coalition included committed atheists and devout religious believers; thugs and intellectuals; utopian communists, confused democrats and fascists; anarchists and authoritarians; past victims of political repression and past perpetrators of that repression. And right from the start, President Yeltsin dismayed many of his own admirers by his apparent indifference to the consortium of enemies that was massing against him. He consistently refused, for example, to put his personal weight and charisma behind the creation of any new political party which might have popularised government policies or countered the opposition's propaganda. He was also strangely reluctant to use the machinery of the law to call to order those opposition newspapers which stirred up hatred against ethnic minorities. Despite occasional threats, he was slow to restrain the growing number of rabble-rousing orators who, in public speeches, began calling for the armed forces to mutiny against the 'treachery' of the Yeltsin regime.

The impression that Yeltsin was oddly negligent in defending the newly captured, and still vulnerable, fortress of Russian democracy was confirmed by his erratic personal behaviour. From autumn 1991 onwards, he developed the alarming habit of disappearing from view for up to two weeks at a time, leaving his aides to explain why appointments had to be cancelled and government business postponed. Some said he was drunk or doting; sympathetic voices tried to explain these absences as a recurrence of the psychosomatic collapse which Yeltsin had suffered after his ejection from the Politburo in 1987.

This appearance of neglect strained the loyalty of those Yeltsin supporters who sincerely believed in the cause of Russian democracy, and assumed that he shared this belief. On the other hand, if that assumption is put aside, and Yeltsin is viewed as a politician with no fixed agenda except the protection and consolidation of his own power, then it is possible to discern a sort of perverse logic in the way he acted, or failed to act.

From Yeltsin's own point of view, it would have been a fatal mistake for him to identify too closely with one ideological camp or political faction. To remain the supreme arbiter of Russia's political development, it was vital to retain some freedom to manoeuvre: the ability to play one side off against the other, to distance himself where necessary from 'bad advisers' and select entirely new ones without compromising his own position as the 'father' of the nation.

As for Yeltsin's apparent slowness to fight back against mounting opposition, here too he had his reasons. It made absolute sense for him to hold back while the state machine, and the institution of the presidency, was still fragile; he could lose everything by playing his hand too early.

As long as that remained the case, his best tactic was to feign weakness or indifference and wait for an opportunity to pull off the ancient oriental trick of turning an opponent's strength to one's own advantage. This trick can be performed in various ways. Most obviously, any leader who is seen to be under threat from a horde of ruthless, vengeful adversaries can justify the taking of almost any measures to save himself – and by extension the peace of the nation and the world – from such deadly danger.

This useful state of affairs will only arise if the opposition is given the opportunity to grow big, ugly and self-confident enough to inspire real fear in the nation and the world. Once that happens, the ruler can do almost anything, employ almost any degree of force, break almost any number of rules, to save himself and the state. If that state becomes more authoritarian as a result, even the most idealistic and fair-minded of people can be relied on to say that there was no other choice.

If the opposition does not grow menacing and ugly of its own accord, then well-tried methods of stimulating this process are available to any master of the Kremlin who wants to use them. Since Tsarist times, Russia's political police has led the world in the art of provocation: meddling in opposition politics with the aim of promoting outrageous, but ultimately controllable, agitators and discrediting sincere campaigners for change.

The Tsarist security police, known as the Okhrana, developed the extraordinary technique of cloning, or manufacturing, tame versions of the trade unions or protest movements which they were supposed to be suppressing.

Police-sponsored opposition and the real thing looked

almost identical, except that the former could always be manipulated by its creators: in other words, discreetly encouraged to raise its voice, stoke political tension, or else relapse into silence, depending on the requirements of the moment.

As well as creating their own opposition movements – a technique that was brilliantly elaborated by the Okhrana's Moscow boss, Sergei Zubatov – the Tsarist police could interfere in the affairs of existing ones by fomenting splits and promoting this or that faction.

In the land of Zubatov, the stand-off between rulers and opposition will never be a simple sort of see-saw, in which the success of one side implies the failure of the other; any regime which hopes to survive has to be present, as it were, on both sides of the see-saw. Russian analysts, faced with any form of political opposition, instinctively ask themselves a question which does not occur so readily to their Western counterparts: is the movement really working to take power from the nation's rulers, or is it playing – consciously or unconsciously – into the rulers' hands?

In 1992, the first full year of the new Russian state's existence, it was probably not necessary for Yeltsin to make frequent recourse to the more machiavellian methods available for conjuring up an extremist opposition. The forces of irreconcilable opposition were gathering momentum of their own accord, and instead of hitting them too early and overplaying his hand, the President had every interest in simply letting them ripen to the point where they could be demonised and destroyed. This does not mean that his apparent slackness and neglect always reflected self-conscious calculation, but these failings were not as disastrous as they appeared.

As for Yeltsin's periodic disappearing acts, they did not do his political fortunes any harm at all. Russian rulers are not American Presidents whose every dental appointment and round of golf has to be relayed in meticulous detail to the public. Caprice and unpredictability had always been the prerogatives of the Kremlin's masters, and they helped to sustain an atmosphere of mystery and fear. Every time the master vanished from sight, his subjects recalled their ancient fear of anarchy; every time he returned, they remembered their dependence on a father with a fist of iron.

So the President's admirers were missing the point, or simply misunderstanding his purpose, when they accused him of faint-heartedness in defence of the new democratic order: first because he had no immutable attachment to that order, or any other ideology, and second because Yeltsin would have doomed himself to early political oblivion if he had relied entirely on the democrats' dwindling ranks.

Between 1988 and mid-1991, when he was staking out a position as the effective leader of the Soviet opposition, Yeltsin had forged a strong partnership with the liberal reformers of Moscow and Leningrad. Yet this proved nothing about his deepest personal convictions, which were unfathomable and in the final analysis irrelevant; and it proved everything about his coalition-building skill.

Even the most passionate admirers of Yeltsin the reformer would be hard pressed to detect anything recognisable as a commitment to liberal democracy in his bitter, rambling resignation speech of 1987, when he was forced out of the Politburo. Indeed, there is still a mystery about who exactly was responsible for leaking Yeltsin's words to the press; one theory holds that it was distributed by provincial conservatives who saw in Yeltsin a possible counter-weight to Gorbachev's liberal pretensions.

If that is the case, the conservatives were – at least for the next five years or so – badly disappointed. Yeltsin's well-tuned instincts told him that the late 1980s, when the decay of the Soviet project was perceptible in every shabby building and potholed road, was not the right time to be playing the conservative card.

So he chose a different strategy: by making himself the standard-bearer of the Moscow intelligentsia, and overcoming their mistrust of his boorish, provincial manners, he tapped into the skills and energy of one of the most articulate and dynamic sections of society; a group whose influence and self-confidence were rising on the tide of reform, and whose presentational skills would be indispensable at a time when Russia's most urgent need was to step back from confrontation with the West.

But Yeltsin never merged his identity with his new friends; he still went to the bathhouse with trusted old cronies from Sverdlovsk, or his chief bodyguard, Aleksandr Korzhakov.

New evidence of Yeltsin's coalition-making genius was displayed in 1990 when he revived the Russian Federation as a political entity and a power base for himself. By securing the leadership of the largest of the fifteen Soviet republics, Yeltsin had placed himself in a sort of alliance – however temporary or artificial – with the leaders of fourteen other republics, as they pressed Gorbachev's central Soviet government to surrender more and more power. For the eighteen months prior to the Soviet Union's final collapse in December 1991, Yeltsin stuck to the principle of 'all [or almost all] power to the republics' with great tenacity.

Under Yeltsin's guidance, the whole Russian democratic movement came to swallow the idea that it was hardly possible for the republics to have too many rights, or the Union authorities too few. Some democrats accepted this principle on the moral ground that the republics were entitled to decide their own future – in those days, idealism was still in fashion. Others, with greater foresight, saw that Russia had more to gain from a break-up of the Union than any other republic, so that a temporary divorce might actually reinforce Russia's ability to impose its will on its neighbours.

For at least a year or so, nationalists from the Soviet republics came to see Yeltsin as their ally, and demonstrations of the pro-Yeltsin democratic movement in Moscow were never complete without the flags of Estonia, Latvia or Ukraine dotted among the sea of Russian tricolours.

Inside the Russian mainstream, Yeltsin tapped into two very different impulses as he built up support for his campaign against the Soviet communist regime. These two sentiments could, and often did, coexist within the same person, but they ran in diametrically opposing directions, and the difference between them was obvious when one looked at individuals who embodied one or other of these impulses in relatively pure form.

There was one small, idealistic group of people – the human rights campaigners and civil libertarians – whose hatred of communism was fuelled by the fact that this doctrine had, at its peak, helped to make the Russian state very strong. In the world of Andrei Sakharov and his fellow dissidents, there was an instinctive suspicion of the ideal of a powerful nation. People in that milieu judged by the evidence of history that any powerful Russian state would mistreat its own subjects and behave aggressively towards other countries. Many of this group were members of ethnic minorities, whose sentiments were informed by family stories of the Ukrainian famine, the annexation of the Baltic states or the anti-Semitic furies unleashed by Stalin.

At the same time, Yeltsin appealed to another, much larger group of people who were turning against the Soviet system for the opposite reason: because, in its recent decadent, half-hearted form, it had become an obstacle to Russian strength. Any competent scientist, industrial manager or military man could see that the country was now failing in its self-imposed task of keeping up with the West, and that the old men in the communist Politburo were the last people who could correct that failure.

The first school of thought hated the Soviet regime because it was cruel; the other did not have a fundamental objection to cruelty, but resented the fact that the regime was incompetent, and was therefore presiding over a disastrous decline in the Soviet Union's position in the world.

Precisely because the Soviet leadership in its final years was both inhumane *and* incompetent, it was bound to be attacked for both these failings; and one of the hallmarks of Yeltsin's rhetoric was the blurring of any distinction between these two critiques. The hundreds of thousands of Muscovites who were prepared to demonstrate for Yeltsin – even when there was a risk of skulls being cracked – included some who longed for freedom from authoritarianism, others who simply wanted their country to be strong again, and perhaps an even greater number who were swayed by both considerations.

The difference between these two sources of dissent is emphasised when a nation faces the possibility of rule that is harsh but economically efficient. In late Soviet Russia, no such option was anywhere in sight. The rulers who imprisoned poets and sent dissidents to psychiatric wards were also guilty of appalling economic mismanagement.

The communist system was failing to meet that criterion by which any ideology, technique and organising principle will stand or fall in Russia: its effectiveness in accumulating, husbanding and consolidating the nation's strength. Among the people who sensed that most strongly were the defence industry bosses who teamed up with Mayor Sobchak in St Petersburg, and the cream of the country's academic economists, epitomised by Yegor Gaidar.

Another category of people who had felt Soviet Russia's weakness acutely were the officers who had fought in Afghanistan. Their experience had made them extremely resentful of a Soviet leadership which had miscalculated the odds when it entered the war, pursued it with incompetence and finally left themselves with no choice but to order a humiliating retreat. Contempt for the old guard was especially pronounced in the élite sections of the Soviet armed forces, whose training and ethos led them to take a dim view of incompetence. In this category were officers of the Airborne Division like Pavel Grachev, whose spectacular operation to relieve the city of Khost in 1987 was rendered pointless a few weeks later by Moscow's announcement that it was pulling out; and his deputy Aleksandr Lebed, who was said to have bellowed battle orders from one end of a canyon to another after his radio equipment failed.

The Afghan veterans were certainly no liberals; theirs was a world where prisoners were tossed over cliffs, or shot in cold blood to give the soldiers some target practice. Nor were they lovers of the West, whose Stinger missiles had claimed the lives of so many of their comrades; but they did acquire a healthy disrespect for the old men in the Kremlin, and in the upper echelons of the defence establishment, who had sent them to Afghanistan.

Yeltsin was appealing to this constituency when – in one of his boldest coalition-making moves – he announced that the former bomber pilot Colonel Aleksandr Rutskoy would be his running mate for the presidential elections of June 1991. Many of the pro-democracy activists who by that time surrounded Yeltsin were astonished by his choice.

Rutskoy was a wild, unpredictable soldier who had exasperated the *zampoliti*, the political and moral watch-dogs of the armed forces, with his recklessness in Afghanistan. Twice – in 1986 and 1988 – he was shot down and had to eject. On the first occasion, he suffered back injuries and had to subject himself to gruelling exercises before returning to the air. On his second tour of duty, he was senior enough to avoid flying altogether, but he insisted on leading sorties deeper and deeper into the territory of the mujahedin, swooping low over their encampments in an effort to draw their fire.

After his second ejection, he was held prisoner in Pakistan. According to Moscow's official story, he had been hit by a Pakistani fighter, but it seems more likely that he was simply downed by rebel anti-aircraft fire, and Moscow found it too embarrassing to admit that someone so senior had been so careless.

It was a disaster for Moscow that such a senior pilot should be in Pakistani hands, and after some hectic negotiations, he was released, and in due course made a Hero of the Soviet Union. In reality, however, there was not much love lost between Rutskoy and his commanders.

Rutskoy entered politics as the gruff voice of the aggrieved generation of war veterans, returning to a country where militarism had gone out of fashion and any idea that Soviet forces in Afghanistan were performing their 'internationalist duty' had become a sick joke. He became deputy head of a movement called *Otechestvo* (Fatherland) whose other activists included old-fashioned communists, religious nationalists and some campaigners for the revival of paganism.

Rutskoy had never been much of a communist himself and certainly was no theoretician. He was a communist in the automatic way that an earlier generation of British officers in Afghanistan had all – with widely varying degrees of personal conviction – been members of the Church of England. At unexpected moments, he used to blurt out the homespun basics of military science as though he were saying something important and original: 'First, you must identify your goal; then you must assess the means available to reach that goal; then you must make a plan.'

Neither the Marxist theory of dialectical materialism nor any other kind of dialectics were much in his line; he resented intellectual acrobats like Gennady Burbulis or Otto Latsis, the respected journalist and former editor of the journal *Kommunist*, who had once been clever Marxists and were now clever anti-Marxists. With his handsome, stocky figure, bulging blue eyes and luxuriant moustache, Rutskoy had a fantastic innocence about him. He also carried round – apparently as a result of some vision or mystical experience in Afghanistan – a quiet conviction that he was destined to play an important role in the history of Russia.

Rutskoy made his first, unsuccessful, attempt to enter national politics during the historic election campaign of 1989, when Yeltsin scored a triumphant victory after campaigning alongside Andrei Sakharov on a platform of democracy and reform.

Rutskoy's campaign manager was a certain Colonel Valery Burkov, who was asked at a voters' meeting what he thought of the doyen of the human rights movement. His reply was short and to the point: 'I'd like to hang that Sakharov.'

This helps to convey the audacity of Yeltsin's move in selecting Rutskoy as his presidential running mate in mid-1991. On one hand, Yeltsin was still a good enough democrat to appeal to the disciples of Sakharov, who had died in December 1989 but remained a guiding light for the Russian reform movement; on the other hand, Yeltsin was drawing into his coalition people who would have killed Sakharov if they had had the chance.

These differences were briefly forgotten during the three rainy days in August when the Russian leadership was boxed into the White House, and it seemed that the building might be stormed by the forces loyal to the new junta.

Rutskoy bustled about the Parliament building, organising volunteers and overseeing the construction of barricades. When a Western television interviewer approached him, he joyfully waved his pistol in the air and declared that he would settle personally with the elderly conspirators who were giving the army such a bad name. If necessary, he would save the last bullet for himself.

Yet any sense of camaraderie between Rutskoy and the other members of the Yeltsin team dissolved very soon after they began taking up the reins of government. Gennady Burbulis, in particular, was contemptuous of Rutskoy's intellectual shortcomimgs, and he did not try to hide his feelings. Burbulis saw to it that Rutskoy was given a small personal staff, and very little to do. In a hapless outburst that caused a great deal of cruel laughter, Rutskoy is said to have pleaded with his rival: 'Genna, let's work things out.'

In early 1992, as Rutskoy became much bolder in criticising Gaidar's economic policy and denouncing the break-up of the Soviet Union, the crafty Burbulis thought of an ingenious way to distract his rival: Rutskoy must be given formal responsibility for reforming Russian agriculture. 'I'm bored with seeing that man pacing up and down the corridor smoking cigarettes', Burbulis had sneered.

A more devious figure would have refused the poisoned cup of answering for this virtually unreformable sector, but Rutskoy duly accepted, and in due course he served up some worthy tomes on the subject of Russian farming.

The Vice-President felt doubly abandoned because Yeltsin hardly bothered to call him, and he was touchingly pleased on the rare occasions when the head of state did make contact. Galina Starovoitova, Yeltsin's tutor in democratic thinking, remembers sitting in Rutskoy's office in early 1992 and watching him almost stand to attention as he received a long-awaited telephone call from his superior. 'Yes, Boris

Nikolayevich', the Vice-President repeated, again and again, like a soldier to his commander. He politely asked the President if he might attend the funeral of a brother officer in the northern Caucasus, and was told that he could, as long as he did not get involved in local politics or address any political meetings; the condition was meekly accepted.

Starovoitova formed the private conclusion that Rutskoy's willingness to fall in with the instructions of strong characters might prove very dangerous. If Yeltsin's neglect drove Rutskoy into outright opposition, the bomber pilot could become an instrument in the hands of very sinister forces. Her foreboding was, of course, borne out only too well.

Eighteen months later, in autumn 1993, Yeltsin and Rutskoy found themselves on opposite sides in a miniature civil war, which culminated in the shelling and seizure of the Russian Parliament where Rutskoy had proclaimed himself head of state.

As he crushed the forces of his rebellious deputy, Yeltsin asked the world to believe that he had made a fateful, yet somehow pardonable, mistake when he chose the air force officer as his running mate.

Was Rutskoy really such a mistake, from Yeltsin's point of view? Any person with Yeltsin's strong, intuitive sense of the realities of political power would have realised from an early stage that whoever walked beside him on his path to supreme office was almost bound, sooner or later, to turn into a rival. Perhaps, at some level, Yeltsin sensed that if some showdown was inevitable, Rutskoy was the right sort of enemy to have: blustering, impulsive, lacking in guile, easy to foil.

The coolness between Yeltsin and Rutskoy cast one shadow over the political landscape of the new Russian state; another ominous sign was the rapid disintegration of the ramshackle but effective coalition of small anti-communist parties which had propelled both men to electoral victory.

The bloc, known as Democratic Russia, included most of the President's most energetic political supporters, though not, of course, his friends in other quarters like the army and the air force. The coalition split apart one freezing weekend in November 1991, at an ill-tempered two-day conference in the central Moscow cinema where the movement had often convened in its glory days to map out its next move against the communists.

Instead of rejoicing over their newly won victory, the democrats found themselves bickering dispiritedly. The enemy had apparently been slain. The Communist Party had been banned and its property confiscated; various tiers of government – national, regional, municipal – were squabbling furiously over who exactly was entitled to the lion's share of the spoils. Half a dozen small groups of dedicated communists were struggling to keep the flame alive, but at that point they did not seem to have any chance of making a come-back.

So there should have been grounds for celebration, and an exchange of constructive ideas on how the new Russia might be built. But Russian politicians, even in those relatively enlightened circles, generally defined themselves in relation to their enemies. Projects of construction would rarely be enough to hold disparate forces together, unless there was somebody cracking the whip from above. Thus the Democratic Russia coalition was doomed to split from the moment its communist enemy expired.

The main catalyst for this divorce was the row between liberals and nationalists over policy towards the non-Russian republics; and in this dispute the contrast between advocates of a strong Russia, and those who were instinctively nervous of that idea, was all too clear.

In the days when it was more or less united in the struggle against communism, the alliance had attracted some of the country's most intelligent and vigorous personalities. It had evolved from a handful of poorly co-ordinated agitators into the first Russia-wide organisation for seventy years that was more or less independent of the Soviet establishment. Yeltsin's election victory in June 1991, which was achieved in defiance of a Communist Party machine which still wielded enormous power in the provinces, was a formidable political feat, perhaps the last great achievement of the amateur style of electioneering that was pioneered in Leningrad and Moscow in the late 1980s.

Before the August coup, Democratic Russia had formed one end of a political spectrum which was easy enough to describe, even if some individuals were hard to place. At one extreme, there were the old-fashioned communists who wanted to bolster the power of the central Soviet authorities, the army and the KGB, to curb the republics' drive for independence, preserve the planned economy and go slow on 'unpatriotic' concessions to the West in foreign policy and arms control.

At the opposite end, broadly occupied by Democratic Russia, there were reformists and liberals who stood for multi-party democracy in politics, a conciliatory stance on foreign policy, free enterprise in economics, curbing the security forces, and upholding the power of the republics.

The dramatic failure of the August coup appeared to herald a victory beyond anyone's wildest dreams for the second camp. But it was not a triumph which could be savoured, because it prompted a horrified sense among many democrats and their supporters, that the pendulum had been allowed to swing too far: so far, in fact, that the very existence of the Russian state seemed to be in question.

As long as the central Soviet authority existed, the slogan of 'all power to the republics' was an axiom for Yeltsin and his followers. However, as soon as the republics attained this power, any notion that all fifteen of them were partners in a single enterprise – that of squeezing the 'centre' – vanished overnight.

Right in the middle of the August 1991 drama, before the outcome was absolutely clear, this point was driven home by an announcement from the barricaded White House which horrified Russia's neighbours: the new Russian state would reserve the right to make territorial claims against any of its neighbours which decided not to join the new confederation, commonwealth or other entity that succeeded the Soviet Union.

This could only be a signal that Russia intended to seize

back from its neighbours such desirable real-estate as Crimea, which had been transferred to Ukraine in 1954; the Russian-speaking areas of northern Kazakhstan, at the southern end of the Urals; or conceivably the Russian-speaking city of Narva in eastern Estonia.

The furore that followed the communiqué from the White House died down after Rutskoy went to assure the leaders of Ukraine and Kazakhstan that Russia would not be pressing any territorial claims for the foreseeable future.

Nevertheless pro-Yeltsin politicians rapidly began reassessing their attitude to the smaller republics. They faced a tricky problem formulating their policy towards the republics of Georgia and Moldova, whose governments were locked in armed stand-off with Russian or pro-Russian minorities. In both these states, nationalist governments had been punished for their zeal in the cause of independence by the mysterious outbreak of local rebellions which enjoyed strong support from the Soviet government. Fomenting these miniature rebellions had been one of the main weapons used by the crumbling Soviet leadership as it tried to stop the republics seceding.

Even if they acknowledged that the Soviet regime was playing dirty tricks on the outer fringes of the empire, many of Yeltsin's democrats baulked at supporting the governments of Georgia and Moldova, which they accused of reproducing in microcosm some of the less attractive features of the Soviet system.

The Georgian leader, an eccentric man of letters and ex-dissident called Zviad Gamsakhurdia, was a particularly dubious figure in the eyes of Russian liberals. In 1978 he had secured his freedom from the KGB by recanting on television and denouncing two American journalists. He said afterwards that he made this recantation with the assent of Merab Kostava, a respected Georgian dissident who died in a mysterious car accident as the independence movement was gathering pace.

A small character with bulging eyes and a neat silver moustache, Gamsakhurdia – like his citizens – was tragically, even childishly, deficient in political judgement. He had some personal grievances against the world: although he had translated some serious English literature into Georgian, he appeared to be deeply resentful of the fact that he had never matched the literary or intellectual status of his novelist father, Konstantin Gamsakhurdia. His rhetoric capitalised on one of his people's collective grievances: the fact that the Soviet regime – as part of an intricate system of checks and balances – had given enhanced political and cultural rights to the ethnic minorities within the republic. Gamsakhurdia promised that in future, Georgia would be for ethnic Georgians. At one point, he suggested confining the vote to those people whose ancestors had lived in the territory before 1801, when it joined the Russian empire.

Gamsakhurdia's fiery speeches could drive to delirium the crowds of admirers who used to gather, on one sultry evening after another, before the arches of Tbilisi's government building. He ranted furiously about the 'tens of thousands of agents of the Kremlin' who were thwarting his drive for independence. However, he played right into the Kremlin's hands by rising instantly to the provocations and local disturbances that Moscow devised.

The collapse of the August 1991 coup gave the leaders of all the ex-Soviet republics the chance to settle local scores. President Mircea Snegur of Moldova gleefully arrested Igor Smirnov, the head of the Russian-speakers in the east of the republic who had proclaimed their own, Moscow-supported statelet. The Georgians redoubled their shelling of Tskhinvali, a once prosperous mountain town which was the headquarters of a rebellion by the Ossetians, a staunchly pro-Russian minority.

The fall-out from the August *putsch* in Georgia was particularly bizarre. It turned out that senior figures in Gamsakhurdia's supposedly freedom-loving government were close to the Soviet hard-liners who instigated the August coup. This ensured that Georgia offered no resistance to the *putsch*; but as soon as the conspiracy in Moscow failed, Gamsakhurdia began to lose power to an armed coalition which had close friends in the Yeltsin camp. All this was symptomatic of the fact that, beneath their furiously nationalist slogans, Georgia's internal battles were often a proxy for power struggles in Moscow.

Gamsakhurdia's populist, anti-élitist tone had struck a chord among those Georgians who had missed out on the corrupt, prosperous and hedonistic world created in their republic by its previous ruler, Eduard Shevardnadze. But the flourishing and precociously talented intelligentsia of Tbilisi had spread the word to its counterpart in Moscow that Gamsakhurdia, despite his own origins, was a crude, heavy-handed and philistine ruler. Few tears were shed in the salons of Moscow when Gamsakhurdia was forced to flee from his underground bunker in the besieged government building, after two grim weeks of shelling which nearly destroyed the historic centre of Tbilisi.

Russia's democrats should have thought harder about the dark precedent that was being set by the shelling of a parliament building, and the violent overthrow of an elected leader. The cultured shrug of the shoulders that followed Gamsakhurdia's demise was an ominous portent for democracy in Russia itself.

Far from fretting over Gamsakhurdia's defeat, many of Yeltsin's democrats shuddered over the fact that a figure like Gamsakhurdia had ever been able to come to power: clearly they had gone too far in conjuring up the republican demon as a weapon against the Soviet regime. Now that the hated centre was rapidly fading from the horizon, it was time for Russia to redress the balance and call its fellow republics to order.

Hence the split in Russia's pro-Yeltsin coalition. An emerging nationalist camp said Russia should stand by its traditional friends, the Ossetians, in the face of 'genocide' by the Georgians, and should also support Prednestrovia, the Russian-speaking statelet on the east bank of the Dnestr River, against the Romanian nationalists who had taken control of Moldova.

Another emotive issue in the winter of 1991 was pressure from some of the autonomous republics within Russia for greater or even total independence. Dzhokhar Dudayev, a former Soviet air force general, had proclaimed his own state after conducting unauthorised elections among the Chechens, the most militant of the warrior races of the northern Caucasus. Tatarstan, another oil-producing territory with a Muslim heritage, was threatening to declare an independent state in central Russia.

Old war-horses of the Moscow democratic movement like Gavriil Popov, the mayor, and Yuri Afanasyev, the iconoclastic historian, insisted that these territories should be given at least one chance to decide whether they wanted to belong to Russia or not. Nationalist figures like Viktor Aksyuchits and Mikhail Astafyev retorted that not an inch of Russian soil should be given up: the break-up of the Soviet Union was proving bad enough already.

It was these national questions, rather than constitutional or economic issues, which created the split in the pro-Yeltsin movement on that sombre weekend in November 1991.

Supporters of the coalition's nationalist wing called on the entire bloc to unite around a new, more nationalist programme. This would urge the government to use all its weight to support the rights of Russian-speaking and pro-Russian minorities in the smaller republics; it would call for fresh efforts to stitch together a full-blooded federation that would cover as much as possible of the territory of the Soviet Union, and would rule out any breaching of the territorial integrity of Russia.

Having failed to persuade the movement as a whole to endorse this platform, about half the delegates walked out of the conference hall.

The activists who were left behind shook their heads in dismay at the 'imperialist' thinking which the walk-out signified. They wanted the movement to concentrate on demands closer to home, including the swift and fair privatisation of housing, businesses and land, without too much rigging of the process in favour of the old élite. They were more worried by the danger of creeping fascism than by the disintegration of the Russian state.

Yet there was an irony here. Of the two wings of the disintegrating democratic movement, one wanted the swiftest possible action to restore Russia's ability to dictate terms to the republics, while the other professed indifference to that issue. Yet it was the latter camp – the camp which wanted Russia to concentrate on reforming its own economy – which performed the best service for the cause of Russian imperialism.

For Russia, the best hope of regaining leverage over the republics did not lie in the use of bully-boy tactics, such as backing the pro-Russian side in local wars; it lay in the pursuit of rational economic policies which would enable Russia to realise its potential strength.

For those Georgians, Balts and Ukrainians who knew their history, the advent of a more nationalist tone in Moscow's political debate gave them an ominous feeling of *déjà vu*. Could this be the second time this century that a Russian opposition movement had used the aspirations of the empire's subject nations as a battering ram to bring the one regime down, only to reinstate the spirit of imperialism once they were in power?

The Bolsheviks, after all, had pronounced themselves in favour of self-determination for all the nations which had laboured under the Tsar and yet, in the end, they had practised Russification more ruthlessly than any Tsar. Stalin himself, the Georgian cobbler's son who could never quite master Russian case endings, personified the communists' journey from friend of the subject nations to masters of the Russian empire.

In 1913, as a young revolutionary on his way to visit Lenin in Cracow, Stalin had, by his own account, compared notes on the cruelty of the Russian empire with a Polish shoemaker who helped to spirit him across the border. Having established that both men came from places with 'plenty of Tsarist gendarmes and no schools in our own tongue' the shoe-maker refused all payment on the grounds that 'sons of oppressed nations should help one another'.

For a few weeks – no more than a few weeks – after the

Bolsheviks seized power in 1917, Stalin appeared to uphold this sentiment. He was a co-signatory with Lenin of the 'declaration of the rights of the peoples of Russia' which was one of the first pronouncements by the victorious Bolsheviks. It guaranteed the subject nations 'free self-determination, even to the point of separating and forming national states'.

Very soon, however, this spirit of fraternity was fading. Just as Catherine the Great had proclaimed herself the protectress of all the Orthodox Christian subjects of Austria and Turkey, revolutionary Petrograd asserted the right to intervene in smaller nations' affairs in the name of the proletariat; and this proved to be an equally effective alibi for imperialism.

In December 1917, Stalin was still insisting, despite the objections of some of his comrades, that the Russian territory of Finland must be allowed full independence, even under a non-socialist government. The following month, with Ukraine in mind, he was arguing that 'the principle of self-determination . . . ought to be subordinated to the principles of socialism'.

As the Civil War intensified, there was an even bigger volte-face in Stalin's attitude to the Islamic peoples of central Russia and central Asia. The Bolsheviks' White enemies were insisting doggedly on the principle of a united and indivisible Russia and this gave Stalin the perfect opportunity to play on the hopes and fears of the empire's Muslim subjects, who were allowed to form a separate Muslim Communist Party and promised the right to establish a large Muslim republic in the Russian heartland.

As soon as the Reds felt confident of victory in the Civil War, these concessions were reversed. The ailing Lenin, observing the ruthless way in which Stalin dealt with questions of nationality, commented famously that his comrade was sliding into Great Russian chauvinism.

The defeated Whites, from their places of exile in China, France and Germany, also observed Stalin's brutal treatment of the empire's unruly subjects, and some of them had to admit that they liked what they saw. The communists' devious, zig-zagging – or to use their sort of language, dialectical – approach had proved more effective in rebuilding the Russian empire than the dogged, simple-minded insistence on a 'single and undivided' fatherland which was the rallying cry of the Whites.

So Russian imperialists with a proper sense of history should not have been unduly alarmed, at the end of 1991, by either the incorrigible impudence of the newly independent republics, or the unsatisfactory borders with which the Russian Federation found itself: there was plenty of evidence from the past to suggest that the most energetic dismantlers of an empire could also be the most ruthless rebuilders.

8

National Salvation: Yeltsin's Enemies Assemble

FEW THINGS ILLUSTRATE the weakness and shallowness of Russia's pro-democracy coalition so vividly as the thoughtless haste with which many of its leading members jumped into the new alliance of communists and nationalists which took shape in early 1992.

In December 1991, the furtive meeting in the forest between the leaders of Russia, Ukraine and Byelorussia, and the death certificate they issued for the Soviet Union, seemed to confirm the darkest forebodings of those nationalist politicians who had marched out of the Democratic Russia conference a month earlier.

Activists like Mikhail Astafyev – whose previous political career had been devoted to denouncing the 'Bolshevik *coup d'état*' of 1917 – moved rapidly and without embarrassment into a new coalition with some of the neo-communist factions who were struggling to recover from the ban imposed on them by Yeltsin.

'I will forgive the communists everything if they restore the state which the democrats have destroyed', Astafyev exclaimed, making plain his view – and it became an increasingly common view – that all the misdeeds of the Soviet regime were a secondary matter compared with the terrible disaster which has just befallen Russia, namely the break-up of the Union.

For Astafyev, these misdeeds lay not merely in the repression and slaughter of tens of millions of people, but also the blunders made by the Soviet regime in the handling of Russia's state interests, which he regarded as numerous and grave. If he was serious about 'forgiving the communists everything' this was remarkable indeed since there was a great deal to forgive, in his view.

Given that he took such a harsh view of the communists' record in office, it is doubly remarkable that he and his kind should have looked to the emerging neo-communists as partners in the struggle to rebuild the Russian state. Yet one of the things that made this new 'red-brown' alliance possible was the rethinking that was going on in the Marxist camp: the rump communists were devising a new version of their own history which played up the empire-building achievements of Stalin and played down the internationalist ideals of Lenin and Marx. Communists of this hue did not have to think twice about their attitude to the break-up of the Soviet Union; they realised at once that it must be denounced as a national disaster, and be used as an opportunity for their party to regain power.

Yet Astafyev and the White Russian revivalists had an easier time of it than the communists when it came to formulating a critique of the Soviet Union's collapse. For the old-fashioned nationalists, Lenin's signature of the Brest-Litovsk Treaty, with its enormous concessions to Germany, was incontrovertible proof that the entire Bolshevik take-over was an exercise in betrayal, cynically financed by the Kaiser. Further evidence of the Reds' treacherous intentions towards the nation was provided later by the 'Bolshevik borders' with which the Soviet regime had endowed the Russian Federation – giving away the Cossack country south of the Urals to Kazakhstan, and as of 1954, granting Crimea to Ukraine. Worse still was the Bolsheviks' decision to allow the Soviet republics – however notionally or theoretically – a constitutional right to secede from the Union. But it was the deal at Brest-Litovsk which first exposed Lenin and Trotsky in their true colours as traitors who would stab Russia in the back.

To anyone who took this one dimensional view of twentieth-century history, it was easy to prove that the new version of Brest-Litovsk – sealed by Yeltsin in December 1991 – was an equally unmitigated disaster, representing the logical outcome of the Bolsheviks' multiple acts of betrayal. The impudent subject nations, exploiting the culpable negligence of the Bolshevik constitution-drafters, had exercised their right to leave the empire, taking with them lands for which rivers of Russian blood had been shed.

Apart from the noisy nationalist orators of post-Soviet politics, a more sophisticated version of this Slavophile critique of the Soviet era had already been advanced by Aleksandr Solzhenitsyn. In the autumn of 1990, he made his ringing appeal, from exile in the United States, for the construction of a new Slavic superstate that would include Russia, Byelorussia, northern Kazakhstan and at least eastern Ukraine. Only by divesting herself of the 'alien' territories of Turkestan and Transcaucasia, and by reincorporating the parts of Kazakhstan and Ukraine which had been artificially disconnected from Russia by Bolsheviks, could the nation begin recovering from the spiritual, cultural and ecological ruin wrought by Lenin and his heirs. Being a man of principle who stood above the fray of post-Soviet politics, Solzhenitsyn could not embrace the view that neo-communists were the most promising allies in the struggle to undo the damage which the country had suffered when the Communist Party of the Soviet Union was in power.

Astafyev, on the other hand, had no scruples about seeking allies among his erstwhile communist enemies; nor did many of his nationalist soul mates. In provincial towns all over Russia, where the number of people who were prepared to agitate in public for any cause was rarely more than a few hundred, the noisiest members of the local pro-Yeltsin movement were often the first to follow Astafyev's lead into the ranks of the hardline opposition.

The complaint of these angry folk was that by letting the republics break free, Yeltsin had thrown out the baby of Greater Russia with the dirty bathwater of communism. All other issues paled into insignificance before the sacred imperative of restoring that statehood, and the duty lay most heavily on those who bore the responsibility of having supported Yeltsin in the first place.

Typical of the petulant souls who made this journey was Ilya Konstantinov, one of the leading lights in the Leningrad pro-democracy movement in the late 1980s. According to colleagues who remember him from that period, there was little to distinguish that burly, black-bearded figure from the other angry young products of Leningrad University who turned the city into a bastion of reform – except that he hopped with unusual frequency from one embryonic party to another, and his intellectual accomplishments were rather modest. Before his election to the Russian Parliament, he was working in the boiler room of a power-station.

Yet by 1992, he had emerged as one of the most vociferous, sharp-tongued figures in the nationalist camp – and he frankly admitted that he was better at making rabble-rousing speeches than the tedious business of drafting laws.

Other early activists in Leningrad's pro-democracy movement made even more dramatic transformations. One extreme example was a former policeman called Yuri Belayev who, having made the acquaintance of an elderly political science teacher who published the works of Hitler as a hobby, became a sort of ultra-nationalist godfather who recruited volunteers to fight in Serbia and the many war zones on Russia's periphery.

Faced with this sort of fluctuating loyalty, one is always tempted to ask whether the people in question had a hidden agenda right from the start. But most of the time, the transition from democratic slogans to nationalist ones reflected the psychological make-up of the restless, non-conformist souls who were attracted to the anti-communist movement in the first place. This cast of mind was well summed up by the Greek Prime Minister, George Papandreou, when he confessed that 'power bores me, only struggle interests me'.

There was no place for malcontents like Konstantinov in the complex and often sordid business of post-communist government; and for those people whose peculiar calling is to denounce the appalling state of what is, and fantasise wildly about what might be, there was no shortage of things to criticise in Russia's new state of affairs.

In the time-honoured way of Russian politics, the ex-democrats were absolutely single-minded in their focus on the enemy – which was now constituted by Yeltsin, Gaidar and the builders of the new Russian economy – and very careless in their choice of friends. They could ill afford such carelessness. A strategist like Yeltsin could make tactical alliances with persons or forces whose purposes diverged sharply from his own – in the confidence that useful fools could always be discarded. But the ex-democrats who ran so feverishly into the arms of the neo-communists were not of that calibre; they were always more likely to be used than users. As things turned out, they were doubly exploited – not only by their neo-communist allies, but also by a Yeltsin administration that was looking for an enemy to demonise.

A different, but perhaps related, sort of laxity began to afflict some of the democrats who remained at Yeltsin's side: people like the dissident priest Father Gleb Yakunin; the human rights activist Lev Ponomaryov; and the Marxist turned civil libertarian Sergei Yushenkov.

As they observed the anti-Yeltsin coalition gathering strength, they began urging the President to take decisive action against his adversaries: to suspend Parliament, declare a state of emergency and purge the security forces. It was easy to understand why some of these high-minded characters felt as they did. They knew that the hardline opposition would show them no mercy if it ever wrested power from Yeltsin, as every day of 'democratic' rule made the opposition's thirst for revenge more keen.

The reformers, therefore, looked nervously to the brute strength of their President as the only thing which might – assuming he bothered to use it – be able to protect them. But they did not stop to reflect, as deeply as they should have done, about the consequences of Yeltsin cracking down on his adversaries. They did not think, as hard as they ought to have done, about the sort of people who would gain influence in the event of Yeltsin turning authoritarian: certainly not saviours of democracy, or friends of the democrats.

Among the activists who abandoned the pro-Yeltsin coalition, there was one who refused to enter fully into an unholy alliance with the communists: Viktor Aksyuchits, an eternal gadfly with a mane of wavy black hair and political ideas that seemed, on the face of things, to correspond rather well to the spirit of the times in newly independent Russia. His ideas were a combination of free-market capitalism, Orthodox Christianity and liberal democracy.

In the late 1980s, he had been fêted in the London *Times* as the 'first Soviet millionaire' – an accolade which was typical of those days, when all forms of opposition to communism, from hunger strikes to the accumulation of private wealth, were cast in the same heroic light.

Unlike many of the glib orators of post-Soviet politics, who invoked the Russian past without saying which period they had in mind, Aksyuchits had at least devoted some thought to locating himself on the Tsarist political spectrum. In the new politics, ultra-nationalists identified with the anti-Jewish death squads and pogrom organisers of the period before the First World War, known as the Black Hundreds; secular, progressive thinkers like Gavriil Popov invoked the memory of Aleksandr Kerensky's liberal government in 1917.

Aksyuchits tried to carve out a position for himself as a sort of progressive monarchist; he admired Aleksandr II, the Tsar-liberator who abolished serfdom, and Pyotr Stolypin, the Prime Minister who tried to broaden the monarchy's power base by creating a new class of independent smallholders. He was fascinated by the Zubatov phenomenon, and he firmly believed that the spirit of Zubatov – in other words, the manufacturing from above of tame and easily provoked opposition parties – was still at large in Russia.

Perhaps because he was too self-willed a character to be manipulated by anybody, Aksyuchits appeared to be a particular target for the dirty tricks of provocateurs. In February 1992, he tried to launch a new, moderate nationalist movement by staging a lavish two-day congress, complete with

Cossacks, folk-dancers and musicians in traditional Russian costume, in one of Moscow's biggest cinemas.

One of the main sponsors of this event was Konstantin Borovoy, the co-founder of one of Moscow's new commodity exchanges. The Moscow correspondent of the London *Jewish Chronicle* asked Borovoy with some astonishment why he, as a prominent businessman of Jewish descent, was prepared to finance an event at which it was almost certain that anti-Semitic slogans would be bandied about. Borovoy replied that his intention was to play his part in channelling nationalist sentiment into relatively harmless outlets, and pre-empt the formation of a strong movement of the extreme right.

If that was the intention, it did not entirely succeed. The meeting was gate-crashed by dozens of scowling, ultra-rightists who booed every speech that showed a hint of moderation, and successfully insisted that their leader, Dmitry Vasilyev, be allowed up to the podium – where he made a furious denunciation of Zionism as the enemy that had brought Russia low.

The claim of the congress to represent moderate nationalism was further undermined by the prominent role played by Nikolai Lysenko, the leader of an ultra-rightist movement based in St Petersburg, who had no scruples about preaching an openly racialist message.

Among the politicians at the congress was Aleksandr Rutskoy, whose speech was interrupted by heckling and laughter. The Vice-President had seen the meeting as an opportunity to establish himself as the leader of a broad nationalist movement which would capitalise on popular distress over the break-up of the Soviet Union and economic hardship.

Having accused the Gaidar cabinet of committing 'genocide' against the Russian people, Rutskoy made the fatal mistake of saying that he was opposed to 'extremism in brown [ie fascist] colours'. This was greeted with catcalls and guffaws; he hastily completed his speech – an over-elaborate piece of rhetoric, peppered with references to Russian philosophers whose names he could barely pronounce – and barely managed to leave the premises before an ugly brawl began between rival factions of the ultra-rightists.

Shaken by that failure, Rutskoy temporarily abandoned the nationalist camp and began forging a new, opportunistic alliance with the emerging 'centre' of post-Soviet politics: the industrial managers led by a sleek veteran of Soviet bureaucracy called Arkady Volsky, and Nikolai Travkin's Democratic Party of Russia (DPR), which was campaigning for a 'strong Russian state' but was more careful than other nationalist factions – in part because several of its most prominent activists were Jewish – to avoid racialist slogans.

As for Aksyuchits, he was forced to admit that he had made 'serious organisational mistakes' in preparing the congress. A movement called the Russian National Assembly was founded at the meeting, but Aksyuchits steadily lost control of it to Ilya Konstantinov, the eternal demagogue. Konstantinov had no scruples about yielding to the obvious temptation of an outright alliance with the neo-communists, whereas Aksyuchits stuck doggedly to his view that communism was 'the most anti-Christian force in history'.

Aksyuchits complained, not without reason, that the new masters of Russian broadcasting went to enormous lengths to exclude from the airwaves those politicians like himself who questioned the notion that there were only two forces in Russian politics: the good President and his bad, communist enemies. Broadcasting, he insisted, was far more rigidly and skilfully controlled under the first year of Yeltsin's rule than it had been during the most liberal periods of Gorbachev's rule. Here too Aksyuchits had a point.

He blamed the Yeltsin government, and in particular the information minister Mikhail Poltoranin, for exaggerating the threat to Russia's new democratic order from the red-brown (communist and fascist) forces. It was certainly true that from the government's point of view, the 'communist-fascist' bogey had its uses. Visiting France in February 1992, Yeltsin gave his hosts a well-calculated *frisson* of horror by telling them he could feel an ugly red-brown dragon breathing down his neck. Yeltsin was duly rewarded with an extra dose of economic aid.

Yet it was no myth that many erstwhile champions of democracy were donning nationalist colours and putting their feverish energy and talent at the disposal of the communist monster which they had worked so hard to slay.

It sometimes seemed as though one group of people was destined always to be bureaucrats, and another, quite small category of people would always be in opposition. In the battleship-grey building which used to house the central committee of the Communist Party, former *apparatchiks* were settling down comfortably to their new role as servants of the Russian Federation. Often, their new tasks were not unrecognisably different from the work they had done under the previous regime, except that the opening up of the economy to competition and foreign investment had led to far bigger opportunities for bribes. At the same time, the fiercest section of the old anti-communist opposition was returning to the places where it felt most comfortable; the streets and the hustings.

It was becoming clearer than ever before that Russian politics were not like the Western variety, where opposition groups could expect to step into their adversaries' shoes as soon as their struggle was successful. In Russia, it was always far more likely that one group of people would act – or be used – as the battering ram to bring down the old regime, and quite another would walk through the newly opened gates of power.

None the less, those Westerners who had lionised the pro-democracy movement were astonished by the ease with which some of their heroes slipped into a new authoritarian discourse, bringing with them all their destructive passion and eloquence. It was a sharp reminder that Russian politicians could abandon the slogans of democracy with the same feverish and impulsive haste with which they originally embraced it.

It did not take Yeltsin's former lieutenants – or least the most pragmatic ones like Konstantinov and Astafyev – very long to find allies. They made friends with a group of tough, practical communists, who understood that their movement would only have a chance of recovering its fortunes if it played the card of Russian nationalism and anti-Westernism and played down the pure Marxist ideology whose time in Russian politics had clearly been and gone.

From the communists' point of view, the advent of these new deserters from the Yeltsin camp could not have been more welcome. Alone, the communists could never have been anything more than a minority, reliant for support on the provinces, the elderly and middle-aged, and those who were destined to be losers in the new order.

Nationalist slogans, which artfully blurred any distinction between communists and anti-communists, had a far better chance of attracting mass support than Marxist ones. Russia was becoming a young person's country, and there were virtually no young communists, except those high-speed cynics who were using the property empire of Komsomol, the Party's youth movement, as the basis on which to build business fortunes. But plenty of young people, dismayed at the dreadful state in which the Soviet regime had left the country, were attracted to the nationalist right.

The communists needed the nationalists, but the nationalists also needed the communists. Activists like Astafyev and Konstantinov, whose personal power base was tiny, were in desperate need of the manpower, the financial and organisational resources, and above all the tactical advice, which the communists – even in their current, vastly depleted state – were uniquely placed to provide.

Before 1991, Yeltsin's anti-communist coalition had rested on a combination of the moral and intellectual power of the Moscow intelligentsia, with the populist appeal – and the all-important insights into the psychology of the ruling élite – provided by Yeltsin himself.

Now a new coalition was forming: the pent-up energy, anger and ambition of the most militant and bitterly disillusioned members of the pro-Yeltsin bloc were being harnessed to the resources, personnel and experience in the manipulation of public opinion which the rump communists could still command.

The sealing of this alliance was soon visible in the strange mixture of symbols which accompanied street demonstrations in Moscow: icons alongside the hammer and sickle; pictures of Nikolai, Aleksandra and the slain Imperial family alongside their killers, Lenin and Stalin; Soviet army uniforms and insignia alongside the Tsarist variety.

The one theme that seemed to fire the enthusiasm of both sides in this strange marriage was anti-Semitism: this was stronger among the Tsarists than the communists, but it was evident enough in both camps. With disturbing frequency, an old Tsarist-era slogan could be heard at public meetings: 'Beat the Jews, and Save Russia.'

The more 'respectable' leaders of the red-brown coalition were careful not to appeal openly to this sentiment, but they did not condemn it either, because to do so would have cut them off from some of their natural constituents. An important part of the opposition leaders' message was an appeal to envy: resentment of anyone who seemed to be taking advantage of the new Russian order to attain commercial or professional success, and nostalgia for the Soviet (and indeed, Tsarist) period when 'upstarts' were kept in place by a political system that placed countless restrictions on self-advancement. Any appeal to these sentiments carried a subtext of hostility to the one section of the population whose traditional values placed a premium on advancement through education, family values and temperance.

An opinion poll in spring 1992 suggested that outright anti-Semitism in Russia was confined to a minority, albeit a significant one. A remarkably high 17 per cent of the respondents assented to the proposition that 'the Jews bear responsibility for the Crucifixion of Christ' while 33 per cent disagreed; however, only 9 per cent said they placed any credence in theories about a 'Zionist conspiracy' aimed at making the Jews a dominant force in the world, while 26 per cent were satisfied that there was no such conspiracy, and 65 per cent said they did not know.

If one form of racialist sentiment *was* increasing rapidly from 1992 onwards, it was resentment of the Caucasian and Transcaucasian peoples – in particular the Chechens, Azerbaijanis and Georgians – who were collectively blamed for a surge in violent crime as well as racketeering and manipulation of the Moscow street markets. One of the quirks of the Soviet system was the fact that it allowed traders from the southern republics to accumulate private wealth, through the sale of flowers and fruit, on a scale that was unimaginable for most ethnic Russians. In the new post-communist world, where money could buy more and more – from hospital beds to hotel rooms to sexual favours – the perceived wealth of the Caucasians was inevitably resented by Russians who were losers in the new system; and this, more than the old-fashioned cause of anti-Semitism, was a sentiment that nationalist orators often drew on, either subliminally or openly.

On the communist side, a confusing variety of factions and cells were struggling to reconstitute themselves out of the battered wreckage of the old ruling party; but by far the biggest group was the former leaders of the Communist Party of the Russian Federation, whose plan was to dress the old faith in clothes which were Russian first and Marxist very much second.

This project had received an enormous boost in early 1990, when Mikhail Gorbachev, searching desperately to find ways to keep the Bolshevik flame from total extinction, made a little gift to the hardline cause. He decreed that since all fourteen of the non-Russian republics had separate communist movements of their own, so should the Russian Federation. The pastures of this new Russian Federation Communist Party were immediately filled with political dinosaurs. Many came from the southern regions of Russia whose giant farms – so well endowed by nature that even under the most irrational of systems, they produced abundant harvests – had always been a bastion of resistance to change.

Liberal-minded Muscovites had observed the RCP's founding congress in a spirit of cultured disdain. The congress heard booming denunciations of the Soviet withdrawal from Eastern Europe – 'the territories that our fathers liberated from fascism' – from the blimpish General Albert Makashov.

Behind the scenes, however, some shrewder, more effective characters in the party were devising a new rhetoric and strategy for communism with a very Russian flavour. The most important of these was Gennady Zyuganov, a thick-set former mathematics teacher from a village deep in central Russia who acted as the builder of bridges between hardline Russian communists and other advocates of a strong, centralised Russia, including the Tsarists. He had worked at the ideological department of the Communist Party of the Soviet Union in its final years and was a bitter adversary of Aleksandr Yakovlev, the theoretician of reform who won widespread acclaim as the architect of *glasnost*.

In mid-1988, the CPSU's ideological machine quietly stopped printing propaganda in favour of classical Soviet communism, as though that ideology had simply died. Instead, the party publishing houses began churning out the words of non-Communist Russian thinkers, from the enlightened to the downright chauvinist. This free-for-all was a symbol of the fact that all ideological questions were being reopened and examined from first principles. Among the first works published in this spirit were the Eurasian theories of Lev Gumilyov, who stated bluntly that Bolshevism had been an alien import into Russia, reflecting Western and Jewish values.

With the help of Gumilyov and others, Zyuganov was able to formulate a sort of Russian communism without Marx, which was uncompromisingly anti-Western and proclaimed the ideal of a grand post-Soviet federation between Orthodox Slavs and Turkic Muslims.

It was under the guidance of Slavophile communists like Zyuganov that the newspaper *Sovyetskaya Rossiya* had been transformed into a forum for nationalist ideas of every kind. His influence was discernible in the paper's decision in December 1989 to publish a landmark manifesto – signed by ten small groups of economic, cultural and environmental protestors – in which a hitherto unfamiliar cluster of slogans was brought together. These included: opposition to the 'anarchy' of the looming market economy, and the sell-off of Russia's riches to foreigners; a return to old-fashioned morality in culture and education; support for the armed forces; support for the Orthodox Church as the guardian of Russia's spiritual life; economic independence for Russia and an end to the 'interference' in Russia's economy by the central Soviet authorities.

(The inclusion of the final demand is a graphic indication that Boris Yeltsin was appealing to at least one school of hardline nationalist thought, as well as liberal reformers, when he proclaimed in June 1990 that the Russian Federation was a sovereign territory.)

Zyuganov, for his part, explicitly rejected some of the key tenets of Western liberal thought, including the notion that anything is permissible unless it is explicitly banned. Russians, he argued, would always yearn for some positive ideological guidance, some particular moral code, by which to direct their lives. In this respect his thinking was much closer to Orthodox theology than to the post-enlightenment world of Voltaire and John Stuart Mill. He believed that Russian communism reflected a collectivist Russian tradition that long predated the revolution: a tradition that was evident in communal systems of land ownership, and also in the Orthodox dogma of *sobornost*, or fellowship, which stresses the submission of the individual to the collective unit.

Zyuganov's version of communism – which avoided such doctrinaire ideas as 'proletarian internationalism' and played down the notion of the class struggle – found willing allies in provincial factory directors who felt they had everything to lose from an economy which became a free-for-all for Western capital. To use his own language, Zyuganov was prepared to make a tactical alliance between the working class – or what remained of it – and the 'national' bourgeoisie.

The theoreticians of the Russian Communist Party were not starting from zero, of course, when they tried to formulate an ideology which was three-quarters Russian nationalist and one-quarter communist. The ghost haunting any such enterprise was that of Stalin, who had drawn ever more deeply on the rhetoric of Russia, and virtually abandoned pure Marxism, as he spurred the nation on to fight the Nazis. As well as the warrior-saint Aleksandr Nevsky, Stalin had invoked the spirit of Dmitry Donskoy, victor of the battle of Kulikovo in 1380; and also Minin and Pozharsky, the folk-heroes who in 1612 emerged from deep in the Russian heartland to drive out the Catholic Poles who had usurped the throne and were trying to impose on Russia their alien, Western ideas about limiting the monarch's power.

Stalin formally endorsed the role of the Russians as the 'elder brother' of all other Soviet nations in 1945, at a reception in the Kremlin for the generals of the triumphant army. At a victory parade a few days earlier, the commanders had cast the banners of the vanquished foe at Stalin's feet, self-consciously imitating General Kutuzov's gesture of fealty to Tsar Aleksandr I after the defeat of Napoleon. It was in the same patriotic spirit that the dictator raised his glass and declared: 'I should like to propose a toast to the health of our Soviet people . . . and above all the Russian people . . . the most outstanding nation of all the nations comprising the Soviet Union'. These comments set the tone for the brutal campaigns against all things foreign and 'cosmopolitan' – a code-word for Jewish – during the final years of the tyrant's rule.

The cause of national-Bolshevism (Russian-flavoured communism) waned under Khrushchev, but reasserted itself strongly in the deeply conservative atmosphere of the Brezhnev era, at least in the intellectual world, where the old nineteenth-century debate between Slavophiles and Westernisers was revived in the pages of prestigious academic journals. The political price for getting on the wrong side of this debate could be considerable; it was for attacking national-Bolshevism that Aleksandr Yakovlev was relegated to the agreeable but powerless post of ambassador to Canada.

The backward-looking climate of the Brezhnev era had

also produced something more stimulating than academic debates about the nineteenth-century: the 'village school' of novelists who articulated with great sincerity and talent the pain that was caused as rural life was destroyed by the forces of modernisation. Officially approved writers of the 1930s had brought a quasi-religious fervour to the idea of dominating nature through the construction of dams, power-stations and factories, thus creating an ideal future, whilst the village writers idealised the past, and the submission to nature which was implied by a life ordered by the seasons.

The greatest product of this literary school is the novel *Farewell to Matyora* by the Siberian novelist Valentin Rasputin, which recounts the story of an island settlement in the year before it is submerged by a hydroelectric dam. Arguably, the greatest 'village writer' of all is Solzhenitsyn; but he is distinguished from the other representatives of this genre by the boldness with which he identified the Soviet regime as the real reason why Russia's modernisation has taken on such a tragic and brutal form. Rasputin and other members of the village school kept their critique within bounds that were broadly acceptable to the communist thought police.

Rasputin's international reputation has been clouded by the racial tinge of his attacks on the *chuzhie* – strangers or outsiders – who have ruined Russian culture. There is, nevertheless, an authenticity and poignancy about his cries of despair over the cost of Russian modernisation which has brought him widespread respect, even among those who are horrified by the political causes with which he has become associated.

It is ironic, in a way, that he should be most fêted by those nationalists for whom nothing is more important than a strong Russia, for his writing is one of the most powerful denunciations one could imagine of the human and ecological damage wrought by the Soviet regime as it sacrificed everything on the altar of crudely defined strength.

Rasputin lived quietly near the shores of Lake Baikal in his native Irkutsk, having never fully recovered from a strange incident in 1980 when a gang of youths beat him up, apparently because they wanted his American jeans. But he was foolish or irresponsible enough to allow a stream of nationalist politicians, of whom Zyuganov was one of the more moderate, to claim him as their ally, and this gave the hard-core opposition the trappings of intellectual credibility which it might otherwise have lacked.

No writer played much of an active role in the emerging movement of opposition to Yeltsin; but through their willingness to appear on podiums, write articles and occasionally make speeches, literary figures such as Rasputin and Vasily Belov proved themselves useful enough servants of the nationalist cause.

A final constituent in the hard-core opposition was epitomised by two clever law lecturers from the provinces: Vladimir Isakov from Sverdlovsk, and Sergei Baburin from the tank-manufacturing city of Omsk. These men, both in their thirties, had supported Yeltsin and at least paid lip-service to his democratic slogans during the very early days of his return to national politics in mid-1990. They abandoned him abruptly when it became clear that the high-sounding slogan of 'sovereignty' for the Russian Federation meant the break-up of the Soviet Union. Both men were often described as communists, but neither had any particular attachment to Marxist ideology: they were polished representatives of Soviet jurisprudence, a discipline which in its Russian form, has little to do with upholding individual rights, but everything to do with the enhancement of the power of the state.

Amid the din of wild nationalist rhetoric which could be heard in the turbulent atmosphere of newly independent Russia, the 'lawyers' provided a calming influence. They understood that the cause of unseating Yeltsin and installing a more openly nationalist regime would be best served by a policy of careful observance of legal niceties and by waiting until the Yeltsin camp wrong-footed itself through some gross violation of the constitution.

In early 1992, it was clear both to opposition strategists like Isakov and Baburin, and also to their adversaries in the Yeltsin camp, that the longer the Russian legislature remained in existence, the better chance there would be of the President being forced out of office by constitutional means. Among the 1,033 members of the Congress of People's Deputies, or full Parliament, perhaps 400 were uncompromising opponents of Yeltsin, and 200 were loyal supporters. The rest were waverers who did not wish to depose the President, but represented regional or industrial lobbies whose short-term interests were being damaged by government policies. Assuming that the President's rating continued to suffer the inevitable attrition of office, it should only be a matter of time before his opponents mustered enough support to dismiss him or reduce his role to that of a figure-head.

The lawyers also counselled realism on another matter: much as they might regret the collapse of the Soviet Federation, and yearn for its early re-establishment, the opposition had to realise that the focus of their struggle for the immediate future must be the Russian republic.

This hard reality was finally driven home on 17 March 1992, when an attempt to reconvene the Soviet Parliament – and hence to re-establish the USSR – was artfully reduced to ridicule by the Yeltsin administration. Making full use of their newly acquired toy – the investigative and enforcement apparatus of the former KGB – the Russian Federation authorities saw to it that not a single premises in Moscow was made available to the would-be remakers of the Soviet Union. The organisers were forced to conduct their proceedings in the dilapidated assembly hall of a dairy farm about an hour's drive from Moscow, where the electricity mysteriously failed and candles had to be found. Barely 100 of the USSR Parliament's 2,250 members attended these lamentable proceedings. The chairwoman, a strikingly beautiful and fiercely conservative Chechen lady called Sazhi Umalatova, maintained a semblance of dignity; but few others could hide their bitterness and despondency.

With this lesson behind them, the so-called 'left-right' opposition worked rapidly to develop a programme for seizing power within Russia. They established a well-disciplined parliamentary caucus called Russian Unity, and they formulated a series of demands which ranged from the absurd to the merely premature. They called for a halt to privatisation – a process which had barely begun – an end to disarmament, and the reintroduction of price controls.

Whether or not they were desirable, these demands were utterly unrealistic: the best that any Russian government could hope to do, in mid-1992, was bring a minimum of order to the run-down of the armed forces and the dismantling of the planned economy. Only if the current period of inexorable, precipitous decline was managed successfully could Russia even consider the rebuilding of its armed forces. But the opposition slogans were not so much a proposal for the real world as a cry of pain from the industrial, agricultural and military lobbies which they represented.

Foreign policy provided further ammunition to fire at the government. The opposition wanted Russia to take a harder line with the republics, especially Moldova, Georgia, and also Ukraine, which was in dispute with Russia over the ownership of the Black Sea Fleet. Another demand was for Moscow to break ranks with the West and support Serbia, which was being subjected to mounting international pressure following the outbreak of war in Bosnia in April 1992.

Most Russian voters were too preoccupied with surviving the country's economic upheavals to care much about Yugoslavia. However, there was one issue on which the opposition's rhetoric did touch a sensitive chord: its demand for much tougher regulation of exports, and the punishment of those who were selling Russia's raw materials cheaply. As Gaidar's economic reformers and the reconstituted KGB were discovering, it was both necessary and extremely difficult to exercise some control over wildcat commodity sales which brought little benefit to the Russian exchequer because the proceeds flowed straight into foreign banks. Apart from the economic arguments, the sale of raw materials touched a sore point in the Russian psyche because of the deep-seated feeling that the nation's resources were a gift from God, to be used sparingly for the collective good, as opposed to enriching opportunistic individuals. Hence the inclusion, in a ten-point opposition manifesto that was issued in July 1992, of a demand for the 'strict punishment of those persons who are guilty of embezzling public property and the sale of natural resources at knock-down prices . . .'

At that time, the opposition was calling for Gaidar to resign and Yeltsin to be reduced to the role of figure-head, with no right to 'interfere' in the economy. By September 1992, they were calling for Yeltsin's impeachment, a procedure that required the support of two-thirds of the members of the full Parliament.

A climax in the opposition's campaign to unseat the President came in October 1992, with the proclamation – at a Moscow conference hall decked out with Tsarist and Communist banners – of a National Salvation Front whose co-chairmen included the former Yeltsin supporters Astafyev and Konstantinov, the communist Zyuganov, and the lawyers Isakov and Baburin. Astafyev seemed thrilled by the thought that the old divisions between Red and White, communist and nationalist, had finally been overcome. 'The question of who was right in 1917 is a purely historical one', he declared. For a moment, it seemed as though Yeltsin had finally succeeded in healing the wounds of the Civil War, by uniting Russians of all ideological persuasions against him.

However, it was also clear from the plethora of feverish resolutions it passed that the Front, having resolved not to live in 1917, was not quite living in 1992 either. It called simultaneously for a halt to economic reform and the restoration of military parity with the United States – as if economic stagnation and conservatism were not the very things which had prompted the Soviet Union to fall behind in the military race.

Another resolution issued a sinister warning to journalists in the state broadcasting system that they would be held responsible for their pro-Yeltsin 'lies' when the NSF came to power. There was also an appeal to the armed forces – verging on the seditious – not to obey any orders they might receive from the Yeltsin administration to crack down on dissent.

Although the NSF's founding charter was careful to state that the movement would work strictly within the framework of the Russian constitution, Yeltsin took the clumsy step of banning the Front – a move that turned out to be unenforceable, given the weakness of the Russian state machine, and was later reversed by the constitutional court.

For the cooler heads within the NSF, the bungled banning order was a thoroughly welcome development; it boded well for the strategy of playing for time until Yeltsin destroyed himself by making too obvious his impatience with constitutional niceties. In late 1992, the opposition seemed at times to be winning the battle for constitutional legitimacy on every front. After a curious, ramshackle sort of 'trial' which took evidence from ex-members of the Politburo, Western historians and former dissidents, the constitutional court conceded that Yeltsin had been within his rights to ban the leadership of the Communist Party, but also found that there was no justification for the ban on grass-roots communist organisations, which should be allowed to reconstitute themselves.

It was hard to imagine what arguments the court could have used to arrive at this decision. The 'constitution' which the court was supposed to spend its time interpreting had been designed with one purpose only; that of legitimising and perpetuating (under a smoke-screen of language about popular sovereignty and freedom), the rule of the Communist Party. There was something odd, if not downright absurd, about studying a communist constitution to see whether the Communist Party was legitimate. Yet these troublesome questions of logic did not, of course, worry the verdict's beneficiaries. The decision gave Zyuganov's Russian communists enough leeway to re-establish themselves in February 1993 as a nation-wide party, claiming 300,000 members.

Although they had lost the property and publishing empire which used to belong to the CPSU, they were still a formidable power in the land. Their programme called for the gradual reconstitution of the Soviet Union by tactical co-operation with the 'national bourgeoisie' which was in power in most of the Union republics – with two giant exceptions: Boris Yeltsin's Russia, and Eduard Shevardnadze's Georgia, both of which were proclaimed to have fallen under the sway of parasitical, pro-Western cliques of *comprador* capitalists; those who made no contribution to their nation's economic welfare.

Whenever non-communist advocates of Russian nationalism fantasised about recreating the Russian empire, their first priority was usually the redrawing of 'Bolshevik frontiers', so as to reincorporate those prized territories which the Soviet regime had been careless enough to leave outside the boundaries of the Russian Federation: places such as Crimea, or at least the port of Sevastopol, where the Black Sea Fleet was based; the pro-Russian enclaves of Georgia, Abkhazia and South Ossetia; Narva, the Russian-speaking city in Estonia; and northern Kazakhstan.

Communist discourse, by contrast, tended to focus not on tinkering with borders, but on the reintegration of entire republics into some kind of new federation, thanks to a rekindling of the community of interest (perhaps more accurately described as a community of ambition and fear) which used to exist between politicians across the Soviet Union.

This difference in emphasis did not constitute any insuperable barrier to co-operation between Zyuganov's communists and Astafyev's nationalists. In practice, these two approaches to rebuilding the empire were complementary, not mutually exclusive. By threatening to redraw borders – either openly or through covert support for local separatists – Russia could put pressure on entire republics to move closer to its embrace.

The most convincing proof that these two approaches to imperialism could be used simultaneously was provided by the fact that the Russian government – the supposedly treacherous, anti-national government whose faint-heartedness was anathema to Reds and Whites alike – was already doing so.

Whether or not the opposition realised it, an important sea-change in the Russian government's attitude to the republics had taken place in mid-June 1992. The turning point came when a small incident – which appeared to be a cunning provocation – led to a sudden flare-up of fighting between forces loyal to the ethnic Romanian government of Moldova, and Russian-speaking separatists in the east of the republic.

Prior to that incident, the Russian foreign ministry had been attempting, in seeming good faith, to settle the conflict in co-operation with the governments of Ukraine, Moldova and Romania. While the cause of the Russian-speaking separatists attracted huge sympathy among all shades of the 'red-brown' coalition, the Russian government had, in theory at least, committed itself to respecting the sovereignty and territorial integrity of Moldova, and eventually to withdrawing its forces from their base in the east of the republic.

On 19 June 1992, however, a furious tank and artillery battle erupted in the town of Bendery, on the front line of the conflict. The fighting began after a Russian army major was arrested by the Moldovan police. They said they were acting on a mysterious – and in retrospect suspicious – tip from a telephone caller who claimed that an incident was under way at a printing press which the officer had just entered. This gave the pro-Russian forces the cue to lay siege to the Moldovan police headquarters, while the Moldovan forces sent for more armour and tried to establish control over the whole town. The Russian garrison based at Tiraspol dropped all pretence of neutrality and sent dozens of tanks thundering across the River Dnestr; several hundred people were killed in two days of fierce fighting.

The flare-up occurred, by accident or design, when Yeltsin was out of the country, and Rutskoy seized the chance to assert that he was taking control. In a chilling television appearance on the night of Saturday, 20 June, the Vice-President solemnly declared that hundreds of civilians and Russian servicemen had died both in eastern Moldova, and in the Georgian enclave of South Ossetia, because of the 'cynical' policies pursued by the governments of those two republics. A government statement issued on the same night declared that Russian forces in the two war zones had been instructed to take 'adequate measures of self-defence' – a formula which clearly portended a much tougher military stance, going far beyond the literal meaning of the words.

A few days later, the Russian garrison in Moldova was taken over by General Aleksandr Lebed, a tough and charismatic paratrooper in his forties who had fought alongside General Pavel Grachev, the defence minister, in Afghanistan. Lebed made it plain from the start that he set no store by the niceties of international law. He regarded the Moldovan government as 'fascists' with no moral right to rule, and made it clear that the 14th Army, as the local Russian garrison was called, was in the region to stay. The Moldovan authorities were forced to abandon indefinitely all hopes of extending their writ to the whole of their territory. Lebed insisted – and there was nobody in Moscow who dared to contradict him – that as a Russian officer, he was subject to higher moral imperatives than any pen-pusher from the foreign ministry, or any other bureaucracy, in Moscow could possibly invoke.

As Lebed was preparing to impose his will in Moldova, Yeltsin signed an accord with Eduard Shevardnadze in which Georgia virtually abandoned hope of reasserting control over South Ossetia. The Russian leader also hammered out with President Leonid Kravchuk of Ukraine the terms of a new Russian-Ukrainian relationship which reflected Moscow's interests far better than the old one. Kravchuk in effect gave up his efforts to assert full Ukrainian control over the Black Sea Fleet, by accepting that the 400 or so ships would be 'jointly owned' for the foreseeable future, and he also promised to tone down Ukraine's support for the Moldovan government in its war with the Russian-speaking separatists. Prior to the Yeltsin-Kravchuk meeting at the Black Sea resort of Dagomys, relations between Moscow and Kiev had been strained to the point where armed conflict seemed possible; but now that crisis had been brought under control.

Andrei Kozyrev, the foreign minister, protested forlornly in an interview with the newspaper *Izvestia* that the 'party of war' was rearing its head in the Russian leadership and dictating a more aggressive policy towards the republics. But the only result of Kozyrev's outcry was to ensure his own isolation for several months, as a shadowy new organ of state, the Security Council, came into being and rapidly became the main forum for the charting of Russia's course in military and external affairs. Only when Kozyrev was prepared to trumpet the hard new line himself did he regain his earlier prominence.

All these developments made it somewhat harder for the communist and nationalist opposition to insist that Russia was failing to assert her own interests, and allowing foreigners to dictate her policy. Yet nothing could diminish the determination of Yeltsin's opponents to bring him down, using every argument they could muster. Every time the government took a step towards asserting Russia's interests, the opposition would suggest going one step further. If the government achieved *de facto* Russian control over most of the Black Sea Fleet, then the opposition would suggest reannexing Crimea, or at least the port of Sevastopol, where a host of pro-Moscow organisations stood ready to act on Russia's bidding. From the authorities' point of view, this opposition pressure was sometimes a positive advantage: it made everything the government did seem moderate and reasonable.

9
Nationalism In High And Low Places

For the cooler, shrewder figures in the hard-core opposition – activists like Baburin, Isakov and Zyuganov – one of the toughest challenges was to find ways of tapping into the pent-up bitterness and frustration that was lurking in Russia's collective consciousness, without formally embracing the cause of racialism or chauvinism.

Another challenge was to keep at arms' length those forces which were fishing in the same emotional waters but often seemed, either consciously or unconsciously, to be playing into Yeltsin's hands by the extremism of their language and behaviour.

One character whom they learned to treat with caution was Viktor Anpilov, a hot-tempered radio journalist who bore a passing resemblance to Mick Jagger. He had held an important post in the Soviet propaganda machine, broadcasting for Radio Moscow in Spanish and then working as a reporter in Nicaragua at the height of the war between the Marxist Sandinista government and their American-backed opponents. His colleagues remembered him as a fanatical communist, who took a keen interest in the ideological soundness of his compatriots in Managua, long after such 'vigilance' against backsliding had ceased to be fashionable. On returning to Moscow, he began proclaiming a political doctrine that was long on chauvinistically-tinged Russian nationalism but, unlike Zyuganov, refused to reject the communist rhetoric of class struggle. Where fainter hearts might have compromised their revolutionary ideals, Anpilov still spoke of the dictatorship of the proletariat and of beating back the counter-attacks of the bourgeoisie. If he had a grievance against Stalin, it lay in the fact that the dictator had not waged class war with sufficient consistency or vigour.

Anpilov was the prime mover in a militant faction that was variously known as Working Russia, Working Moscow and the Russian Communist Workers' Party; at a Revolution Day demonstration in November 1992, he seemed to be calling on the army to rebel. Events in which Anpilov was involved had a way of turning violent. One of these was a picket of Moscow's main television building in June 1992 by a hysterical crowd whose main demand was an end to 'Zionist influence' on the airwaves. The one thing which distinguished Anpilov from other opposition agitators was the fact he had a hard-core of 10,000 or so supporters who could be called on to the streets at short notice. Any event he organised could always be sure of *massovost* – that untranslatable communist word which means a mass presence, a large, single-minded crowd.

Another figure of whom the hard-core communist-nationalist opposition became wary was Aleksandr Sterligov, a KGB general who was working as an aide to Vice-President Rutskoy at the time of the August 1991 coup. In that capacity he had been in charge of handing out weapons to the volunteers defending the White House: this fact alone is a graphic illustration of the way the KGB was present on both sides of the barricades during the August events. When the coup collapsed, Sterligov was a member of the party which flew down to Gorbachev's place of captivity in Crimea and arrested the architects of the putsch, who included the KGB chairman Vladimir Kryuchkov. Sterligov said afterwards that in helping to arrest his notional boss, he was merely acting on instructions from Rutskoy, an associate on whom he does not look back with any particular affection.

With his taut, pinched and intensely alert features Sterligov could inspire greater fear in the average Russian onlooker than most of the noisy malcontents who made up the opposition.

In February 1992, Sterligov came into the news as the organiser of a well-financed congress in Nizhny Novgorod, which under its old name of Gorky had been a bastion of the Soviet military-industrial complex. This meeting proclaimed the foundation of a Russian National Council or Sobor which, to judge by the blaze of publicity it attracted, was making a strong bid to turn itself into the main vehicle for anti-reform, anti-Western agitation in Russia. It called for a powerful state machine to restore at least part of the planned economy, complete with price controls and a ban on foreign exchange transactions. At that time, such demands belonged – regardless of their desirability – to the realm of fantasy: the Russian state was still far too feeble to claw back any of its former control over the economy. However, this state of affairs would not last for ever, and Sterligov spoke for those sections of the Russian establishment which believed that the reconstruction of a mighty state could not come a moment too soon.

The Sobor's supporters were a strange mixture of the highly 'respectable' (in the sense that it clearly had backers who were well placed in the Soviet industrial and political world), and the downright murky. Formally speaking, it was an offshoot of a group called the Slavic Council (Slavynasky Sobor) which had been formed a year earlier out of a cluster of groups on the outermost fringes of the far right, some of which were dabbling in Nazism. In January 1992, General Sterligov had appeared like a *deus ex machina* at a meeting of this Slavic Council and persuaded it to bless the creation of the RNC, a much higher-profile organisation which would form a kind of bridge between the ultra-rightist fringe movements and the respectable world.

Viktor Aksyuchits took the foundation of this Sobor as a personal insult to himself. He felt that its real purpose was to put a spoke in the wheels of his own movement. Was it a coincidence, he asked, that the formation of his Russkoye Natsionalnoe Sobranie (Russian National Assembly) should be followed only days later by the creation of a movement with a confusingly similar name, the Russkiye Natsionalny Sobor, or Russian National Council? For Aksyuchits, a conspiracy theorist in a country which compels even the most sceptical of people to believe in conspiracies, the Sobor and the blackshirts who heckled and disrupted his own congress were all part of a single campaign to prevent the emergence of a genuinely independent opposition movement.

In June 1992, as Anpilov's mob was chanting its slogans outside the Moscow television centre, Sterligov's Sobor held another congress in one of the grandest neo-classical buildings in central Moscow, and liberal Muscovite opinion was acutely alarmed by the movement's self-confidence, lavish funding and the sinister edge to Sterligov's rhetoric. It became a commonplace to say that in any scenario involving a sudden switch to a more authoritarian form of rule, Sterligov was likely to be among the protagonists.

Rasputin and several other conservative writers were all roped into the RNC; so was the communist theoretician Gennady Zyuganov, and the head of a chemical factory in the Siberian city of Krasnoyarsk with the evocative name of Pyotr Romanov. However, many of the general's early associates, including Zyuganov, later quarrelled with him because of his seeming determination to have the nationalist cause to himself. Sterligov was a co-signatory of the founding documents of the National Salvation Front, but he took no part in the founding congress, apparently because he was unable to establish himself as the most influential figure in the new movement.

In other quarters, however, the general was more successful. There was one very well-known young man who supported Sterligov's movement quite consistently, and that was the self-described young millionaire, German Sterligov, who turned out to be a kinsman of the general, although the proximity of the relationship was not clear.

The story of German Sterligov provides a cautionary tale for all Western observers who are inclined to jump to conclusions about who is who, and who is what, in Russia. A pale, bespectacled and unprepossessing 24-year-old, he attracted a blaze of publicity in 1990 by the ingenious, provocative act of starting a Young Millionaires Club, at a time when it appeared to the West that almost all Russians were pathetically poor.

Oddly enough, it was never possible to pin down much precise information about the club, or the identity of any of its members besides German and his brother; but the very idea of a 'young millionaire' was enough to bring a trail of reporters to the young man's office where they heard his outrageous story. In the surly, insolent tone that bright young Russians adopt when talking to people they regard as half-wits, this brash young man would tell his incredulous visitors how he had built up a giant commodity exchange, with about fifty subsidiaries, from show business to horse-racing, whose names he could not be bothered to remember.

German's exchange was called Alisa 'after his dog'. Only a few years previously, this precocious Russian yuppie – who might have stepped out of the movie, *Wall Street* – had by his own account been a penniless high school drop-out, who got the idea of acting as a middleman in the building trade because he was 'bored with being poor'.

Young Sterligov's emergence in mid-1992 as a kinsman, admirer and sponsor of a politically ambitious KGB general was not much mentioned in the Western press; it was too hard to square with the image that Western readers had been served up a couple of years earlier, of German as a brash but generally admirable hero of the Gorbachev revolution. Clearly, he was not quite the friendless waif he suggested when he launched his business career and the fact he was contemptuously dismissive of communism and all its works did not in any way imply that he took a negative view of the other pillar of the Soviet state, which was the political police.

The stories of the Sterligovs – just like that of the Leningrad TV star Nevzorov – made a mockery of the old rule of thumb by which Westerners had analysed Soviet politics. On the one hand there were supposed to be 'bad' conservatives who wanted to keep as much as possible of the old system intact –

the empire, the security forces, a confrontational relationship with the West, the command economy (with its strict limits on the role of money), the communist monopoly on political power and information.

On the other hand, there were the 'good' reformers who wanted to dismantle all those things and replace them with a Western system which allowed for open competition in the realm of ideas and in economic life: the freedom to speak one's mind, and to grow personally rich.

When Russia's first self-described young millionaire popped up out of nowhere, it was assumed that he must be a member of the second camp. Yet there was no reason why a youthful tycoon should not be a supporter, and a very sophisticated and effective one, of at least certain aspects of the old order, a friend of the security forces, and a determined enemy of the West. German Sterligov was certainly the latter. In mid-1992, he started complaining furiously that the CIA was trying to recruit him – but he had flatly refused, because contrary to what the cynical Americans believed, 'not everything or everyone in Russia was for sale'.

When private money first started trickling into Russian politics in the late 1980s, it was assumed that it would be used on the side of the reformers, the people who supported private enterprise and improved relations with the West. The Democratic Russia coalition, for example, was generously funded by the world chess champion Garri Kasparov, one of the few Soviet citizens who did not have to apologise for being personally wealthy. The communist establishment tried to resist the bourgeois tide by using the non-monetary privileges which it still enjoyed: control of printing presses, a virtual monopoly of the provincial media, and the ability to manipulate opinion by regulating the supply of food and other essentials to the major cities.

By 1992, people were recalling the cynical adage that money has no smell. There was no reason why private funds should not be deployed in a hardline cause; at least the more conservative parts of the Russian business world would have every interest in supporting parties that favoured domestic rather than foreign capital, and authoritarian government, even dictatorship, over democracy.

This was one of the ironies of the economic reforms undertaken by Gaidar. His policies were speeding up the commercialisation and monetisation of the economy, the establishment of money as a store of utility and token of power. Yet many of the powerful persons who stood to benefit from this process – if only because their consent would have to be bought, somewhere along the way – were political conservatives, like the old-guard industrial bosses of Nizhny Novgorod who welcomed General Sterligov and his Sobor to their city.

While the Sobor's economic programme reflected the fantasies of its industrial backers, there were parts of its manifesto which showed a much firmer grip on reality than many of the wilder outpourings of the red-brown family. Their author appeared to be well aware that he was writing in 1992 – as opposed to 1982 or 1912 – and to be in close touch with the Eurasian theories of Lev Gumilyov which had become so fashionable in the Russian establishment.

In external policy, the manifesto said, Russia should focus her energies on the restoration of her influence in the former Soviet Union, and the consolidation of her position in Asia. She should seek the help of India and China in countering the 'aggressive hegemonism' of the United States.

The three main threats to Russian security were identified very coolly and precisely:

> . . . the growth of nationalism and fundamentalist tendencies in Central Asia and Transcaucasia, leading to tension in several regions inside Russia which are inhabited by Muslims; the active penetration of Central Asia and Transcaucasia by foreign governments, calculated to undermine the influence of Russia in that region; the growth of militant anti-Russian nationalism in Ukraine and Moldova, causing a threat to Russian interests in the Black Sea . . .

These were not the outpourings of Soviet or Tsarist nostalgia; they were hard-headed assessments made by hard-headed men from the very core of the establishment.

A close analysis of Sterligov's political strategy confirmed the impression of an organisation that is trying to influence political events from inside, rather than outside, the ruling élite.

He suggested a period of emergency rule in which the Supreme Soviet or standing Parliament would continue to function, while the Congress of People's Deputies, or full Parliament, which was the main bastion of opposition to Yeltsin, would go into abeyance. The judicial system would continue to function, and so significantly, would the President. If the President proved uncooperative about changing the cabinet, it might be necessary to threaten him with impeachment; but in principle, the President's authority should remain intact.

Once the immediate political and economic crisis was over, the country's future would be decided by a Zemsky Sobor (Council of the Land), drawn from representatives of Russia's regions and its different social classes. This Sobor would take over from the Congress of People's Deputies as the arbiter of Russia's future. In the interim period before the Zemsky Sobor was assembled, executive and legislative power would be concentrated in a National Salvation Committee. However, there was no suggestion that the President would lose his prerogatives during this crucial period. The more closely these proposals are examined, the more it looks as though Sterligov's proposals were not a fantasy about time travel, or a strategy to remove Yeltsin, but a twinkle in the eye of the hardest men inside the governing apparatus.

Small wonder, then, that Sterligov and the NSF leaders like Konstantinov, Astafyev and Zyuganov could not easily find a common language; the general was proposing to shore up Yeltsin's presidency while the NSF was furiously determined to bring him down.

In early 1993, Sterligov made it even plainer than before that there was a place for Yeltsin in his political strategy: there were also people in the Yeltsin entourage, such as Oleg

Lobov, the old *apparatchik* and presidential crony from Sverdlovsk, with whom the general was sure he could work.

If Sterligov had friends, or at least potential associates, in the heart of Russia's government, he was also a familiar figure on the extremist fringes of Russian politics. It appeared that one of the functions of his Sobor was to act as a conduit, for ideas, tactics, and personnel, between the highest and lowest places in public life.

The ideas which travelled along this conduit were often to do with race. For example, the Sobor debated the principle of 'proportional representation' for ethnic groups in government, science, culture and the media. This meant that Jews, Georgians, Armenians and so on would be subject to quotas limiting their share of jobs in proportion with their community's share of the Russian population. The group most immediately affected by this measure would be the Jews, who accounted for barely 1 per cent of the total population but were well represented in academia, the arts and the liberal professions – despite the operation in the Brezhnev era of an elaborate system of restrictions which prevented Jewish entry to many of the country's most prestigious institutions of higher education.

One of the first people to use the words 'proportional representation' in this very specific sense was Konstantin Smirnov-Ostashvili, a far-right agitator who died mysteriously in prison in spring 1991 while serving a sentence for stirring up racial hatred. His associates were among the co-founders of the Slavic Council, out of which Sterligov's Russian National Council was eventually formed.

Another of the RNC's proposals was the establishment of a national Congress, confined to ethnic Russians, which would somehow be more legitimate than the existing Russian legislature, for which all citizens, including ethnic minorities, had voted. This Congress could decide which of the smaller nations on Russian soil could be viewed as 'friendly' and which could not. This idea of *ad hoc*, ethnically defined assemblies, incidentally, did not enter post-Soviet politics via

Russia; it had already surfaced in most of the non-Russian republics during their struggle for independence.

A further twist on Sterligov's theory was that if Yeltsin somehow managed to dissolve the existing Parliament, then this all-Russian Congress would be called on to play an important role in 'counter-balancing' the President's authority and charting Russia's future.

It is worth reflecting for a moment on who was making these proposals: not some obscure eccentric but the former right-hand man of the Russian Vice-President; a man who had played a central role on the winning side of the August 1991 drama, which the world had hailed as the start of a new, democratic era for Russia. Some very un-Western ideas had a toe-hold in the highest echelons of the new Russian state, during its early days.

Equally, it should not be assumed that Sterligov had broken all his links with the Russian leadership by 1992; or that his proposals – at least on the constitutional question – were anathema to the Yeltsin team. The President's interests could be quite well served by a situation in which the only rival to his authority was not a full-blown Parliament, whose constitutional position he could hardly deny, but some self-appointed repository of ethnic purity.

Nor were Sterligov's supporters on the margins of Russian society. As a sympathetic report in the daily *Rossiskaya Gazeta* observed:

> At previous patriotic gatherings, one could not help noticing a fair number of very peculiar persons with unpleasant clothing, unwashed hair, and inflamed eyes . . . but at patriotic gatherings organised by General Sterligov, there is a preponderance of quiet, solid, thoughtful, intelligent people with a certain sadness in their eyes.

It went on to say that the Moscow branch of Sterligov's Assembly included professors, entrepreneurs, army officers, city councillors and at least one priest.

Despite this graphically drawn contrast, the distance between the unwashed and ill-dressed on one hand, and the solid and well-established on the other, has never been very great in Russian politics. Both have their place in the hard-line, anti-Western, anti-democratic camp and if the unwashed and ill-dressed have any real significance at all, it is generally because they serve the purposes of the solid and well-established and are therefore given a helping hand.

The final years of the Soviet era had seen the emergence of several ultra-nationalist forces whose distinguishing feature was not the extent of their grass-roots support but the friendly treatment which they manifestly received from the very highest levels of officialdom.

One such phenomenon was the absurdly named Liberal Democratic party headed by an eccentric, multilingual lawyer named Vladimir Zhirinovsky, who had astonished most observers by winning six million votes in the June 1991 elections. He was a strange, restless, petulant person with a coarse sort of charisma, whose brief political career had been devoted to a peculiar variety of causes.

After abandoning his career as a legal adviser to the Soviet Peace Committee and, later, the Mir Publishing House – both important cogs in the Soviet propaganda machine – Zhirinovksy had made brief appearances in the Democratic Union, the first and most utopian of the reformist parties; in a short-lived Jewish cultural organisation; and then shared a platform at a public meeting with an obscure grouping of the ultra-right.

The creation of his Liberal Democratic party in mid-1990 was given a blaze of sympathetic publicity by those organs of the Soviet press – Tass news agency, *Pravda*, state television – which were still subject to ideological guidance from the authorities.

Then the Soviet justice ministry showed indecent haste in registering the new party, although the membership lists turned out to be lists of names of a community of ethnic Turks which had been subject to racial violence in Uzbekistan. The LDP's first public noises were all about the market economy and rolling back communism; accurate and even witty imitations of the language that most of the other tiny new parties were spouting. But in autumn 1990, as the self-appointed head of a shadowy bloc of 'centrist' parties, Zhirinovsky began proposing the suspension of the democratic process and the declaration of a state of emergency. He was allowed to make this appeal in the lavish surroundings of the Oktyabrskaya, the Communist Party's grandest hotel – a place that the ruling élite would rarely make available to anyone but its closest friends.

Anatoly Lukyanov, the hardline Soviet parliamentary chairman, seemed not to be troubled by the fact that most of the parties in the centrist bloc did not exist, and he received the bloc's so-called representatives, including Zhirinovsky, for high-profile discussions on the country's future. Zhirinovsky approved heartily of the January 1991 crackdown on the Baltic states, and in February he was an enthusiastic participant in a conference on a 'great, united Russia' that was organised by the newspaper *Sovyetskaya Rossiya* under the benign gaze of Gennady Zyuganov and other luminaries of nationalism.

Zhirinovsky's campaign for the June 1991 presidential elections was sympathetically covered by state television, and he was clearly well briefed on the state of popular psychology. One of his best-publicised promises was to slash the price of vodka: this persuaded the chattering classes to treat him as a joke, which was a foolish mistake. Like Sterligov, his discourse was a mixture of wild extremism, and hard, practical politics. For example, one of his campaign promises in the presidential elections was to encourage the use of Russian soldiers in UN peace-keeping missions, as a way of gaining hard currency and expanding Russian influence on the cheap. This was to emerge two years later as a key strategy in post-Soviet foreign policy, and Zhirinovsky was merely ahead of his time in transmitting it from the inner circle of the policy-makers to the electorate.

He seemed briefly disoriented by the failure of the August 1991 coup, but he was soon back on the streets again, threatening to declare war on Pakistan and blast the Baltic states into submission by using giant fans to blow nuclear waste in their direction. He fished in the same waters as the mainstream nationalist opposition, but they were intensely suspicious of him. He was unprepared to co-operate with others, endlessly self-centred and ambitious and seemed to have friends in very high places.

Another 'opposition' force on whom the powerful clearly smiled was the shadowy and disputatious movement of blackshirted chauvinists who went under the generic name of Pamyat, or memory. At least eleven factions of this movement have been identified, ranging in size from a few dozen members to a few hundred; they include everything from ostentatiously devout Orthodox Christians to pagan factions who view Christianity as a Jewish heresy, and St Vladimir – who baptised Russia in 988 – as a crypto-Hebrew.

Pamyat had emerged as a visible force in the streets in 1987, just as reformist political groups were starting to come out into the open. The black shirts and peaked hats of its supporters were very similar to those worn by the ultra-rightist movements which flourished among the Russian diaspora in Germany and China in the 1930s.

At a time when reformist and, above all, Jewish demonstrations still ran the risk of violent dispersal by the police, Pamyat meetings enjoyed impunity, even protection from the authorities. In May 1987, Pamyat staged a demonstration in Red Square – something which would have required consent at the highest level – and held a meeting with the Communist Party boss of Moscow, a certain Boris Yeltsin. This does not imply that he had any particular sympathy for their cause, but it does suggest that they had good connections in the municipality.

Their rhetoric was an emotional mixture of cultural grievances – for example, the ruined state of Russia's churches, monasteries and graveyards – filled with dark ethnic overtones. At public meetings, they would read out the names of prominent Bolsheviks, lingering over those with Jewish names and implying that they were primarily responsible for destroying Russia's heritage. An obvious target was Lazar Kaganovich, the Jewish commissar who, in 1933, had dynamited Moscow's greatest place of worship, the Cathedral of Christ the Saviour, which was built to celebrate the victory over Napoleon.

The best known of Pamyat's quarrelsome leaders was Dmitry Vasilyev, a stout, balding man in his forties who was well read in pre-revolutionary history and a skilful orator. A former photographer, he had played the part of Pyotr Stolypin in a film, and also worked as an assistant to the nationalist painter Ilya Glazunov, whose religious and patriotic subject matter was tolerated by the Brezhnev regime in the spirit of national-Bolshevism.

In the early months of the Gorbachev era, Vasilyev gave a public reading of *The Protocols of the Elders of Zion*, a nineteenth-century work of propaganda which purports to tell the story of a Zionist plot to take over the world through the devious stratagems of socialism and liberal democracy. Although the work originated in Western Europe – it was based on a German novel of the 1860s entitled *Biarritz* – it had been widely distributed in Imperial Russia as part of the Tsarist regime's effort to discredit the revolutionary movement. The re-emergence of *The Protocols* in late Soviet politics suggested that very old-fashioned methods were being used as a counter-point to the freer expression of pro-Western ideas.

Vasilyev initially presented himself as a loyal Leninist who supported Gorbachev's *perestroika*, and suggested that his blackshirted marchers were merely doing their bit to keep that worthy enterprise on track. The rhetoric of *perestroika* was so vague and woolly in those days that almost anybody could claim to be its friend. In common with the propagandists of the Soviet regime, he carefully directed his attacks to the political doctrine of Zionism, as opposed to the Jewish race.

From 1991 onwards, however, Vasilyev's diatribes changed tack, and he started describing himself as a monarchist, a devout and theologically conservative Orthodox Christian, and a fascist. Fascism, he said, was a spiritual phenomenon that should not be confused with Nazism, which he disowned.

His school of monarchism gave no truck to the claims of the Grand Duke Vladimir Kirillovich or his daughter; he wanted a Zemsky Sobor – Council of the Land – to select a new dynasty, and rivals within the nationalist movement said he did not discourage the idea that he himself might be a candidate for the throne. Instead of focusing on Zionism as the enemy, he now said his greatest foe was the Jewish religion and he had nothing but praise for ethnic Jews who converted to Christianity. Vasilyev was a skilful manipulator of historical arguments, and of historical and religious symbols that could strike a chord in those sections of the Russian public who were fascinated by the past but woefully ignorant of its details. Like many other, more respectable voices in the nationalist camp, Vasilyev fashioned a discourse which was designed to appeal to people who had welcomed the demise of communism but were bitterly disillusioned with what followed: further economic dislocation, the break-up of the Soviet Union and wars on Russia's periphery.

From a radio station acquired by the movement in October 1991, Pamyat broadcast the message that the communists and the democrats were part of the same, diabolical phenomenon. 'Communism has simply stretched a sickly-sweet mask of democracy over its bestial countenance', the listeners were told. As for Marxism, it was 'a brainchild of Judaism' which was a religion based on racial superiority, striving for world power and hatred of humanity. 'Only in order to popularise its ideas was Marxism forced to don the mask of the altruist', the radio insisted. In a world where communist bosses from deep in the Urals suddenly metamorphosed into champions of human rights and reform, the theory of 'masks' had an obvious appeal to simple and confused souls, struggling to read the signs of the times.

Indeed if Vasilyev's outpourings were right about anything, it was the fact that Russian reality could not be decoded at all without an ability to see behind masks; he had worn several of them himself, from architecture and history buff, to street protestor, to mystic. Western analysts – being unaccustomed to this phenomenon of masks – generally asked the wrong questions when the blackshirts first appeared on the streets in the late 1980s.

Ultra-rightists in the Vasilyev mould were not the precursors of a mass movement of fascists, who might organise themselves in opposition to the government, and conceivably overthrow it. Nor was it helpful to view them simply as one more beneficiary, along with so many others, of the freedom of speech granted by Mikhail Gorbachev. Whatever the blackshirts were, they were not just a mirror-image of the reformist and pro-Western movements which were gathering strength: a caricature perhaps, but not a mirror-image. When the blackshirts emerged from obscurity on to the streets, with police protection and their own, peculiar discourse, this was not a sign of frustration, pent-up ethnic prejudice or anything else welling up from the grass-roots of society. The hierarchical way in which Soviet society was organised made that virtually unthinkable. Pamyat could only have manifested itself if people at the very top of the Soviet power structure had, for some reason, smiled on the enterprise and smoothed its path. The right question to ask is not which popular grievances Pamyat might have articulated, but why powerful figures considered its emergence to be desirable.

An obvious – but not quite adequate – explanation is that Pamyat was a way of warning the pro-Western camp in politics that they did not have the field to themselves, and they should not go too far. Another possibility, perhaps nearer the mark, is that Pamyat's ideology was only a slight caricature of the personal convictions of highly-placed persons amongst the Soviet élite who wanted these ideas to be aired in public. A third theory, more far-fetched but in the Soviet context entirely conceivable, is that Pamyat was a way of reminding the rest of the world of the fragility of Soviet reforms, and of the terrible forces which might be unleashed if the project were allowed to fail. Finally, ultra-nationalist groups which operate with the blessing of the authorities can be a useful way of frustrating the efforts of any genuine opposition forces who are becoming a thorn in the government's side; that, at any rate, was the complaint of Viktor Aksyuchits.

At election meetings in Moscow, he was repeatedly taken to task by a woman who claimed to speak for Pamyat. Again and again, she would taunt him over the fact that he had been expelled from Riga naval academy, one month before his graduation, after a fist-fight with an official from Komsomol. He would shout back at her that only a person with very good access to the police files could be so familiar with the details of his early life. He faced another provocation when self-proclaimed supporters started handing out his election leaflets in the metro and showering him with unwanted 'compliments': 'Vote for Viktor Aksyuchits, he's an anti-Semite, he'll kick out all the Jews!'

The authorities' sporadic efforts to rein in Pamyat were never very convincing. In January 1990, liberal Muscovite opinion was horrified by a violent rampage carried out by Pamyat supporters, led by Smirnov-Ostashvili, at a meeting of liberal writers. The following month and again in May, there were rumours all over the country that an anti-Jewish pogrom by Pamyat supporters was imminent. The rumours spread like wildfire through cities thousands of miles apart, and it was hard to avoid the conclusion that officialdom was involved in fomenting them. The possibility of pogroms was very much in the air already because of the horrific anti-Armenian violence that had shaken Baku the previous month, paving the way for a Soviet army crackdown in the republic of Azerbaijan. Like the last Tsarist regime, the Soviet authorities came under strong international pressure to do something about anti-Semitism, and they duly arrested Ostashvili, a disturbed character who was dismissed by most of his rivals on the far-right, including Vasilyev, as a provocateur or worse. In October 1990, Ostashvili was sentenced to two years' hard labour under the Soviet law – a poorly enforced one – that penalised the spreading of ethnic hatred. His apparent suicide the following spring gave the ultra-rightists a martyr, and a new figure around whom elaborate conspiracy theories could be woven.

However, nothing in the Ostashvili case – which left the more effective figures in Pamyat very much at liberty – diminished the impression that the movement had powerful friends. The chairman of the KGB, Vladimir Kryuchkov, had aroused the suspicion that he might be a supporter when he said in December 1990 that there were many 'fine patriots' in Pamyat's ranks.

For most of the eighties, Vasilyev's bodyguard, and chief instructor to the blackshirts in physical education, was a former special forces officer called Aleksandr Barkashov. Barkashov used to tell interviewers that he had been schooled in the evils of Zionism by a favourite uncle who worked in the ideology department of Stalin's Communist Party. The biggest disappointment of Barkashov's military career was the Soviet-Egyptian split of 1973, which robbed him of the chance to go to help Egypt in its war against Israel. In 1990, Barkashov split with Vasilyev and took with him at least fifty of the youths he had been training. Like many godfather figures on the extreme right, Barkashov ostensibly provided instruction in the martial arts, but he never discouraged the idea that he was dabbling in firearms as well.

On abandoning Vasilyev, he briefly teamed up with a young economics graduate called Viktor Yakushev who was making a determined bid to establish himself as the most extreme of Russia's extremists. Yakushev, who was articulate and well read in the Nazi classics, claimed to be grooming about 150 well-disciplined followers for the task of seizing power and creating a Russian Nazi super-state in which 95 per cent of the population would be slaves, subject to the order of an Aryan élite.

Yakushev was militantly anti-Christian, and he said he was instructing his followers in Tibetan Buddhism because that religion was the closest to Russian culture. He believed that the Russians and Germans formed a single race, and predicted a major war which would lead to a Russian-dominated Europe. The partnership between Barkashov and

Yakushev broke up after a few weeks, and Barkashov took sole charge of his miniature private army which called itself Russian National Unity. Like many other, more respectable, figures on the Slavophile right, Barkashov believed strongly in the natural friendship between the Russians and the Germans, and he viewed Eisenstein's film *Aleksandr Nevsky* as part of a Zionist plot to undermine this partnership.

Barkashov was a co-founder of the Slavic Council. His followers made up the security guards for that organisation and, much more important, for the lavish and high-profile meetings of the Russian National Council which were organised by General Sterligov in 1992.

In an opposition movement that was in danger of splitting under the strain of over-sized egos, doctrinal squabbling and clashing agendas, a vital, unifying role was played by the talented wordsmith Aleksandr Prokhanov.

More than any other figure in the Russian nationalist world, Prokhanov was fired by a passionate, non-sectarian devotion to the cause of imperialism. He stated frankly that he was prepared to make use of any principle, ideology or religion as long as it contributed to the higher cause of rebuilding and consolidating the Russian empire: from communism to rightist authoritarianism, Eastern Christianity to Islam, neo-paganism to numerological conspiracy theory.

Prokhanov grew up in Transcaucasia, and his ancestors were members of an exclusive sect of zealous Russian Christians known as the *molokane*, or milk-drinkers, for their practice of consuming dairy products on fasting days.

When the Soviet literary establishment split into liberal and nationalist camps during the Gorbachev years, Prokhanov was one of the toughest and most articulate figures on the nationalist side, helping to turn the Russian Federation Writers' Union into a bastion of opposition to *perestroika*.

Veterans of the union remember him in the 1970s as a shy, furtive character who described himself as a Christian but was nervous of the thought police. At some point, however,

Prokhanov seems to have made his peace with the Soviet Union's military and ideological establishment, for he became a semi-official chronicler of the army's campaign in Afghanistan. He was fantastically prolific, turning out more than thirty books. They ranged from a war novel called *A Tree in Central Kabul* to an apologia for the Soviet Union's long-range missiles, entitled *Nuclear Shield*. He was variously described as the Soviet Kipling or the songbird of the General Staff.

As the Soviet Union started to disintegrate, Prokhanov consistently played the role of co-ordinator and unifier between various brands of nationalist, imperialist, anti-Western, anti-Catholic and anti-Jewish ideology. In December 1989 he caused a minor sensation with an essay in *Literaturnaya Rossiya*, the journal of the Russian Writers' Union, in which he lauded the empire-building achievements of both Stalin and the Tsars, and painted a ghastly picture of what would happen as Russia continued to disintegrate: a civil war with nuclear and chemical weapons. In July 1991, he was co-author and initiator of the 'Word to the People' published in the daily *Sovyetskaya Rossiya*, which foreshadowed the August coup by warning darkly of the dreadful morass into which the country was sliding.

It was after the coup's failure, and especially after the break-up of the Soviet Union, that Prokhanov was able to cast himself in the role that he most relished: that of uncompromising, indefatigable warrior against the traitors and thieves who made up the 'temporary occupying regime', as he called the Yeltsin administration. To a political camp that was stunned and demoralised, Prokhanov brought energy, self-confidence, verbal dexterity and a certain relish. He was fanatical and he enjoyed his fanaticism; he thrilled to the challenge of taunting and wrong-footing an opponent which was clumsy and brutal in the manner of all Russian regimes.

Prokhanov took over an official publication of the Writers' Union and renamed it *Dyen* (*The Day*) after a conservative journal of the nineteenth century. He filled it with anti-Yeltsin and anti-Western outpourings from every quarter: diatribes, essays, poems, sermons and dirty jokes. There was something in its pages to appeal to every sort of activist in Russia's diverse, anti-democratic family: superannuated teachers of Marxism from the outer provinces, seminarians in Zagorsk, homeless army officers returning from Germany or the Baltic states, malcontents who had taken to the streets in favour of Yeltsin and were looking for a new cause to demonstrate against.

Prokhanov was an important ally in the attempt by former pro-Yeltsin democrats and Zyuganov's Russian communists to come together as a 'left-right' opposition; but he also spread his net much wider than that.

He took the view that there were no enemies on the far-right: Zhirinovsky and Pamyat received sympathetic mentions, as did Viktor Anpilov's ultra-militant communists.

Prokhanov was suspicious of the qualified nationalism preached by Viktor Aksyuchits; but those politicians who had truly repented of their democratic past, such as Mikhail Astafyev and Ilya Konstantinov, were prominent figures on the *Dyen* editorial board. The board's other members provide an impressive indication of the breadth of the hardline coalition. They included Aleksandr Nevzorov, the pioneer of 'investigative journalism' from Leningrad; conservative writers such as Valentin Rasputin and Stanislav Kunyaev; Father Dmitry Dudko, a former dissident priest; the Russian communists Zyuganov and General Albert Makashov; and the KGB's General Sterligov.

It was clear – if only from the scoops it obtained – that *Dyen* had sympathisers at high levels in the army, the foreign ministry and the security police. It took particular glee in publishing material that was calculated to embarrass Andrei Kozyrev, the foreign minister. In late 1992, for example, it published what it claimed was a letter to Kozyrev from James Baker, the US Secretary of State, which began 'Dear Andrew . . .' and continued in a similarly cosy style. The newspaper also carried comments on arms control which took a hawkish line and were based on detailed knowledge of the subject. For example, it argued that Russia was left at a severe disadvantage by Start-2, the treaty on limiting long-range nuclear rockets which was concluded by Yeltsin and Bush in 1992.

In pitching its emotional appeal, *Dyen* drew heavily on the images of the Second World War. When, in the early hours of 22 June 1992, policemen dispersed the mob of Anpilov's followers who were picketing the headquarters of Russian television, *Dyen* reported the event as though the police action was an assault on the Russian nation of similar dimensions to the Nazi onslaught of exactly fifty-one years earlier.

As well as appealing to memories of the 'anti-fascist struggle' against Hitler, the pro-fascist doctrines that flourished in the White Russian diaspora during the 1930s were also dusted down and given their first airing for sixty years. Through the pages of *Dyen*, readers were reintroduced to figures like Anastas Vosniyatsky, a resident of Connecticut who set himself up as the head of a fascist community.

For those who cared to notice them, the pages of *Dyen* were full of smutty jokes and word games. The President, for example, was always described as EBN, an anagram of his initials (Yeltsin, Boris Nikolayevich) which instantly recalled the word *yebenye*, one of the coarsest Russian terms for the sexual act. The use of these puns helped to create a kind of sniggering, winking, familiarity between paper and readers, just like the obscure nicknames and euphemisms used by the British weekly *Private Eye*.

Moreover, in person one of the first impressions conveyed by Prokhanov – a man with long, slightly unkempt black hair and restless dark eyes – is that of a louche, rib-digging character, a journalists' journalist who enjoys winkling out the foibles of others, puncturing their pomposity and gossiping about them. At the same time, Prokhanov is an indefatigable zealot, a person who can become quite carried away by his own rhetoric, as he holds forth on the wonderful political prospects that are opening up and the breadth of the coalition he is building. He has more political nous and a broader field of vision than most of the narrow constituencies whose support he invokes. Only his tendency to run away with his own rhetoric seems to prevent him from being a really formidable political strategist.

Interviewed in summer 1993, Prokhanov gleefully predicted that the President's demise – physical or political – was imminent. If Yeltsin violated the existing constitution in a bid to impose his will, he could find himself arrested, along with the entire government. Otherwise his demise 'might happen in the most unexpected way . . .'

> He might have a stroke, which would be the best way to go, because as you can see, he is very unwell. He is constantly under intensive care, it reminds me of Chernenko. The way he speaks, the rasping, heavy breath, the inability to put words together . . .
>
> How will Yeltsin leave the scene? If we are talking about ideology, about his general policy, then Yeltsin has gone already, because his policy no longer exists, the potential of Yeltsin's democracy has been exhausted. When Yeltsin came to power, trains still ran on time, and there was still enough fuel to keep the planes flying – but now the government has no economic capacity left. And its political capacity has been exhausted, along with its economic and moral capacity.

Nobody could have accused Prokhanov of suffering from an inability to put words together. He welcomed the fact that Rutskoy was moving into a position of uncompromising opposition, even though his personal relations with Rutskoy were strained and he took a dim view of the Vice-President's intelligence.

Although his small, bare office was dotted with icons, Prokhanov went on to make some comments on the subject of religion which were fractionally more broad-minded in tone than many of the columnists who filled his pages.

For example, Prokhanov stated frankly that he did not think it realistic or desirable that Orthodox Christianity should become Russia's official religion. The Catholic Church was the dominant religion in France and half of Germany, and he respected its role in those countries. On the other hand, it did have to be admitted that Catholic expansionism was having a bad effect on the former Soviet Union. By opening new parishes and dioceses in Ukraine and Byelorussia, it was fomenting the break-up of those republics. As for Russian Baptists, who were strictly apolitical, and other Protestants, Prokhanov said – and this was an amazingly tolerant statement for a member of the far right – that he could see 'little harm' in their activities. He went on to describe Judaism as 'a normal religion, a form of spiritual existence that is essential to the Jewish Diaspora, so let them have it . . .'

But a comment like that, from a man in Prokhanov's political corner, could not be left without a sting in the tail. 'The whole Jewish Diaspora is in such a state of excitement, it's alternately stricken with an inferiority complex which expresses itself as aggression towards Russia, or afflicted with fits of depression which makes them want to leave the country . . .' He went on to say, as a kind of aside that was reeled off without great conviction, that he himself accepted the theory that 'the anti-Christ will emerge from Jewish circles, that he will at a certain point take over the world and turn it into his kingdom, but then he will be defeated by God and the Christian ideal of the new Jerusalem'. So much for eschatology, then; Prokhanov seemed to abandon the subject with relief, and he brought somewhat greater conviction to his admission that 'the mysteries of the end of the world are somewhat remote to me, when we are so engaged in political struggle . . .' But was it worth engaging in political struggle if the end of the world was nigh? To this question, Prokhanov gave a sniggering answer that seemed to come straight from the gut: 'You might as well ask what's the point of having sex when we are all going to die.'

One of *Dyen*'s most frequent contributors was the author Eduard Limonov, who had enjoyed a *succès de scandale* with his sexually explicit novel of New York low-life, entitled *It's Me, Eddy.* This bitter-sweet tale of a penniless, bisexual Russian youth in Manhattan provided an image of the capitalist world as a hard, sordid and mercenary place, very different from the open-hearted, problem-free Nirvana which the West had seemed to offer when Russians caught their first real glimpse of it in the Gorbachev era. Limonov's contributions to *Dyen* were in a somewhat different vein. An instinctive hater of conventional wisdom who loved to shock, Limonov sought out a political position that was as far as possible from the pro-Western, pro-Yeltsin consensus that had recently been in fashion. He became a noisy advocate of the Serb cause in former Yugoslavia, and the war waged by the Abkhaz minority, with moral and material support from Russia, against Eduard Shevardnadze's Georgia. Limonov found a new outlet for his literary talent in touring the conflict zones and romanticising his new-found causes. When Zhirinovsky, in a characteristic publicity stunt, announced the formation of a shadow cabinet, he put Limonov in notional charge of the KGB, but Limonov later became disillusioned with the LDP leader.

The paper's lewd puns and the checkered background of its contributors did not seem to dissuade the most conservative wing of the Church from taking advantage of the generous amount of space which Prokhanov offered them. Just as a small number of liberal clerics had shared a common cause with secular reformers and had joined the colours of Boris Yeltsin, conservatives like Father Dmitry Dudko seemed happy to join ranks with communists and other advocates of authoritarianism to form a united anti-Western, anti-modern and anti-democratic front.

In April 1993, *Dyen* and other hardline newspapers soared high into the realm of conspiracy theory following the macabre Easter Day murder of three much-loved monks at the newly restored Optina monastery, which before the revolution had been one of the greatest centres of Russian spirituality.

The only details which emerged were the fact that the killer was an Afghan veteran, apparently deranged; and he had used a dagger with a symbol suggestive of devil-worship carved into the handle.

Dyen told its readers that Russia's 'Zionised' media were doing their best to cover up a crime committed by dark forces that were bent on subverting Russia's Orthodox heritage. On the same page, an account of the theological significance of the Council of Nicaea in 325 slid into a furious diatribe against Jewish proselytising in the Roman empire and then into an argument that drew generalised anti-Semitic conclusions from Christ's outbursts against the scribes and Pharisees. The Hebrew claim to be a chosen people 'conceals the true blood connections of the Jewish race, which are Satanic ones . . .'

However, *Dyen*'s foaming wrath over the Optina murders did not, apparently, extend to the Soviet ruler who consigned hundreds of thousands of Christian believers to incarceration or death, before reviving the Church to suit his own purposes. An entire page in *Dyen* devoted to the 'mysteries of history' turned out to be an elaborate and insidious hymn of praise to Stalin, relying on subliminal as well as intellectual forms of persuasion.

The page included historical essays, which argued that Stalin – uniquely wise among the Bolsheviks – had seen through the motives of the American capitalists who tried desperately to prop up Kerensky's provisional government in 1917; and also a quote from Winston Churchill, marvelling at the 'energy, erudition and unbending will' he observed in the Soviet tyrant. The most eerie touch was provided by four grainy photographs, forming a square on one side of the page. Kerensky and Yeltsin were placed side by side, as though to imply that like Kerensky, the current Russian leader was a temporary, provisional figure. Below Kerensky there was the young Stalin, looking full of confidence and guile, and below Yeltsin there was a figure in a greatcoat whose head had been blacked out. In other words, there was another great tyrant, as formidable as Stalin, waiting in the wings; but his name could not yet be revealed.

Perhaps these shadowy intimations were not Prokhanov's most important contribution to the broader hardline cause. Of greater significance was the platform his newspaper provided for a younger generation of 'new right' ideologists who were trying to elaborate a new school of anti-modern, authoritarian thought which transcended the anti-Semitic and monarchist themes of traditional Russian conservatism.

Among the most prominent of these was Aleksandr Dugin, a former Pamyat activist who joined Prokhanov in forging links with the far right in France, Germany, Belgium and Spain. Drawing in part on theories that were evolved in the Axis powers in the 1930s, the Russian rightists drew a contrast between the old-world civilisations of continental Europe which were rooted in the soil, and the cold, calculating rationalism of the Atlanticist powers – the United States and also Britain – where traditional values, hierarchies and totems were powerless against the logic of capital.

As Dr Walter Laqueur, the distinguished analyst of the Russian right, has pointed out, this school of ultra-conservatism tends to be neo-pagan, and is often anti-Christian. It admires primitive cultures and sees in their rites and customs a healthy expression of primal urges, the collective unconscious postulated by Jung. It despises egalitarianism and sees merit in the idea of warrior élites.

Among the West European ideologists whom Prokhanov and Dugin came to admire was Alain de Benoist, the exponent of anti-modern, anti-American and anti-capitalist thinking who has commanded some attention on both the extreme left and the extreme right of French politics – although his ideas are so far beyond the pale of respectability that even to write about him is considered suspect.

Another neo-rightist theoretician whom Prokhanov helped to publicise was Sergei Kurginyan, an actor with a scientific training who argued that Russia could not copy the West's model of industrialisation because that would finally destroy the world's ecosystem. Instead, some compromise must be found between high technology and the structure and values of traditional society.

Kurginyan finally broke with Dugin on the grounds that his colleague had become too obsessed with the fantasy of a continental empire which did not coincide with Russia's own interests. Kurginyan, whose name and appearance reflect his Armenian roots, ran into difficulties of a more prosaic kind in his tentative relationship with General Sterligov. On his arrival at the grand Moscow meeting of Sterligov's Council, he was roughly manhandled by the security guards, trained by Aleksandr Barkashov. 'What's a black arse [the standard Russian insult for Transcaucasians] like you doing here?' they demanded to know. Kurginyan complained rather vigorously to the general.

In more rarefied circles – academics, politicians, journalists – the theories of Kurginyan and other new-rightist ideologues fared better. Two former Soviet Prime Ministers, Valentin Pavlov and Nikolai Ryzhkov, and Yeltsin's spokesman Pavel Voschanov were members of an informal think-tank, the Experimental Creative Centre, in which Kurginyan was a leading light.

The diverse bundle of ideas aired by the new Russian right included Lev Gumilyov's theory that the ethnos or nation is the principal agent of history; and the notion that Eurasia forms a single geographical and geopolitical space which Russia – as a unique, self-sufficient ethnos belonging neither to East or West – is destined to dominate.

There was some confusion, however, as to what the ideas of Eurasia and the ethnos implied in practice. When neo-nationalists like Prokhanov and the communist leader Zyuganov described Russia as a Eurasian state, they sometimes appeared to mean that there was a political and cultural affinity between the East Christian Slavs and the Turkic Muslims. In other words, Orthodox Russia had more in common with the traditional, authoritarian values of Central Asia than it had with the individualist, humanist West. It should therefore attach the highest priority to rebuilding links (on Russia's terms, of course) with the Kazakhs, Uzbeks and other Turkic nations which were cut off from Moscow by the Soviet break-up. As well as giving space to ultra-conservative Orthodox clerics, Prokhanov offered whole pages of his newspaper to Muslim ideologues from Tatarstan and the northern Caucasus, who explained how Islam's God-centred and communal values differed from the humanism and individualism of Western Europe.

Both Zhirinovsky and Pamyat's Dmitry Vasilyev had been flanked for part of their careers by deputies whose names pointed clearly to Soviet Muslim origin. So it was already well established that there was no inconsistency in professing Slav nationalism and a version of Muslim authoritarianism. On the face of things, the idea of the Slav-Turkic alliance could draw much inspiration from Gumilyov, who believed that the eastern Slavs flourished under the so-called Tatar-Mongol yoke; that Aleksandr Nevsky was a blood-brother of one of the princes of the Golden Horde; and that the modern Russian nation was as much a product of Tatar and Mongol influences as it was of Christendom.

It was also possible to read Gumilyov in a different way. If it was true that the fusion between the early Slavs and the early Tatar-Mongols into a 'super-ethnos' called Greater Russia had taken place hundreds of years ago, then those Turkic peoples whose identities had remained distinct – the Uzbeks, Kazakhs and perhaps even the pure-blooded Tatars, Bashkirs and Chechens, who lived inside Russia – were an alien presence which might actually 'contaminate' the almighty super-ethnos. So it was possible to draw isolationist, as well as expansionist, conclusions from Gumilyov's teaching.

These contradictions did not greatly trouble Prokhanov, whose self-imposed mission was to be a unifier, a healer of divisions within the ultra-right; a closer of ranks against the Western (or pro-Western) enemy. Any ideology, any religion or anti-religion was worthy of propagation, in his view, if it served the cause which he never hesitated to describe as imperialism. Without discrimination, he gave a platform to both the main impulses which drove the Russian nationalist cause.

The first of these was the longing for a traditional Russia, a Russian Russia, the warmth and cruelty of communal life which was articulated with such dexterity by the village writers, and in a different way, by the conservative wing of the clergy and even the old-fashioned communists. The second was a keen desire for a strong Russia, a Russia which compensated for its lack of Western sophistication with sheer, brute strength on a scale that would fill outsiders with fear and therefore respect. This was the nationalism of the *Dyen* writers who railed against the Start-2 treaty because it would strip Russia of the deadly SS-18 missile, the showpiece of its arsenal. These two impulses – the traditionalism of the Slavophiles and the power-worship of the militarists and pan-Slavists – were profoundly different, although a great deal of Russian nationalist discourse is aimed at blurring that distinction. It is a long way from Rasputin's villages to the silo of an SS-18; but Prokhanov played his part in reducing that distance.

He had only one blind spot, only one serious limit to his flexibility. So passionate was his hatred of Yeltsin and all his works that he simply could not entertain the idea that the Russian President, the hated EBN, could be as good an instrument in the sacred cause of imperialism as any other.

10

Riding The Roller-coaster

From the winter of 1992 till the autumn of 1993, Russia – or at least official Russia – was on a kind of roller-coaster, which frightened the world and filled its own people with emotions that ranged from excitement to dread, passionate engagement to shoulder-shrugging indifference.

The 'irreconcilable opposition' – and for some reason there seemed to be no other kind – became wilder and more desperate as it scented the blood of Yeltsin and his entourage. The President's supporters pressed him harder and harder to strike back against the foe whose countenance was darkening with every passing day; and they cared less and less about how black their own faces might grow in the course of this life-or-death struggle.

For the second time in less than two years, the country faced a legal and constitutional crisis which could not have a legal or constitutional outcome, and therefore could only be resolved when one party or other broke the shackles of the law and rewrote the rules in its own favour.

The first insoluble crisis of state had occurred in mid-summer 1991, when it became clear that nothing except a *putsch*, or possibly even a series of *putsches*, would settle the future of the disintegrating Soviet Union. This was because there was no conceivable arrangement that would win the assent of both the assemblies which were competing for supreme authority over the same physical space: the Soviet Parliament and the Parliament of the Russian Federation.

Anything which satisfied one would be unacceptable to the other. Under Yeltsin's chairmanship, the Russian assembly had embarked on a quest for power which acknowledged no limits; and because the Russian legislature was so boundlessly ambitious, the Soviet one grew more and more obstinate in its determination to keep whatever remained of its own crumbling authority.

Assuming they could overcome their intense dislike of one another, it was conceivable for Gorbachev as Soviet leader, and Yeltsin as senior politician of the Russian Federation, to strike their own man-to-man agreement on how to resolve the crisis, but it was hard to imagine any peace terms which both men could sell to their respective constituencies. The new Union treaty which was supposed to be signed on 20 August 1991 was the fruit of one such high-level deal between Gorbachev, Yeltsin and the other republican leaders. It would have kept the Soviet Union in existence as a loosely structured federation whilst devolving most economic power to Russia and the other republics.

It is, however, perfectly clear in retrospect – and it was fairly clear to certain prescient observers at the time – that this treaty could never have gained acceptance. Precisely because it gave so much power to the republics, there was no possibility that the Soviet Parliament would ratify it, and thus terminate its own life; in contrast there were many politicians in the Russian Federation who felt that it did not give *enough* power to the republics.

The only thing that could break this deadlock was some kind of coup; and as it turned out, there was a double coup. The hard men on the 'Union' side were clumsy enough to jump first – by isolating Gorbachev and declaring a state of emergency on 19 August 1991 – and their failure duly triggered a sort of counter-*putsch* by Yeltsin which led to the Union's total collapse.

By the end of 1992, a similar sort of deadly impasse between two rival authorities was taking hold. Again, neither party saw any reason to exercise the self-restraint, or the deference to some universally acknowledged adjudicator, which underpins the functioning of democracy in the West. On the contrary, each camp steadily fed the extremism of the other, and waverers were forced to make their choice.

On one side of this new deadlock was the Russian Parliament, which had initially provided Yeltsin with a power base, but was now turning away from him, and on the other, a fragile but steadily consolidating Russian administration, with the President at the top.

The head of the former faction was the parliamentary speaker Ruslan Hasbulatov, the clever, sharp-tongued economist who had entered the top ranks of Russian politics in mid-1990 at Yeltsin's side. It soon became clear why Yeltsin had chosen him as a lieutenant. As deputy chairman of the Russian Parliament, Hasbulatov proved himself a relentless and resourceful warrior in the cause of squeezing the Soviet government into oblivion and establishing a new state called Russia.

Hasbulatov was a Chechen, a member of the largest and most formidable of the Muslim races who inhabit the northern slopes of the Caucasus mountains. He was often described as a 'pipe-smoking economics professor' which was literally accurate but misleading: it suggested a carefree affability which nobody of Hasbulatov's background could be expected to have. His childhood was blighted by Stalin's decision in 1944 to deport every Chechen man, woman and child from their mountain homeland to Kazakhstan, more than a thousand miles to the east. For a boy who grew up in the grinding hardship of exile in Alma-Ata, the Kazakh capital, to have risen to high rank in Muscovite academia was a formidable achievement; it required something more than tweedy good nature. Hasbulatov had the pale complexion and strong physiognomy of his race, but as the strains of the political struggle began to take their toll, a haunted look seemed to enter his eyes.

'I will die a violent death,' he used to predict, full of bitterness and resignation. Those who knew him well said this was not a premonition that his struggle with Yeltsin would turn bloody, but a cry of alarm over the feuding in his native Chechnya. In the immediate aftermath of the August 1991 coup (during which he behaved with exemplary courage) he welcomed the move by Dzhokhar Dudayev, the maverick air force commander, to seize power from the local communists in Grozny, the Chechen capital. Yet Hasbulatov very quickly came to realise that the self-proclaimed Chechen republic could be a sharp thorn in the side of the newly independent Russian Federation, and so later he supported calls for the rebel state's suppression. This prompted fighters loyal to Dudayev to pledge on their Chechen honour that they would punish their compatriot for his treachery: hence the parliamentary chairman's paranoia and some of his more surprising decisions – such as an order to Moscow hotels instructing them not to accept Chechen guests.

Hasbulatov was a tough manipulator of parliamentary procedure, and his acerbic macho manner had more than once reduced women deputies to the point of tears. With characteristic double standards, the reformist deputies who voted Hasbulatov into office were only too pleased in the early days when he used his sarcasm on parliamentarians like Svetlana Goryacheva, a starchy communist lady from Vladivostok; while later, when Hasbulatov had shown his colours as a hardliner, the democrats bristled with indignation over his verbal battles with Bella Denisenko, the health minister who was one of their own. A low point in Hasbulatov's fortunes seemed to come in late 1992 when he appeared before Parliament in a state of virtual collapse, which an official statement attributed to overwork and 'excessive smoking'. Denisenko accused him of being under the influence of alcohol or some other stimulant, and he replied unprintably.

Hasbulatov served Yeltsin well when both men were engaged in wearing down the Union, but once this purpose had been achieved, these two power-hungry men were almost doomed to become rivals. Hasbulatov – who formally succeeded Yeltsin as chairman of the Russian Parliament in October 1991 – was a more substantial figure than Vice-President Aleksandr Rutskoy, Yeltsin's other mutinous lieutenant. From spring 1992 onwards, Hasbulatov gradually began constructing his own power base, working patiently and meticulously to build up a network of supporters within Parliament, and beyond. The parliamentary chairman had an appetite for quiet, systematic work which Yeltsin, who thrived on crises but became bored in quiet times, entirely lacked. As a member of a race which – to judge by opinion polls – was becoming more and more unpopular in Russia, Hasbulatov could never hope to be freely elected to supreme power in Russia; but he apparently saw a real chance of becoming the country's most powerful figure through discreet manipulation of the vagaries of the constitution.

As chairman of the Russian legislature, he stood at the apex of a network of soviets or councils which extended from Moscow to the smallest village. Every region, city, town and neighbourhood had its own soviet; these were the bodies which gave the USSR its name.

The executive branch of government which Yeltsin headed was strong in the cities of Moscow and St Petersburg, thanks to their charismatic mayors, but the further one went into the provinces, the weaker the executive looked. Yeltsin had named a governor (usually a senior official of the Communist Party) as his representative in each of Russia's seventy regions, but in places where the soviet was strong, conservative and loyal to Hasbulatov, the President's men could be very lonely figures. In several cases, the governors simply broke ranks with Yeltsin and became advocates for the regions they ruled and there was not much anybody in Moscow could do about this. From Hasbulatov's point of view, it was tempting to believe that the Russian presidency, and the entire administrative branch of the Russian government, could be neutralised or even abolished, for this would leave Hasbulatov as the most important person in the land.

To this end, the speaker had steadily built up a large permanent apparatus. Many of the most conservative figures in Gorbachev's personal staff – the ones who had betrayed him during the August coup – were recruited by Hasbulatov. His military adviser was General Vladislav Achalov, the paratroop commander who had backed the conspirators during the August 1991 events while his young subordinates Pavel Grachev and Aleksandr Lebed were rallying to the other side. Another senior, hardline figure who joined the 'parliamentary' staff was Filipp Bobkov, a former deputy head of the KGB who had once been in charge of surveillance over dissidents.

Westerners were too quick to imagine that they understood the Yeltsin-Hasbulatov stand-off because it was, among many other things, a battle between a government and a parliament and Western countries, notably the United States, have those battles too. On one hand there are the makers of executive decisions, on the other the setters of general rules; in between them, as a referee and definer of boundary lines, the judiciary. For the Western political scientist, some degree of healthy, creative tension along these lines is the very stuff of which democracy is made. But like most comparisons between Russia and the West involving persons or institutions, this parallel misleads as much as it enlightens.

As the struggle between Yeltsin's government and Hasbulatov's Parliament gathered pace, it became clear that both sides wanted a monopoly on all forms of power; neither believed in the Western principle that power should be divided between executive, legislative and judicial forms of authority. Hasbulatov's Parliament – or rather the enormously powerful presidium which steered parliamentary business – was not so much a law-making body as a rival source of executive power. It was in direct competition with the government for the right to spend money, command soldiers and policemen, and of course reap the benefits of the enormous corruption which the fitful move to market economics was opening up.

The Russian Parliament should have set general guidelines for government spending, and it failed to do that effectively; yet through its presidium it could, and often did, allocate money to specific regions, enterprises or persons. The central bank was, in theory, subordinate to the legislature, and it was sometimes in response to the instructions of Hasbulatov's people that it doled out soft credits to this or that favoured customer. More often the bank was yet another centre of barely accountable and capriciously exercised power.

The Parliament was near enough the levers of power to frustrate the efforts of those people who were trying to manage the nation's crisis – and far enough away to avoid responsibility for the consequences of anything that happened. It was powerful enough to plunge the country into hyperinflation, and detached enough not to blamed.

Hasbulatov's trump card was a dog-eared old document, endlessly amended in the power struggles of the previous two years, called the Russian constitution. This made it clear, in so far as it made anything at all clear, that the Congress of People's Deputies, or full Parliament, was the highest authority in the land, and that all questions of national life, from the most particular to the most general, lay within its competence. This was a legacy of its role as a rubber-stamp for the decisions of the Communist Party; if the party was to be all-powerful, then so must its chosen instruments of governance. In principle, therefore, there was simply nothing that a president, prime minister or cabinet minister could do that the Congress might not instantly undo; and there was no obligation on the legislature to do anything at all that was constructive or beneficial to the national interest.

The only body that could change the constitution was the Congress itself. Everyone agreed in principle that the constitution – drawn up in 1977 when Russia was still a communist republic in a communist state – was outdated and bristling with internal contradictions; but there was no reason to imagine that the Congress would ever agree to constitutional changes which implied the watering-down of its own potentially unlimited power.

Yeltsin had some strong cards too. His own personal charisma, his reputation as a valiant warrior for democracy, was bound to suffer attrition as the post-communist world failed to produce the expected miracles and his own fallibility became more obvious. But he was still on balance more popular than Hasbulatov's Parliament, and certainly more popular than the stiff-necked communists who formed the Assembly's largest and loudest faction. By the winter of 1992/3, his personal popularity rating might have been little more than 25 per cent; but if he could somehow convince the public that he was the only alternative to a communist come-back, he would be almost certain of prevailing.

Therefore Yeltsin's best hope was to break the constitutional impasse by holding a referendum with a question to which there could be only one answer, even from those people who had once admired him and were now badly disappointed. The question must force people to choose between Yeltsin and the reformers or Hasbulatov and the communists; presidential power or parliamentary power; a presidential constitution or a parliamentary one. The sooner a referendum could be held, the better it would be for Yeltsin; the longer such a poll could be put off, the better it would be for Hasbulatov, because with every day of political paralysis, Yeltsin's charisma was fading. The President's biggest problem was that only the legislature was entitled to call a referendum, and it was very unlikely to do so, unless it could somehow be trapped or bounced into signing its own death warrant, just as the institutions of the USSR had found themselves trapped after the August coup.

In late 1992, the crisis was moving onto a high gear. At the beginning of December, a twelve-month period in which Yeltsin had secured 'special powers' to name ministers and run the economy was due to expire. Even with its special powers intact, the administration had experienced the greatest difficulty in imposing its will on the economy. It had not been able, for example, to stop the central bank from issuing credits to industry and the other republics to the tune of about 40 per cent of Russia's GDP. Without these special powers, Yeltsin was in danger of being reduced to the status of a figure-head, like the British monarch.

If he was to go on ruling the country, he needed even more power than he had enjoyed over the previous year and unless he was very artful, he could find himself with considerably less. It was a hard situation – the sort Yeltsin relished – but there was more than one option open to him.

He could have bought off, literally or metaphorically, enough of the 1,033 members of the full Parliament to blunt the influence of the 400 or so irreconcilable opponents of his rule. This would not have been excessively difficult: it would have been enough to entice them with jobs, flattery and privileges. Most members of the Congress were modest provincial characters whose greatest fear was the loss of the few scraps of privilege that went with parliamentary status: a car, a flat in Moscow, free travel round the country, a modest salary and expenses. To put it very cynically, they would have come fairly cheap, and Yeltsin did have some scope for parrying the hostility of the legislature by sweet-talking some of its members.

The state of public finances, on the other hand, did not leave much room for compromise over policy. The achievements of the year had been substantial, but they were fragile. At nearly 30 per cent a month, inflation was about as high as it could be without tipping over into hyperinflation, which would render the country unmanageable. So there was little enough scope for warding off the hostility of Congress by throwing more money at this or that lobby.

Yet Prime Minister Gaidar, whom nobody could accuse of lacking a sense of purpose, felt in late 1992 that a minimum of tactical concessions should be made in order to be sure of reaching the strategic goal of irreversible market reform. He had already made clear his view that it was worth courting the support of the most competent and potentially competitive of the country's industrial managers in order to drive a wedge between their interests and those of the incorrigible dinosaurs.

In this spirit, he believed there was room for some political compromise with the parliamentary caucus known as the Civic Union, which comprised the supporters of Vice-President Rutskoy; the industrial managers on whose behalf the veteran bureaucrat Arkady Volsky claimed to speak; and Nikolai Travkin's Democratic Party of Russia, the biggest of the minnow parties which had abandoned the pro-Yeltsin coalition. The Civic Union was supposed in theory to account for about half the members of the 1,033-strong Congress, so that any deal that involved both them and the 200 or so parliamentarians who were committed supporters of the President should have been rock-solid. The practical consequences of such a deal would mean a new sort of coalition cabinet dominated by Gaidar, Volsky and their protégés.

All this sounded fine in theory, but it rested on the highly dubious assumption that Russia's political scene was occupied by neat, shiny building blocks which only needed putting together with ingenuity and care. In reality, the landscape was peopled with a morass of confused, opportunistic individuals; neither the Civic Union nor anybody else could deliver legislators' votes in decisive numbers. For an intensely political, power-conscious animal like Yeltsin, the real challenge did not lie in squeezing worthy policies through a narrow parliamentary door; it lay in gaining some mastery over a dull, featureless landscape by picking fights and winning them, and in that way reacquiring the ancient and indispensable technique of inculcating fear.

Consciously or unconsciously, Yeltsin fumbled any opportunity there was during his first set-piece confrontation with Parliament, in December 1992, to broke a sensible compromise based on salvaging the most important policies. He began by offering legislators the chance to choose four key ministers – of foreign affairs, defence, the interior and security – on the understanding that the government would have a free hand over economics. This was too much for Yeltsin to offer – he risked forfeiting the support of the current holders of those key portfolios – and it was not enough to satisfy the Congress. Its rejection merely demonstrated the legislators' bad faith, which may have been the intention. A week later, after much bickering, stalemate and a sordid televised fist-fight in which Yeltsin's parliamentary supporters hardly distinguished themselves, the President mounted his first political offensive against the Congress. This too was mismanaged.

On the morning of 10 December, he told legislators that he had given up trying to work with them, and pledged to hold a referendum in the spring on whether he or Hasbulatov should be entrusted with nursing Russia back to health. Yeltsin then marched out of the Congress and made a dramatic appearance at a Moscow factory, driving home his point that he had an obligation to the ordinary Russian people that was more important than any legal niceties. To the exasperation of the President's advisers, his speech failed to include any clear call to his own supporters in Congress to leave the assembly hall after him. If as many as 300 had done so, the assembly would have been left without a quorum and he would have scored an instant victory.

Instead, he left the Congress in the condition of a wounded bull, frightened, angry but very much alive. A wave of panic-stricken rumours had many deputies almost convinced that an army unit had arrived at the Kremlin to disband their assembly by force. Blind to the political damage they were doing themselves, they passed a resolution forbidding the President to call a referendum, and threatening him with instant and automatic removal from office if he tried to dissolve the legislature. The deputies' fear of immediate disbandment receded slightly when the ministers of defence, the interior and security came to address them and all three (not surprisingly, in view of the President's earlier willingness to jettison them) stopped short of supporting Yeltsin's initiative. But the stage had been set for a confrontation in which one side or the other would eventually win. Many deputies who had once considered themselves supporters of the President now gravitated towards the clutches of Mr Hasbulatov. The speaker seemed to represent their only hope of avoiding the terrible prospect of early elections, which for many of them would spell defeat, poverty and obscurity.

The first wrangle between President and Parliament was resolved by Judge Valery Zorkin, the chairman of the constitutional court whose profile as an arbiter of the nation's affairs had risen as a result of the trial which ended in a partial reversal of Yeltsin's ban on the Communist Party.

Zorkin was a soft-spoken but self-important man with a strong belief in his own contribution to shaping Russia's destiny. As a scholar of Russian legal history, he belonged to a Marxist (and Orthodox Christian) tradition which rejects the Western idea of 'cold law' – the dogged application to all situations of a finite set of rules – and looks on the state, including the judiciary, as a moral force and social engineer.

Zorkin's belief in his own historic mission was fuelled as he brought Yeltsin and Hasbulatov together and brokered a compromise: each side in the dispute would reverse its most recent moves to neutralise the power of the other, Parliament would have a say in choosing the next Prime Minister, and a referendum would be held in April on a new constitution. Yeltsin appeared to be the winner in the medium term – a referendum was still in prospect – but in the short term he paid a humiliating price. From the list of candidates he suggested for Prime Minister, the legislators rejected Gaidar in favour of Viktor Chernomyrdin, a thick-set technocrat of the Soviet school who for the last seven years had been in charge of the country's gas industry.

Chernomyrdin was, at it turned out, one of the most competent representatives of that school. The gas industry was a success story. It was laying new pipelines, buying up foreign subsidiaries and performing with unique success the very trick which the country as a whole so badly needed to play: the conversion of old-fashioned forms of influence afforded by the command economy into a new sort of commercial power that was tradable in the international market-place. The first signals sent by Chernomyrdin as Prime Minister were conservative ones. He tried to reintroduce price controls and spoke contemptuously of the 'bazaar' which Russia's first steps towards a market system had created. But he steadily showed his colours as man who was well in tune with the requirements of the moment: an economic reformer and practitioner of a new and sophisticated form of regional power politics in which energy flows would play a vital part.

In theory, the producers of oil, gas and coal ought to have been natural believers in bringing a dose of reason to the

Russian economy. They were among the most obvious losers in a communist system which forced them to deliver their output to rickety old factories, or to regional bosses with political muscle, for a fraction of the world price. Things were not quite as simple as that, because any transaction which was conducted at artificially low prices provided both parties with handsome opportunities for freelance profit-taking. The scale on which this took place is shown up by the remarkable revelation, early in 1993, that at least one-quarter of the oil delivered by Russia to Ukraine the previous year had been illegally diverted.

As Prime Minister, Chernomyrdin seemed at first to be wedded to the old-fashioned communist view that the interests of energy and industry were indivisible, but it soon became obvious to captains of energy like himself that Russia could not afford, either commercially or strategically, to go on supplying all of its Soviet customers with fuel at knock-down prices. As a first step – made almost inevitable by a steep decline in the output of many forms of energy – Russia had sharply to reduce its supplies of subsidised energy to the republics; a measure which would have the happy side-effect of deepening their political dependence on Moscow. In second place, Russia had gradually to ratchet up the price at which its own industries and cities were supplied with fuel. This, together with the privatisation process which was just beginning, would gradually sort out the viable bits of industry from the unviable, and weed out what Chermomyrdin learned to call 'unnecessary production'.

So Chernomyrdin soon turned out to be a better economic reformer than the Gaidar team dared to hope; and a practitioner of a more effective form of imperialism than the red-brown campaigners for national salvation dared to imagine possible as long as Yeltsin remained President.

Uncommitted members of the Russian legislature – the so-called 'marshland' whose inhabitants were neither firm supporters, nor unconditional enemies, of the President – praised the compromise brokered by Zorkin as a victory for common sense, a step backwards from the brink of civil war.

But that was an excessively unrealistic view: at best, Zorkin's deal had merely allowed both ends of the spectrum – the President's men on one hand, Hasbulatov and the communists on the other – a short breathing space in which to lick their wounds and prepare to lock horns once again.

If common sense had prevailed, the Congress would have ended by making the deal that had been almost concluded beforehand: Gaidar would have remained as Prime Minister, and some relatively enlightened factory boss would have been installed as his deputy. But no such victory for moderation took place. What happened instead was that very Russian phenomenon, a peculiar and unexpected synthesis which is born out of the clash between two extremes. The advent of Chernomyrdin – who was voted into power by parliamentary hardliners, and then turned quite rapidly into an effective reformer – was a reminder that in politics as well as nature, the coming together of two entirely different substances can force into being an alloy that is more durable than either.

Although Yeltsin had almost wilfully fluffed his own lines in the December 1992 drama, his stand-off with Parliament had highlighted at least one important political fact: support for the President tended to fall off sharply in quiet times, when people had nothing to think about except the daily grind of survival, but it rose sharply when tension with his parliamentary enemies was at its height. Public opinion was easily bored by quiet, depressing times, but it responded with alacrity to the prospect of a fight. Exactly the same thing could be said of Yeltsin himself.

World opinion seemed to lose interest in the complexities of Russia for the first two months of 1993, and when it opened its eyes again, it was horrified by what it saw. A distracted and vacillating President seemed to be losing ground by the day to an uncompromising red-brown coalition that was determined to bring an abrupt end to economic reform, reconstruct the Soviet Union and put together a new coalition of anti-Western states, from Iraq to Serbia.

The agreement with Yeltsin to hold a referendum on constitutional change was renounced by Hasbulatov, and then by Zorkin. Hasbulatov gave up all pretence of being a social democrat, who might hope to mediate between various extremes. He embarked instead on a close, if loveless, relationship with the resurgent communists, who blamed the West for destroying the Soviet Union and were determined to undo the damage. Egged on by strategists like Baburin and Isakov, the parliamentary hardliners were confident that Yeltsin could be emasculated at least, impeached and disgraced at most. When Yeltsin appeared before Congress on 10 March, it contemptuously rejected all his proposals for a way out of the constitutional crisis. Western leaders wondered where they had gone wrong, as they contemplated a picture of seemingly unrelieved disaster.

Yeltsin was certainly in a tight corner, but the situation was not, from his point of view, quite as unsatisfactory as it seemed to his Western friends. As the spectre of red-brown opposition drew closer, the world was steadily browbeaten into accepting the Manichaean view of Russia which Yeltsin presented them. *The Economist*, editorialising on Moscow's power struggle, abandoned its usual scepticism and accepted the view that this was nothing less than a fight between light and darkness.

> At stake is not just who rules Russia, but what sort of place it will be: prosperous, or poverty-stricken, open or inward-looking, a force for good or ill. If Russia's second great revolution goes wrong, its people will this time have a lot more to lose than their chains.

At that time, the smugness that descended on the Western world in the aftermath of its Cold and Gulf War victories was still very much intact; it was still assumed that a Russia which was prosperous, as the West defined prosperity, would be a force for good in the world, as the West defined goodness. The Yeltsin administration would have been foolish if it had not capitalised on that sentiment for all it was worth.

If Yeltsin was the repository of all the world's hope for 'goodness' in Russia, it followed that helping his administration, and forgiving it any minor peccadilloes, was an overwhelming political imperative. The Group of Seven capitalist leaders fell to bickering furiously among themselves over how exactly Russia could be assisted. France and Germany shamed a sceptical Japan, which was holder that year of the Group's rotating presidency, into playing its part as a co-ordinator of aid to Russia. The newly elected President Clinton scrambled to prepare an aid package for Yeltsin in time for their first meeting in Vancouver in early April, although there were moments when it seemed unclear whether the Russian leader would last that long. President Mitterrand tried unsuccessfully to turn the Vancouver meeting into a summit of the Group of Seven (or Eight) with aid to Russia as the sole item on the agenda.

Somewhere in the course of these frantic discussions, it came to be accepted by everyone that for reasons of historical necessity, Russia must be given a uniquely privileged sort of treatment by the International Monetary Fund and the World Bank. From an attitude towards Russia that was unrealistically tough – in the sense that it had no mandate to take any account of internal political constraints – the international financial institutions duly somersaulted, under urgent instructions from the leading Western governments, and switched to an entirely different posture: one that virtually exempted Russia from the financial conditions which were expected of any other country. For the bankers and economists who worked at those institutions and had spent a lifetime schooling unruly nations in the ways of financial rectitude, it was a bemusing experience, at once comical and exasperating, to watch Russia's leaders cheerfully rewrite the rules of the capitalist club before they had even joined. High-flying bureaucrats, used to laying down the law in every semi-bankrupt finance ministry in the world, found to their astonishment that Russian officialdom treated them with condescension: the condescension of borrowers who know that their banker has no real choice, because the political cost of meanness is even higher than the financial risks of profligacy.

The sheer political ugliness of Yeltsin's enemies meant that

Western politicians, as well as financial institutions, had no option but to view him in the most charitable of lights. James Baker, newly retired from the job of US Secretary of State, used a signed article in *Newsweek* magazine to describe the dreadfulness of the Russian opposition: they were extremists who 'would draw their power not from what they stand for but from what they stand against . . .' Baker added:

> The one objective they would stand for, is the return of empire, to defend the rights [of] and even reunite the 25 million Russians who live in Kazakhstan, Ukraine, the Baltic states and the other independent states of the former Soviet Union. Anyone who cares about the freedom of Ukrainians, Estonians, Latvians, Lithuanians and the other formerly captive nations of the Soviet Union cannot easily dismiss the dangers. The fervent hope for these anti-democratic, anti-Semitic, anti-modern and anti-Western reactionaries would be to find Russia's future in its past.

In the face of such appalling dangers, it seemed to be almost carping for anyone to point out that Russia was already involved in armed stand-offs in at least three republics: in Moldova, where General Lebed's garrison was firmly entrenched; in Tajikistan, where Russian forces were shoring up a communist regime in its conflict with Islamic and secular opponents; and, with increasing openness, in Abkhazia, the north-western region of Georgia.

War had been raging in that beautiful and potentially prosperous territory since autumn 1992. Under the Soviet system, the ethnic Abkhazians – an ancient race which made up less than 20 per cent of the population – had dominated the region's administration, with Moscow's blessing. Just like the Slav community of eastern Moldova, Abkhazia had served the Kremlin as a time-bomb that was primed to explode in the event of the surrounding republic (in this case, Georgia) making a serious bid to free itself from Moscow's shackles. Fighting erupted amid the orange groves and holiday camps on 14 August, when Eduard Shevardnadze sent a Georgian force, so poorly-disciplined that it could hardly be described as an army, into the region, ostensibly in pursuit of rebels loyal to his predecessor, Zviad Gamsakhurdia. Shevardnadze said afterwards his forces had been promised safe passage by Vladislav Ardzinba, the scholar of Oriental history and staunch friend of Moscow who headed the Abkhazian government. If any such promise was given, it was not respected: the war between the Abkhaz leadership and the Georgian government evolved rapidly into one of the dirtiest and bloodiest on former Soviet soil.

At first, the most conspicuous allies of the Abkhaz cause were volunteers from the Muslim nations of the northern Caucasus, who streamed southwards over the Russian-Georgian border to join the battle against Shevardnadze's forces. By early 1993, however, the anti-Georgian coalition had a new and far more powerful friend in the shape of the Russian air force which repeatedly bombed Sukhumi, the Georgians' main stronghold. General Grachev, the defence minister, initially denied that these raids were happening; then asserted that the Georgians were bombing themselves; and finally confirmed that Russia was carrying out the raids, in retaliation for attacks on its own forces in the region. He made it plain that for strategic reasons – the need for maximum access to the Black Sea – Russia would maintain a garrison in Georgia indefinitely, regardless of any objections that the government in Tbilisi might have. Grachev did not, for any practical purposes, regard Georgia as an independent state, any more than his old comrade General Lebed recognised the independence of Moldova.

On 28 February 1993, only a few days after the bombs started falling on Sukhumi, Yeltsin put his strategic cards on the table, more clearly than before: 'The time has come,' he said 'for the relevant international organisations, including the UN, to grant Russia special powers as a guarantor of peace and stability in the former Soviet Union.' The government of Ukraine (no longer, by this stage, in a mood to pick fights with Russia) was horrified: it described Yeltsin's proposal as a 'gross violation of the norms of international law, including the principles of the United Nations charter'.

But Western governments paid little attention to Kiev's complaint, or to Shevardnadze's protests over the bombing of Sukhumi: they were too busy trying to head off the advent of a government in Moscow which might commit the terrible sin of imperialism.

It would, of course, be an over-simplification to say that there was no difference at all between Yeltsin and his opponents over policy towards the republics. Under Grachev's tutelage, Russian aircraft had at least confined their attacks to the Abkhazian war zone; if Rutskoy had had his way, they would have bombed Tbilisi, the Georgian capital, as well. It was also true that the wars on Russia's periphery were providing a training ground for Yeltsin's domestic enemies; a fact which gave the President and his supporters in the West genuine cause for concern.

In 1992, many police commandos and soldiers of fortune who had taken part in the unsuccessful struggle to thwart the independence of the Baltic states found a new home among the separatist Slav forces of eastern Moldova. In the Georgian war, many of the ethnic Russian fighters who volunteered their services to the Abkhaz cause stated openly that their wages were being paid from an account in the rebel Slav enclave of Moldova. The soldiers, both serving and retired, who made up this network of Russian nationalism were natural adversaries of the Yeltsin government; even the arrival in Moldova of General Lebed had not convinced them that Moscow had a genuinely 'patriotic' government.

Yeltsin's best hope of neutralising the threat from these forces lay in incorporating them, which meant endorsing their activities as semi-official warriors for the nationalist cause; by early 1993, this process was already under way. It was wishful thinking for the politicians of the capitalist world to view Yeltsin as a besieged paragon of virtue and the opposition as the only source of extremism.

Yeltsin, as it turned out, had his own mysterious way of denying victory to his domestic political enemies, and it was one that owed little to the advice, or the financial support, of his Western friends. By the middle of March 1993, he was looking so bruised and battered by the blows raining down on his head that even his sympathisers, at home and abroad, were writing him off as a spent force, who might at best be able to limp on for a few more months. This created a suitably dramatic background for his second political offensive, which proved to be far more successful than the one he had attempted in December.

On Saturday, 20 March, he struck back, going on television to inform the nation that he was introducing a period of 'special rule' – a term that was carefully left undefined – in which Parliament would no longer be able to obstruct his work. Economic reform would be speeded up. The referendum, which legislators had desperately and cynically tried to prevent, would now be held on 25 April: it would ask voters to give the verdict on the President, Parliament and a new constitution.

The reaction of Yeltsin's opponents to this speech was every bit as hysterical and ill-considered as the presidential team had hoped. As the December stand-off had shown, Yeltsin had little chance of prevailing over Congress in a head-on confrontation. What he could do, though, was goad and madden his enemies into destroying themselves, and his address of 20 March went a long way towards achieving that purpose.

One of the wildest early reactions to the speech came from Vice-President Rutskoy. This was a surprise, though not an unwelcome one, for the Yeltsin camp had been calculating that Rutskoy, after all his blustering, would eventually fall into line with the President. Within hours of Yeltsin's broadcast, Rutskoy was harrumphing furiously before the presidium of Parliament: Yeltsin's speech was a 'state crime' which had rendered the President unfit to rule a single day longer.

The cooler heads among the Vice-President's supporters had to take him aside and urge him to show restraint. To them, at least, it was clear that there were certain presentational difficulties in using the term 'state crime' – in other words, treason – to describe a decision to consult the electorate. Rutskoy's advisers also realised that he could fatally damage his own fortunes by jumping too quickly on the anti-Yeltsin bandwagon and proclaiming himself head of state; if these moves were only half-successful, and Russia was left with two presidents, the electorate might not forgive him. Unfortunately for his own career, Rutskoy was not inclined to take proper account of this advice – either in the political crisis of spring 1993, or in the far bloodier one which followed.

Judge Valery Zorkin's reaction to the 20 March speech was equally ill-considered, and from Yeltsin's point of view, equally satisfactory. Zorkin instantly and permanently wrecked his own credibility as a neutral or disinterested arbiter of Russian life by denouncing the presidential initiative as a *coup d'état* before he had even seen the text of Yeltsin's decree. Hasbulatov was generally credited with a calmer temperament than either Zorkin or Rutskoy, but he too was swept along in the general hysteria and set about moves to impeach Yeltsin, in the belief that he could secure the necessary amount of votes – 689, or two-thirds of the full Parliament's 1,033 members.

The impeachment moves had a curious psychological effect, which took most Western observers by surprise. Far from dealing Yeltsin a final *coup de grâce*, the campaign to topple him set off a surge of public support, even among those who were deeply disappointed with his performance. It was the reaction of a family, quarrelsome but also close-knit, which instinctively closes ranks when the father-figure is under threat – however wayward, whimsical, cruel or ineffective the paterfamilias might be.

Yeltsin's rating in the opinion polls duly soared, and that of his opponents tumbled. Fate played an uncanny part in this process. Shortly after Yeltsin's address of 20 March was broadcast, news came that a heart attack had claimed the life of his 85–year-old mother Klavdiya, whom he remembered as the only source of gentleness in a brutal Siberian childhood. According to his memoirs, she was the only person who saved the young Boris from the beatings administered by his own wayward, whimsical and cruel father.

On Tuesday, 23 March 1993, Russia's television viewers saw the President, red-eyed and distraught, bending over his mother's open coffin. The audience also observed that both Zorkin and Rutskoy – in a clumsy effort to show their magnanimity – had attended the funeral and offered the President their condolences. But this gesture merely confirmed public opinion in the feeling that the President's enemies were hypocritical as well as malicious.

The following day, the presidential decree ushering in a new form of administration was finally published. To the grave embarrassment of all those who had rushed to accuse the President of treason, this text turned out to be far milder than the television address of five days earlier had led the world to expect. It merely stated that Parliament could not countermand the President's decrees unless Zorkin's court also declared them to be unconstitutional. It was hard for Judge Zorkin to object to that, and he tried feverishly to formulate a new position which was more sympathetic to the President. However, he had already exposed himself as an impulsive and partisan figure by the stridency of his initial reaction to Yeltsin's broadcast. Hasbulatov tried vainly to put the brakes on the impeachment move, sensing that it would now fail, but it was too late.

With tens of thousands of Yeltsin supporters demonstrating nearby, an impeachment resolution was moved in the Grand Kremlin Palace, and it fell short by seventy votes. Sensing that they had overplayed their hand, many legislators turned their fury on Hasbulatov, and he narrowly escaped removal. The Congress then set about amending the questions for the forthcoming referendum, and it appeared at one point that two rival plebiscites might be held. The important fact was this: it was no longer in question that the electorate would be given the opportunity to pronounce on Russia's political crisis, and it steadily became clearer that almost any recourse to the ballot-box would work to Yeltsin's advantage.

On 3 April, Yeltsin arrived in Vancouver to see Bill Clinton and take delivery of a $1.6 billion aid package, which was presented as a sort of down payment on the $40 billion worth of debt forgiveness, grants and loans that he could expect from the Tokyo summit of the Group of Seven later that year. Walking through the Canadian woods, the two Presidents made an emphatic, if not wholly convincing, display of their personal friendship. 'Win, Boris, win!' Clinton stage-whispered in Yeltsin's ear, pledging his personal support for the Russian leader in Moscow's power struggle; but in fact Yeltsin had won already, with a strategy so devious that nobody in Arkansas would ever have dreamed of it.

Yeltsin was no longer in such desperate need of his Western friends to help him deal with the Russian hardliners; but he did, in a sense, need the Russian hardliners to help him deal with the West – that much was clear from some of the comments made in Vancouver. He told the Americans Russia could not go any further in pressing the Bosnian Serbs to accept a peace plan, because that would expose him to further complaints in Moscow that he was betraying Russia's Orthodox Slav brothers. For similar reasons, Yeltsin asked Clinton to understand Moscow's concerns over the Russian minorities in the Baltic states.

Rutskoy, interviewed on the day Yeltsin returned from Vancouver, was spluttering with contempt for the President's achievements, and for the aid package just announced. 'What does $1.6 billion amount to, when in 1992 alone, between $17 billion and $40 billion was illegally exported from Russia, simply stolen!'

'I love figures,' Rutskoy confessed, notwithstanding the vagueness of the ones he had just cited. He went on to calculate out loud, somewhat laboriously, that Prime Minister Chernomyrdin's cabinet had churned out an average of six decrees per day during its three months in office. 'Can you implement that many decisions? No, you can't. They should have restricted themselves to about four documents, but good ones.'

Buried in the Vice-President's curious numerology, there is an important point about capital flight, although it is not one that would readily occur to Rutskoy. As long as Russia's emerging capitalists – whether they were shady export kings, directors of newly privatised industries or launderers of Communist Party assets – had more faith in Swiss banks than in Russia's embryonic financial system, it would be virtually impossible for foreign funds to have any significant effect on the economy; they too would find their way to Switzerland. At the same time, it was plain that a huge amount of money was building up in Russian hands, ready to come gushing back from Zurich to Moscow or Yetakerinburg as soon as conditions existed in which it was rational to invest; creating these conditions was far more important than attracting foreign loans. But Rutskoy, surrounded by hardliners who explicitly opposed the creation of favourable conditions for investment, did not see that far ahead.

Rutskoy was at pains, however, to stress that his doubts about American loans were nothing personal.

> I know a lot of Americans, especially the ones who fought in Vietnam. They are good guys, excellent guys, and I sincerely feel for them. Ask any one of them: if someone cringes and abases himself before you, will you respect that person?
>
> No you won't, because it is not a man's trait. Even a woman who has self-esteem will never cringe before anyone and seek a relationship of dependence . . . because she respects herself not only as a woman, but as a human being.

There was one thing that spurred Rutskoy to even greater heights of indignation than capital flight, hyperactive governments, or self-abasement by persons of either sex, and that was turncoats; people like Burbulis, Gaidar and Yeltsin who had once belonged to the heart of the communist establishment, and were now militant anti-communists. 'They say that if Yeltsin and his government step aside, the reds will come back – but who is really a red?' Rutskoy demanded to know. These comments were reminiscent of another *bon mot* which was ascribed to Rutskoy around the same time: 'A real politician does not change his views, he changes reality.'

Yeltsin, by contrast, understood that plodding adherence

to the same dogmas and opinions was no virtue at a time when reality – with or without the intervention of politicians – was changing faster than almost anybody could comprehend. On the Saturday after his return from Vancouver, he used the opening of a new international telephone network to begin his referendum campaign.

In a style that was very much his own, he created an atmosphere that was simultaneously modern and old-fashioned, comically Soviet yet also very post-Soviet. The occasion itself – a fifteen-fold increase in the number of telephone lines linking Moscow with the West – was a vivid metaphor for everything that was new. But Yeltsin, addressing the Prime Minister of Denmark, Nyrup Rasmussen, over a newly installed video-telephone link, burbled out a piece of ill-digested history in a way that was reminiscent of Brezhnev at his haziest. 'Six hundred years ago, in 1493, Peter the Great opened up a window on Europe via Denmark,' he declared, confusing Peter the Great with Ivan the Great, and Denmark with the Netherlands. It was rather like saying that Abraham Lincoln had won the War of Independence against the French.

History lessons were left behind, however, as the President plunged into a small crowd of well-wishers who had no doubt as to where their sympathies lay in Yeltsin's stand-off with Hasbulatov, Rutskoy and the like. 'Hit them, Boris Nikolayevich!' 'Hit them harder'. 'Be more decisive'. A middle-aged woman interrupted in a high-pitched monotone to make it clear she did not share the general mood of adulation. 'I'm an engineer, and I only get 10,000 roubles a month [less than $15 at the current rate] and bread costs thirty-four roubles a loaf, and as for milk . . .' Yeltsin's features melted into a look of indescribable tenderness. 'Yes, I know 10,000 isn't a lot, but it's better than 5,000', he murmured, in the homely manner of someone who was in roughly the same income bracket himself. When the lady insisted, he tried teasing her instead, pointing at her warm scarlet anorak and synthetic woollen hat. 'From the way you are dressed, I wouldn't say you are in poverty . . . I was in

Vancouver last week, and people there weren't dressed any better than you.'

Yeltsin – who claimed to have spent a year of his life sleeping rough in railway stations and other makeshift accommodation – could get away with such banter, in a way that Gorbachev never could. Teasing people about their material circumstances did not come so easily to a man who looked as though he was born to wear Western suits.

The results of the 25 April referendum were not perfect for Yeltsin, but they were incomparably better than anybody would have dared to predict five weeks earlier. After much wrangling between Yeltsin, Parliament and Zorkin's court, it was agreed that voters should be asked four questions: whether they trusted the President; whether they agreed with his economic policies; whether they favoured early presidential elections; and whether they favoured early parliamentary elections. The answers to the last two questions would carry no legal force unless an outright majority of registered voters – very difficult to muster in any democracy – gave their assent. Among those who voted, 59 per cent expressed confidence in the President, while a surprisingly high 54 per cent voiced support for his economic reforms. The idea of early parliamentary elections was favoured by 43 per cent of the total electorate – in other words, not quite enough to ensure that they took place – while 33 per cent wanted early presidential elections.

Yeltsin would still have to live, for the time being, with the existing legislature, but his high personal vote meant that he had recaptured the political initiative. The whole atmosphere was now more favourable to the President, and his chances of winning approval for a new constitution, tailored to his own requirements, were vastly improved. The President's high scores belied the impression which had gained ground only a few months earlier of a nation that was suffering almost unbearable pain as a result of economic transition.

By late spring 1993, many Russian city-dwellers were, in fact, a good deal better off than they had been in the worst throes of the 1991/2 economic crisis; food shortages were a fading memory, and the real value of wages had risen significantly. In dollar terms, the average monthly pay packet had gone up three- or four-fold since the start of reforms in January 1992. A crash programme for privatising large and medium-sized enterprises had been in progress since December 1992. More than 300 such companies had been sold off by mid-March, on terms which were attractive to existing managers and workers, without sacrificing the principle of outside investors' rights.

Anatoly Chubais, the deputy Prime Minister who had once figured among the brightest luminaries of the Leningrad fold, shielded the privatisation programme from the sniping of Parliament and the initial scepticism of Prime Minister Chernomyrdin. The second problem, in any case, was rapidly disappearing as Chernomyrdin's experience of office, and his dealings with Western governments, convinced him that there was no alternative to market reform.

Perhaps more important, hundreds of thousands of young Russians were mastering the tricks of capitalism on a small scale with an alacrity which left their parents and grandparents bewildered. Some of these tricks could not have been gleaned from any Western manual: how to buy off the racketeers who preyed on every small business; how to hire a debt collector who could terrorise the most recalcitrant of creditors; how to dodge the taxes which would choke any business which seriously tried to pay them all.

One of the net results of all this frantic, sordid activity was to generate wealth and raise living standards – not just among the tiny élite of the 'super-rich', but among millions of people who benefited, directly and indirectly, from the new economy. There were also millions of tragic exceptions: pensioners who had no hustling grandchildren, or shares in newly privatised industries, to support them in their old age; alcoholics, the mentally ill and other flotsam and jetsam whom the new system would surely drown. But those people tend not to vote; they are living confirmation of the Russian theory of conservatism – much in evidence among the columnists of the weekly *Dyen* – which views democracy as a conspiracy of the articulate and able-bodied over the simple and disadvantaged.

All this helps to explain why, in April 1993, Yeltsin managed to win a 59 per cent approval rating – an improvement on the 57 per cent score with which he swept into office as Russia's first elected President two years earlier.

It would be an exaggeration, of course, to claim that all or even most of the citizens who supported Yeltsin in the referendum were clear-sighted beneficiaries of Westernising, liberal reforms. Any incumbent Russian ruler has a wide range of stratagems at his disposal to boost his own electoral fortunes, including the manipulation of the media and appeals to old-fashioned sentiments of deference. Yeltsin also curried the support of forces that were anything but pro-Western, such as the Cossacks, the ancient caste of warrior-peasants which was re-emerging rapidly in the wheatfields of southern Russia and had provided hundreds of volunteers for the cause of the Slav separatists in eastern Moldova.

The Cossacks' demands included the restoration of their historic lands, freedom to practise their traditional forms of communal government and justice – in which public whippings featured heavily – and the right to establish separate Cossack units in the army. Yeltsin and his parliamentary enemies competed furiously for Cossack favour, and in mid-March, the President issued a decree which went much further than any previous decision towards meeting the community's demands. He was rewarded instantly with an offer by the White or anti-communist wing of the Cossacks to turn out on the streets of Moscow and thwart the President's enemies by force.

Fortunately it never came to that, but the President's willingness to court the Cossacks was a firm signal that he would look for support wherever he could get it – including places that were well beyond the Westernising liberals' ken. Yeltsin was to find himself keeping even odder company when the next phase of his political struggle began: a frenetic exchange of corruption charges which shook the body politic to its foundations.

11

ARTILLERY PREPARATIONS

VIEWED FROM ANY distance, there was a terrible symmetry about the two sides – 'presidential' and 'parliamentary' – which were struggling for control of Russia in early September 1993. The number of people who were seriously involved in playing this deadly political game was quite small, perhaps a few dozen on each side. Their past careers were intertwined in a confusing way: many of those people who had stood by Yeltsin during the August 1991 *putsch* were now among his leading opponents; while Yeltsin's toughest supporters included several recent defectors from the parliamentary side.

Each side was looking desperately for a stratagem that would end the stalemate and tilt the balance of advantage in its own favour. They sensed the approach of another moment, like those in 1917 and 1921, when a handful of cunning individuals could, if they played their cards correctly, gain decisive leverage over the fate of millions of people, and thus over the history of the world.

It was getting harder to distinguish the two sides' policy aims, even if there was some difference in the routes they proposed. Each side said the other was engaged in destroying the country, and was about to deliver a *coup de grâce*. The leaders of each faction seemed hell-bent on 'saving' the country from the depredations of the other, if necessary by engaging in a little precautionary destruction themselves.

Both factions claimed to have out worked out their own, disinterested and uniquely effective recipe for breaking Russia's political deadlock. An assembly hand-picked by Yeltsin had elaborated and endorsed one draft constitution, which predictably enough vested wide-ranging powers in the presidency. His rivals in the legislature were touting their own, alternative version which would, of course, give Parliament the main say in running the country. Yeltsin had long since been forced to abandon the moral high ground which he had briefly managed to capture in the immediate aftermath of the April referendum; there was now a complete stalemate.

The whole debate over the constitution had been overshadowed, in the public mind, by another sort of political battle, which was equally arcane but much more spiteful: a furious exchange of corruption charges in which each side accused the other of malpractice on a staggering scale. The opening shot in this war had been fired by Rutskoy, who in April, in a vain effort to influence the result of the referendum, made the bizarre claim that he possessed eleven suitcases full of documents which proved that the Yeltsin administration was incorrigibly dishonest. Among a torrent of other charges, he said that army commanders had made fortunes by selling off naval bases and airfields. In this claim, at least, he was not alone: Yuri Boldyrev, a popular young reformer from St Petersburg, had recently been forced to resign from his job as Yeltsin's chief corruption-fighter after daring to suggest that Russian generals had lined their pockets as they pulled out of East Germany.

Rutskoy also accused two senior Yeltsin aides of involvement in the sale of red mercury, a mysterious substance which is supposed to facilitate the production of nuclear weapons, but is viewed by most Western experts as a giant confidence trick. He asserted that Yeltsin's information chief, the stocky newspaper-man Mikhail Poltoranin, had acted improperly over the sale of a Russian cultural centre in Berlin. Rutskoy also directed a stream of charges, including that of mishandling money earmarked for humanitarian aid, at one of Yeltsin's deputy Prime Ministers, Vladimir Shumeiko, a fresh-faced factory boss from southern Russia.

Swinging his axe even wider, Rutskoy took Gaidar to task

for selling off Russia's gold reserves and granting export licences too freely. Of the people named by Rutskoy, it was Gaidar who made the most dignified response: he challenged the Vice-President to a televised debate and forced him to withdraw his allegations. Other members of the Yeltsin entourage decided that attack was the best form of defence; they started delving into Rutskoy's past with a view to discrediting him.

Nikolai Makarov, the deputy prosecutor-general, advised parliamentarians in late June that some of Rutskoy's allegations appeared to be well founded, and they would therefore be justified in launching a campaign for the removal of Shumeiko and Poltoranin from office. This advice was instantly accepted. A few days later, the Yeltsin faction responded in kind by appointing a flamboyant Moscow lawyer named Andrei Makarov (no relation of Nikolai) to take charge of a new anti-corruption panel whose obvious, if unstated, mission was to find skeletons in Rutskoy's cupboard.

Each side had its own Makarov, and soon enough, each side had the services of its own shadowy *émigré* businessman who had dabbled in high politics as well as commerce. One of these characters was Boris Birshtein, the head of a successful Zurich trading company who had left the USSR in 1979, and – in contrast with the fate of many Soviet Jews who emigrated in those days – was able to retain cordial ties with the land of his birth. By his own account, he 'spent a lot of time . . . meeting a lot of people, building connections and relations' in the Soviet leadership.

By mid-1992, he was well enough connected to play a crucial role in bringing a halt to the war in Moldova, where he was part-owner of a luxury hotel. When Rutskoy and Viktor Barannikov, the security minister (in other words, head of the ex-KGB) flew down to that republic for peace talks with President Snegur, it was at Birshtein's behest and in his corporate jet. As Rutskoy moved into open opposition to Yeltsin, Birshtein found himself drawn deeper into a power struggle in Moscow where peace would not be so easy to arrange.

In July 1993, as the media became obsessed with the issue of corruption, viewers of state-controlled television were treated no less than four times within a single week to the sound of a tape in which Birshtein's voice was heard to remark that 'Sasha' (Rutskoy) wanted to 'exterminate' the careers of Poltoranin, Burbulis and Shumeiko.

Birshtein's interlocutor was his erstwhile business partner Dmitry Yakubovsky, the other mysterious millionaire who was thrust into the public eye that summer: he too was based abroad, in Canada, but his departure from Russia was much more recent.

Yakubovsky must rank as one of the most astonishing figures of the post-Soviet state, and he epitomised many of its features: he was young – barely thirty – street-smart, opportunistic, fascinated by guns and money. His personality left a strong impression with anyone who met him and he was full of earthy, cynical humour. Yakubovsky was sometimes described as unprincipled, but this was not quite true: whatever other motives may have driven him, he had strong political opinions, and they were those of a trenchantly authoritarian nationalist. He was too much a product of his own time to be a communist, but he despised Gorbachev for half-destroying the machinery of the Soviet state, and above all the state's capacity to inculcate fear. 'How can anyone claim to have been wrong for the first thirty years of his career, when he was a communist, and right for the final five?' he used to sneer, referring to Gorbachev.

Like any good Soviet prosecutor, he was fascinated by the law as an instrument of repression. He also suffered from a sort of compulsion to test the law's ability to restrain his own behaviour. In December 1994 he was arrested for stealing priceless manuscripts.

He was perceived as a Yeltsin ally, and therefore his activities were covered sympathetically, even fawningly, by the liberal press, but he actually despised liberal ideas. In 1990, he had won the confidence of two of the most conservative members of the USSR leadership (defence minister Dmitry Yazov and parliamentary chairman Anatoly Lukyanov) by devising elaborate legal arguments in support of Moscow's demand to be compensated financially for the property it was abandoning in Germany. This led to a bitter conflict with Gorbachev, who insisted on handling the German question personally, and Yakubovsky found it healthier to live for a couple of years in Switzerland, where he consolidated his connection with Birshtein. In spring 1992, however, he returned to Moscow, and managed with extraordinary speed to win the confidence and personal friendship of several senior figures in the new Russian leadership: deputy Prime Minister Shumeiko, the security minister Barannikov, and Valentin Stepankov, the prosecutor-general.

Among other posts, Yakubovsky became head of the weirdly named 'information agency of the committee for military reform' which was authorised to trade in weapons rather than press releases. He was promoted, that summer, from the rank of captain to colonel, although it was never quite clear which branch of the security forces he served. At one point he was named special representative to the cabinet of the security forces as a whole.

He had many political friends, and one adversary: an invisible technocrat called Yuri Skokov, who as secretary of the newly formed security council, was also engaged in empire-building, in more than one sense. After a summer of hobnobbing in the holiday *dachas* of the high and mighty, Yakubovsky was forced in September 1992 to leave the country again, fearing possible attempts to prosecute him and the hostility of Skokov. From his place of exile – a suburban mansion in Toronto – he remained in frequent and friendly telephone contact with all his high-ranking friends. He therefore found himself in a unique, pivotal role when those friends became bitterly divided into 'presidential' and 'anti-presidential' camps.

Twice in the summer of 1993 Yakubovsky was spirited back to Moscow in conditions of great secrecy. In June, he was brought home by members of the Rutskoy faction, who hoped that the young adventurer would be willing to betray his friend Shumeiko, and were sorely disappointed when this request was refused. In July, he was smuggled into Moscow by the other side who anticipated – accurately this time – that Yakubovsky would help them construct a case against Rutskoy.

Having served as a business partner of Birshtein, Yakubovsky knew a great deal about the Swiss connections of the Russian leadership. He knew, for example, about a trip to Switzerland made by the wives of Barannikov and deputy interior minister Andrei Dunayev, in which both ladies had been plied with jewellery, fur coats and trinkets to the tune of hundreds of thousands of dollars. The reason he knew all this was that his brother Stas, a resident of Zurich, had helped to look after the extravagant pair. Information of this kind was invaluable for the 'uncompromising' members of the presidential camp, whose purpose was to steer Yeltsin away from giving any ground to his critics. Details of the shopping trip were used to convince Yeltsin that both Barannikov – whom the President had always regarded as a friend – and Dunayev had to go. Both were abruptly dismissed on grounds of 'ethical shortcomings' and with them, the President lost two ministers who might have served as a bridge between himself and his adversaries.

By August 1993, Russia's public life was turning rapidly into a sordid and poorly scripted melodrama. Yakubovsky, back in Canada, reported that he had found a bullet-hole in his BMW and a note in his driveway warning him not to disturb 'AV' – presumably Aleksandr Vladimirovich Rutskoy – as badly as he had already disturbed 'Uncle Vitya' – presumably Viktor Barannikov. Then the Russian media was supplied with another remarkable tape-recording: a telephone conversation in which Valentin Stepankov, the (pro-Rutskoy) prosecutor-general, was heard to make dark hints about the 'treatment' which might be meted out to Andrei Makarov, the Yeltsin camp's newly appointed corruption-hunter. The prosecutor was egged on during this conversation by Yakubovsky, whom he was foolish enough to trust and view as a possible accomplice in the administration of 'treatment' to the presidential investigator.

In any case, neither Yakubovsky nor Andrei Makarov seem to have been swayed by these dark hints. On 18 August, Yeltsin's investigators alleged that Rutskoy was involved with a suspicious Swiss bank account into which state money had been diverted. To their disappointment, however, these allegations, which stopped fractionally short of an outright charge of embezzlement, did not greatly impress the public, which had grown thoroughly punch-drunk with the issue of dishonesty in high places. Even if only a quarter of the charges flying about were true, it was a lamentable comment on Russian democracy that virtually every member of the team which had stood together in the besieged White House against the August 1991 conspiracy was now to be found on one side or other of a sleazy shouting match.

The authorities' habit of creating new institutions out of thin air, like the Andrei Makarov panel, did not bode at all well for the establishment of a law-based state either. But perhaps the most disturbing aspect of the summer of scandals was the manner in which Yakubovsky had to be spirited in and out of Russia, and the light this shed on the divided loyalties of the security forces. When he flew into Moscow on 23 July, he had to be rushed past the airport security service – who as part of Russia's border guard were still run by Barannikov from the Lubyanka, and would in all probability have arrested Yakubovsky – and was bundled into an armour-plated car by members of the presidential guard. The latter guard was the former Ninth Administration of the KGB which since late 1991 had been placed under the direct orders of the head of state, and was now commanded by a little-known figure called General Mikhail Barsukov. Yeltsin himself may well have been ignorant of the fact that such furious competition was going on between different sections of the security forces. He seems to have been genuinely reluctant to believe the evidence against Barannikov (or rather Mrs Barannikov) when it was presented to him a few days later.

The story of Yakubovsky's departure on 30 July, which emerged in the Russian press several months later, was even more dramatic. Together with the head of Yeltsin's legal department, General Aleksandr Kotenkov, Yakubovsky and his two bodyguards made a hectic drive from Moscow to Armenia, which was seen as the safest exit route. Despite the fact that Barannikov – the person who had most reason to resent Yakubovsky – had by then been dismissed, the party still had to wait at Yerevan airport for a tense couple of days to establish whether the border guards there, who also took orders from the Lubyanka in Moscow, would allow them all to fly away in a private jet.

A highly dangerous situation had arisen in which two of the most prestigious and well-armed divisions of the former KGB were taking orders from different masters. For members of the presidential apparatus, this underlined the need to bring as many as possible of these élite forces under the Kremlin's direct control: the Lubyanka, even under the direction of an ostensible friend of the President, like Barannikov, could never be fully trusted.

The fact that Russia's leaders, political and military, were so divided served to intensify the feeling that a single source of authority was desperately needed. The American idea that a political system requires checks and balances had never been less fashionable.

By squabbling over the constitution, the 'presidential' and 'parliamentary' sides in Russia's power struggle were in danger of letting all authority drift away from Moscow and towards the regions; and by hurling corruption charges at one another, they were contributing to a general breakdown in the credibility of the state. Observing this, fewer and fewer people doubted the desirability of having one unquestioned fount of authority, capable of imposing its will on every region, every branch of the security forces, every wrong-doer.

Therefore, the rhetoric of all political factions was peppered with strident calls for the creation of a strong and well-ordered state, covering Russia and as much as possible of the rest of the former Soviet Union. In a sense, however, the presidential camp had one advantage; the fact that its plan was already unfolding. On 10 September, the presidential spokesman, Vyacheslav Kostikov, used the columns of *Komsomolskaya Pravda* to celebrate the strides which had already been taken, and the excellent prospects that now existed for the lofty cause of reconstructing the Union.

'The age of democratic romanticism in Russia has come to an end', he wrote, admonishing any citizens who still flirted with the ideals of Yelena Bonner. He added that it was 'only a matter of time' before the re-emerging economic relationship between Russia and the smaller republics translated into some closer sort of political association. In plain language, most of the republics were in a desperate state, economically and militarily; they realised that the West would not or could not be of decisive help, and this gave them little choice but to re-enter the Russian embrace.

A few days earlier, five republics had agreed to surrender some of their financial independence to Russia in return for the recreation of a new monetary zone, based on the Russian rouble. Their own attempts to establish separate currencies had been failures.

That monetary agreement fell through, as it turned out, because the terms were not quite favourable enough to Russia to reflect its real economic weight; it became obvious that it was not yet in Russia's interest to readmit those ramshackle states into its monetary system. But the whole texture of the relationship between Russia and other republics had been transformed since the collapse of the Soviet Union. Far from straining to escape Moscow's leash, many of the republics were now imploring Russia to reincorporate them, at least economically.

They had suffered a devastating blow in July, when Prime Minister Chernomyrdin hit the nation with the sledgehammer of a 'monetary reform' under which all rouble banknotes issued prior to 1993 were declared worthless. This was widely condemned at the time as a harsh and unexpected blow to the interests of Russian citizens, at the very moment when their living standards, and confidence in the future, were starting to rise again. President Yeltsin, apparently caught unawares by his Prime Minister's move, mitigated its effects by raising (from 35,000 to 100,000) the amount of roubles that each citizen of the Russian Federation was allowed to exchange. But the measure's most important purpose was not tempered: that of pitching the republics into the financial wilderness by rendering worthless most of the Russian currency which was still circulating in their territory as the main, or even sole, form of money. At a stroke, Chernomyrdin's move had further enfeebled the economies of the republics, and hence their political bargaining power, and boosted Russia's prospects for investing its currency with value. It looked clear enough that the republics would reintegrate with Russia, sooner or later, but the process would be strictly on Russia's terms.

Ruslan Hasbulatov, for his part, had a different scenario for the remaking of the Soviet Union – with himself at the top. He wanted to remove all power from the mayors, governors and presidents who wielded, or were trying to wield, executive authority in many parts of the former Union. He would then restore untrammelled power to the network of soviets (republican parliaments, regional assemblies, town and village councils) which, in most cases, still existed. Although few people were aware of its existence, Hasbulatov was also chairman of an association which grouped the parliaments or soviets in most of the ex-Soviet republics. In his capacity as president of this Inter-Parliamentary Assembly, he already considered himself the highest-ranking official on former Soviet territory.

Thus both sides were committed to the creation of a powerful, flourishing and firmly governed post-Soviet state; and both sides acknowledged the importance, for any leader trying to maintain such a state, of a mighty political police force.

In late August there had been a muffled cry of alarm from human rights groups as they realised the implications of a change in the law which had been approved, very quietly, by both President and Parliament a month earlier. The 1992 law on security was amended so that officers of the former KGB would no longer need a warrant to search homes or offices; the only requirement was to inform the public prosecutor twenty-four hours after making an entry.

Democratic ideals had receded a long way since mid-1990, when an ambitious young politician called Oleg Rumyantsev had turned his eager mind, and his South Korean laptop computer, to drafting a constitution for Russia. In those days, Rumyantsev had tried – with the warm encouragement of the whole Yeltsin team, including the Russian leader himself – to find a formula that would make it virtually impossible for the KGB to interfere in the private affairs of citizens. Now the last remnants of that idealism were being abandoned, with scarcely a murmur of dissent from anyone on the political scene. The argument was no longer about whether there should be a powerful security police, but whose security police it would be.

Yet even as they outbid one another in calling for a strong and toughly policed state, politicians on both sides of the divide were often prepared, for opportunistic reasons, to espouse policies that ran in the opposite direction. They competed feverishly for the favours of power-hungry bosses in the Russian regions, with little apparent regard for the country's survival as a coherent political space; and they flirted with economic policies which, if pursued consistently enough, would have driven the whole of Russia to ruin.

It has to be admitted that in this respect the symmetry between the two sides was not total. Parliament was far more consistent in the pursuit of economic disaster, as though it calculated that it would not be held responsible, and might indeed reap some benefit when catastrophe struck.

In August, Hasbulatov's Parliament voted through a budget amendment, calling for extra spending, that would have sent the rouble's value crashing through the floor, and undone the substantial but precarious economic achievements of the previous eighteen months. Parliament had also done its best, albeit without lasting success, to sabotage the crash privatisation programme under which 5,000 large businesses were due to be sold off by the end of 1993. But the enemies of Anatoly Chubais, the deputy Prime Minister, who masterminded the privatisation programme with extraordinary doggedness, were as numerous inside the government as they were in the legislature.

The economic signals from the government as a whole were desperately confused. The cabinet included Oleg Lobov, a Yeltsin crony from Yekaterinburg who was no friend of Chubais or the market, and an internationally respected reformer in the figure of Boris Fyodorov.

Western economists had become sceptical, perhaps excessively so, about the net effect over the past eighteen months. The attitude to newly independent Russia among the international financial institutions had tended to go in waves: from politically inspired enthusiasm to disappointment when things happened more slowly, or in a different order, than was indicated by the script. In early September 1993, sentiments towards Russia among the monetary mandarins were at a low ebb; the International Monetary Fund said it had virtually given up hope of Moscow adopting policies that would justify any further credits.

As for Hasbulatov's men, they may have been extremely bad economists – so bad as to make the government look positively virtuous – but they had some good constitutional lawyers and political strategists on their side. Ironically, one of them was Rumyantsev, the young, self-confident character who had originally been encouraged by Yeltsin in his work: For the past three years he had been involved in one project after another to give Russia a proper constitution. With his neatly trimmed beard, well-cut suits, fluent English and penchant for modern technology, he was one of the few opposition figures who was capable of presenting a more or less acceptable face to Westerners.

Having co-founded a tiny Social Democratic Party, Rumyantsev had followed the same trajectory as another confident young man, Sergei Stankevich: from keen, bustling Westerniser to staunch defender of Russian statehood and the Slav cause in Serbia and Moldova. Stankevich had practised his new-found nationalist faith inside the Kremlin, as an adviser to Yeltsin, while Rumyantsev put his talent for debate and sophistry at the service of the opposition. Each seemed perfectly comfortable in his new home.

Rumyantsev was one of those who saw clearly how the land of Russian politics lay at the beginning of September 1993. For all the similarities between the two political camps, there was one important difference: the Yeltsin team had a declared interest in forcing an early confrontation, while his opponents' interests would be best served if they could somehow exercise self-restraint. Rumyantsev had taken very seriously indeed a bizarre image used by Yeltsin on 19 August, the second anniversary of the coup. The President had made it plain how badly he wanted to hold new legislative elections, in defiance of the existing Parliament, by the end of the year, and he claimed to have a strategy for doing so: 'It will cover about two and a half months', he said. 'Part of August – I call it the artillery preparation – then September, the crucial month, then October and probably part of November.'

With Yeltsin in this frame of mind, it was vital that legislators should remain calm and keep their nerve; and if they did so, they would stand a good chance of demonstrating to the country and world that they were the representatives of 'moderation' in the face of a rash and cynical President.

Moreover, one political prize after another should, without too much effort, fall into the parliamentary side's lap quite soon. Yeltsin's fitful manoeuvring to fix the constitution had not altered the fact that Hasbulatov's Congress was the highest organ of government, and the only body which was entitled to change Russia's political system. In spring, the Congress had narrowly failed to impeach Yeltsin; now, with bitterness running higher on both sides, it might be induced to abolish the presidency altogether. All that was necessary was somehow to keep the old legislature alive for a few more months.

So long as things were not forced to a head any earlier, it would be possible, in Rumyantsev's view, to 'put Yeltsin under control' by amending the existing constitution in November, and then passing an entirely new constitution – with no presidency at all, or only a token one – in March. Rumyantsev's hopes had been boosted by visits to over thirty regions. These trips made it clear to him that Yeltsin's midsummer tactic of creating a federation council, grouping together all of Russia's regional bosses, had boomeranged. The President had hoped that the council – suitably bribed by promises of devolution – would act as a counter-weight to Hasbulatov's Parliament, and would support his proposals for a new constitution; but these hopes had not been realised.

Parliament, emboldened by its freedom to make wild promises and take no responsibility for the consequences, had done a better job of wooing the regions. Of the two drafts for a new constitution that were in circulation by mid-September, most of the regional bosses much preferred the parliamentary one, which was the brainchild of Rumyantsev.

With support like that, it seemed to Rumyantsev that all Parliament needed to do was make reasonable proposals for a 'compromise' between its own ideas on the constitution and those of the President; it could still be confident of emasculating the presidency, if not actually abolishing it.

Other voices on the parliamentary side were calling for a swifter method of removing Yeltsin. Zorkin's constitutional court, which was more and more openly allied to Hasbulatov, might be induced to declare null and void the December 1991 agreements by which the Soviet Union was dissolved; and 'Soviet power' with Hasbulatov at the summit would automatically be restored.

This route – preferred by the communists – was a riskier and more confrontational one; the opposition's interests, whether they realised it or not, would certainly be better served by letting parliamentary procedures take their gradual, devastating course.

Yeltsin, on the other hand, found himself in the opposite situation. He wanted confrontation to be as early and total as possible, so that all those who were reluctant to take sides

– in high places and low, in Russia and abroad – would be forced to make their choice: the President or his enemies.

There was also a seasonal factor to bear in mind. The strange but almost unfailing rule of Russian politics is that the forces of authoritarianism fare better in winter, as though the violence of nature somehow demonstrated the need for a similar degree of toughness in human affairs. As things stood, the loudest advocates of an iron fist were to be found in the ranks of the opposition, among the communists and nationalists who dominated the legislature. Only by seizing the initiative quickly could Yeltsin make sure that it was he, and not his enemies, who rode the wave of authoritarian sentiment which the coming winter would assuredly bring.

On 16 September, Yeltsin went to visit the Dzerzhinsky Division at its headquarters outside Moscow. It was the high point in a series of visits to important military units in the Moscow area. Unlike most of the regular army, which was still desperately undermanned, the politically sensitive units based near the capital were kept at full strength and their pay packets were regularly topped up.

Having undergone several changes of master in recent years, the Dzerzhinsky Division was now under the authority of the interior minister, Viktor Yerin. After all the recent upheavals in the security forces – the sacking of Barannikov and Dunayev, the waves made by Yakubovsky – Yerin was one of the few figures that Yeltsin wholeheartedly trusted. This confidence was to be tested severely in the coming weeks.

The President joked with the Dzerzhinsky soldiers, trying on one of their red berets, and conferred quietly with their commanders. And in the midst of these jocular scenes, he dropped a political bombshell.

He told the reporters trailing after him that after a nine-month absence, Yegor Gaidar was being reappointed to the cabinet, with the rank of deputy Prime Minister. At the very moment when Westerners had written off Russia's economy as a lost cause, the brightest star of the reformist ranks was being restored to office. Around the world, the news was greeted with bemused satisfaction. 'Yeltsin swings in favour of the liberals', said a headline in *Le Monde*.

To those Westerners who still looked at Russian affairs in the old way, there was something odd about heralding Gaidar's return during a visit to a military barracks. Gaidar, in the Western mind, stood for an intelligent, rational, open, accountable way of administering Russia. He stood for economic freedom, and therefore presumably for political freedom. He was forward-looking and enlightened, whilst Yeltsin's opponents, and some of his supporters, were reactionary and dark.

The Dzerzhinsky Division, veterans of Afghanistan and Lithuania and Azerbaijan, seemed to epitomise the old ways: the use of force to impose the Kremlin's will on the outer limits of empire, in defiance of the West.

But on reflection, the contradiction was not really so stark. Gaidar stood for competence in economic affairs; the fact that he was prepared to face down every sectional interest in Russia – industrial, agricultural or military – was a reflection not of some secret compact with foreign powers, but of his passionate commitment to Russia's strategic interest, defined in the broadest way. The Dzerzhinsky Division stood for competence in military affairs, and not just brute force either. Like the Pole whose name they bore, and like the suppressors of the Kronstadt rebellion, they were adept practitioners, when properly deployed, of subterfuge and stratagem: the creation of deceptive impressions, the spreading of false information, the art of deceit which is known in Russian military handbooks as *maskirovka*.

In the last days of the communist regime, Vladimir Kryuchkov had discovered to his frustration that soldiers alone, even very resourceful soldiers, were not capable of holding his dominions together when the economic foundations of the empire were crumbling.

Yeltsin, at some gut level, understood things better: the cunning of a crack regiment needs to be combined, in a carefully calibrated mixture, with the high brow of a first-class economist. That sort of combination – between academic brain and skilfully applied brawn – is absolutely unbeatable, and the President realised this better than his critics. If there was any fundamental distinction between Russia's presidential and parliamentary factions, it perhaps lay simply in the fact that the former had far more intelligence, broadly defined.

Satisfied that the artillery was in place, Yeltsin launched his offensive on the evening of Tuesday, 21 September 1993. In a broadcast to the nation, he declared that he was suspending the Russian Parliament: elections would be held for a new legislature in December. In his memoirs, Yeltsin says that he had taken a firm decision at the beginning of September that 'Russia is not going to have a Parliament like this any longer . . .'

The first person he informed was his only real confidant in political matters: a discreet, efficient mandarin who served Yeltsin loyally in the Communist Party machine of Yekaterinburg but was virtually unknown to the world. His name was Viktor Ilyushin.

In a phrase that spoke volumes about Russian attitudes to law, he told Ilyushin to prepare a 'proper juridical basis' for an action whose illegality was absolutely plain. A week later, Yeltsin's chief legal adviser, Yuri Baturin, was brought into the discussion.

On Sunday, 12 September, he disclosed his plan to the key members of the government: Yerin, Pavel Grachev, Andrei Kozyrev, and Nikolai Golushko – respectively ministers of the interior, defence, foreign affairs and security. Golushko had been placed in charge of the Lubyanka after Barannikov's dismissal. He was a safe choice – a solid, bespectacled product of the KGB mainstream with a long record of monitoring and curbing dissent in both Russia and his native Ukraine. The experience of Bakatin and Barannikov had doubtless made Yeltsin wary of attempting to put his own man in charge of the Lubyanka. At any rate, this was not the moment for experiments.

Describing the meeting with his four subordinates, Yeltsin delivers a paean of praise for Yerin, the police chief. He recalls that Rutskoy, Skokov and Barannikov had tried to have Yerin dismissed for failing to deal with organised crime; Yeltsin had then intervened in mitigation, and 'let him off with a severe reprimand' which he accepted stoically.

Later, Yeltsin continues, he came to see in Yerin a 'profound mind, an intelligent man, of eminent integrity . . . to say nothing of the respect in which he is held by the militia and generally, his professional qualities. He was a remarkable man.'

The President admits he was nervous about the loyalty of Golushko, wondering whether this erstwhile scourge of dissenters might see something 'contrary to his human and political principles' in the closure of Parliament. Not quite so absurdly, Yeltsin mused that 'it might be a good thing to have a chance to test this man in extreme circumstances'.

In any case, all four of his interlocutors agreed with the proposed action, and Kozyrev piped up with the comment that the closure of Parliament should have been made much earlier.

The following day, Yeltsin briefed Prime Minister Chernomyrdin, who had just returned from the United States. The visit had been delayed because of a bad-tempered US-Russian row about the proposed sale of Russian rocket technology to India. It now looks clear that the resolution of this row, as well as the reinstatement of Gaidar, was part of a general mending of fences with the West ahead of the internal showdown, when Yeltsin would need friends in every possible quarter.

Yeltsin says he initially planned to impose the crackdown on Sunday, 19 September, when the White House would be empty and could be sealed up without difficulty. But on 17 September, he was persuaded to postpone the move by some of his ministers on the following grounds:

- the emergency regime might make it impossible to hold the planned summit of the Commonwealth of Independent States in Moscow on 24 September, and the Kremlin would lose face;

- the date – the 19th – was too reminiscent of the previous occasion when the Russian legislature was suspended, in 1991;
- most important, Hasbulatov and Rutskoy had learned of the impending crackdown; they knew it was coming on Sunday and could be expected to arrange counter-demonstrations.

Yeltsin says that faced with these arguments, he agreed to defer the crackdown, but only by two days, till 21 September. Nothing in this account of the grounds for the 48-hour postponement rings true. If anything, the reasons cited might have justified bringing forward the crackdown; and the first and third objections would certainly not have been addressed by a two-day deferral.

Yeltsin, vulnerable to charges that he failed to avert bloodshed, is understandably at pains to insist that he wanted a peaceful closure of the White House. Nevertheless one of the reasons he is obliged to protest so much is the very fact that the final, violent denouement brought him far greater political advantage than any peaceful outcome would have done. Whatever Yeltsin might say, the possibility of casualties was clearly anticipated by the authorities from an early stage. From 19 September onwards, Moscow's hospitals were told to prepare for a large number of emergency admissions.

In a page of his memoirs that rings true in spirit, even if the details are fuzzy, Yeltsin recalls that he was taken to task, just as the September crisis was beginning, by Barsukov, the head of the Kremlin guard, for failing to make sufficient preparation for the possibility of armed resistance by the parliamentarians. There were at least some people in the Kremlin who anticipated right from the beginning that the closure of Parliament, whatever its precise timing, would have its price in blood.

12

A Terrible Ugliness

THERE IS AN uncanny sweetness and serenity about the manner of academician Dmitry Likhachov, Russia's greatest scholar of medieval history, even when he is recounting the unspeakable horrors of the Arctic prison camp where he was incarcerated in 1928. But his fine, octagenarian features grow animated when he remembers the rebellion against the Bolsheviks by the seamen at the Kronstadt naval base in 1921.

He was the teenage son of a respected St Petersburg engineer, but by that time the comfort and high culture of his childhood environment had given way to the hunger and hardship of civil war. As well as bourgeois families like his own, the food shortages were ravaging the workers and servicemen who were supposed to be the vanguard of the new order.

Kronstadt was one of the crucibles of Russian protest; as individuals or *en masse*, sailors from the base had taken part in the Decembrist rising of 1825, the People's Will insurgency in 1882, and all the upheavals of 1917, including the Bolshevik takeover.

By early 1921, the seamen were protesting under new slogans: an end to the dictatorship of the Bolsheviks and the Cheka, political freedom and civil rights, the release of non-Bolshevik socialists from prison. Within a few weeks, the sailors were crushed by the forces of Leon Trotsky, who had been hardened by their civil war victory and boosted by an influx of veterans from the Tsarist army. Any rebels who failed to flee across the ice to Finland were slaughtered.

Before this happened, however, the rebellion had won tremendous support among the workers of St Petersburg. Likhachov remembers one giant factory after another downing tools and he is convinced that the only thing which averted a march against the Smolny buildings, and the possible overthrow of the Bolsheviks, was a Cheka trick.

The secret police, he recalls, spread a rumour round the working-class districts of the city that the organisers of the uprising supposedly wanted their supporters to march forward when they heard three loud shots in the city centre.

Hours later, the first shot was heard; after a few more hours there came a second. The crowd waited and waited for the third shot but it never came.

It was not the balance of class interests, or even a straight contest of military prowess, which saved the Bolsheviks; but the low cunning of some faceless men whose intrigues had previously been at the service of the Tsar and could in principle be placed at the disposal of any regime.

If Likhachov is right, then many things about the way his compatriots have been taught to view history for the past seventy years must be wrong. Victory, at this crucial moment, went not to the brave, or the class-conscious, or even to the well-armed, but to the devious.

The bare facts of what happened in Moscow in the second half of September 1993 have burned themselves into the memory of the world, although many Russians have tried very hard to forget them. Hours after Yeltsin's announcement on the closure of the legislature, several hundred parliamentarians – meeting in the White House in 'emergency session' – voted to impeach Yeltsin, proclaimed Rutskoy President and placed their own 'ministers' in notional charge of Russia's armed forces.

The new 'defence minister' was General Vladislav Achalov, a protagonist in the August 1991 conspiracy and for the past year chief military adviser to Hasbulatov. Viktor Barannikov and Andrei Dunayev, the policemen with the extravagant wives, were notionally restored to their old fiefdoms at the Lubyanka and the interior ministry.

Although the first few sessions of the defiant Parliament made a reasonable effort to maintain decorum and respect procedure, the White House rapidly started to resemble an armed camp, as volunteers and soldiers of fortune came to the building's defence. Prominent among these was the network of Russian nationalist warriors, somewhere between mercenaries and regular soldiers, which was born in the Baltic states, later extended to Moldova and was now engaged in the final stages of a vicious and successful war against Georgia.

The most conspicuous group of fighters at the Russian Parliament, however, was a private army commanded by Aleksandr Barkashov, who at various times had been chief bodyguard to Dmitry Vasilyev, right-hand man of the Nazi ideologue Viktor Yakushev and chief security officer for Aleksandr Sterligov's Russian National Assembly.

Unembarrassed by the company they were keeping, the parliamentarians began appealing for support from regional bosses and military commands around the country. The former were encouraging, the latter non-committal. It is likely that many senior military chiefs sympathised with the parliamentary cause, preferring the full-blooded sort of imperialism preached by Hasbulatov's men to the more sophisticated variety practised by the President. But military men had become wary of political gaffes; their instinct told them to lie low and see which way the wind was blowing.

On 24 September, Yuri Luzhkov – the mayor of Moscow who enjoys vast power over the infrastructure and the security forces of the capital – cut off the electricity and hot water from the White House. Mayor Luzhkov emerged as a vital presidential ally during the crisis – repaying the loyalty Yeltsin had shown him when he firmly instructed his first corruption investigator, Yuri Boldyrev, not to touch the issue of wrong-doing at city hall. Among Luzhkov's prerogatives was the provision of utilities and accommodation to the security forces in the Moscow area, including the Dzerzhinsky Division; he was uniquely well placed, therefore, to win hearts and minds.

He and Yerin worked together to organise a cordon of paramilitary police round the building, making it possible to leave but virtually impossible to enter. With Yerin's co-operation, thousands of riot police from provincial Russia were brought into the capital to back up the government side.

On the same day, in a propaganda coup for Yeltsin, the CIS summit went ahead and proved, in Yeltsin's words, to be very productive. The President seemed to be beating his adversaries in the race to put the Union back together again.

The authorities also announced the foiling of a plot to seize the Moscow military headquarters of the CIS, following a shooting incident the previous night in which a policeman and an old lady were killed.

After two weeks of mounting tension, and abortive attempts at reconciliation, the stalemate was finally broken on 3 October, when a crowd of demonstrators broke through the cordon round the White House with unexpected ease, and some of the pro-Yeltsin forces in the vicinity appeared to switch their loyalty.

Egged on by Rutskoy and Hasbulatov, armed volunteers from the White House took over the mayor's office, a high-rise glass-fronted building next to the Parliament. Rutskoy and Hasbulatov also urged their supporters, before the television cameras of the world, to storm the Kremlin.

There was no attempt to do that, but the parliamentary forces, armed with bazookas and automatic weapons, did try to storm the Ostankino television centre, which was the main source of news for over 200 million viewers all over the CIS.

Control of the country appeared to teeter in the balance for several hours as a furious gun-battle raged around the broadcasting facility and Yegor Gaidar used the one channel which was still functioning to make a passionate appeal for Yeltsin supporters to rally at the city council.

The well-known Russian journalist, Sergei Parkhomenko,

reported from the Kremlin that there were scenes of panic among the staff, which did not completely subside even after Yeltsin arrived by helicopter from his weekend *dacha*, early on the evening of 3 October.

After a tense night of negotiations between Yeltsin and the army, tanks appeared outside the White House at dawn and began bombarding the building with highly accurate shells that penetrated windows and killed dozens of people.

As the shelling began, Yeltsin made a broadcast to the nation in which he begged the people's pardon for being so lenient and tardy in dealing with the 'fascist-communist' plot. After about seven hours of bombardment, the political leaders of the Parliamentary faction surrendered and were taken to the old KGB jail at Lefortovo. Meanwhile Yeltsin used the state-of-emergency regulations, imposed the previous night, to ban about a dozen newspapers which had supported the parliamentary side, and impose a temporary regime of censorship on the remainder of the press.

That is the outline of the story as it impressed itself on a dazed country and a bewildered world; and those bare facts were enough to convince most Russians, and most of the world's politicians and opinion-makers, that Yeltsin had no choice but to act as he did. Clinton, showing more loyalty than was really necessary, suggested that Yeltsin had 'bent over backwards' to avoid bloodshed.

In retrospect, this was about as fitting a response as the foolish public giggle with which he greeted the first news of Yeltsin's crackdown on 21 September. But at the time, there was in most Western quarters a powerful sense of relief that the worst had been avoided, and that Russia would not be plunged after all into a new totalitarian regime by a bloodthirsty gaggle of neo-Nazis, blimpish generals and war junkies.

There could be no doubting the fact that the most prominent of the Parliament's armed defenders were members of a private army whose leader had dabbled in neo-Nazism; and the whole world had seen the frenzied, contorted features of

Rutskoy and Hasbulatov as they issued their battle-cry to storm the Kremlin.

The wickedness of one side, however, does not imply the virtue of the other and to judge the conduct of the presidential faction, it is necessary to look more closely, both at the details of what happened and the political context in which the events unfolded.

First of all, the fighting around the television centre on the night of Sunday 3 October, was not nearly such a close-run thing as it was made to appear. It was less a battle than a killing field, in which more than sixty very good, very bad and very ugly people – from brave and distinguished journalists to neo-fascist thugs – were shot by soldiers from the Vityaz unit, a semi-secret section of the Dzerzhinsky Division whose normal job was to suppress prison mutinies, or race riots in Central Asia, without too many questions asked about the rules of engagement.

It seemed to the world that the television centre was poorly defended, and the sense of drama was heightened when, at an early stage in the battle, the Ostankino news service suddenly stopped broadcasting. The building was, in fact, packed with Vityaz men, but they were not visible to the benighted fools outside who thought they were about to recapture the Soviet Union.

The raggle-taggle army of fascists, Stalinists and drunken old women, warbling the communist songs of their youth, was led to the television centre by the bumbling blimp, General Albert Makashov. All the regular soldiers and police in the vicinity pointedly disappeared from view as Makashov approached the small glass-and-concrete edifice where most news bulletins were prepared. Opposite, on the other side of a broad avenue, stood a similar but much bigger building, where the remaining broadcasting facilities were housed. The space in between these two structures was transformed, for the next seven or eight hours, into a piece of hell, as Vityaz men poured fire down from both buildings.

The first shot, which seemed to come from nowhere, injured one of Makashov's men in the knee. Then, a few minutes later, a man standing beside Makashov fired a grenade launcher into the building, which virtually decapitated a young Vityaz soldier. That was the only casualty which the defenders of the building suffered during the entire night. The other sixty deaths were either attackers, passers-by or journalists.

Vyacheslav Bragin, the Ostankino director who was also an undistinguished pro-Yeltsin politician, was heavily criticised for his decision to stop broadcasting as the battle began – even by those who had no other quibble with the presidential side's behaviour during the October crisis.

As many people pointed out, there was no technical reason why the station's journalists should not have continued broadcasting from a reserve studio, if its main facilities had been damaged. There was certainly no shortage of awesomely brave cameramen who were willing to risk their lives to capture what appeared to be one of the deciding moments of history, on a par with the storming of the Winter Palace in 1917.

But Bragin, with sudden and uncharacteristic concern for the safety of men who were regularly assigned to war zones, explicitly forbad his reporters from filming, and kept their equipment under lock and key. By that time, the entire world had been subjected to television images of Rutskoy and Hasbulatov calling for an assault on the Kremlin. They had also seen footage of the security forces around the White House surrendering to the rebels – a scene that was frightening enough to convince even the calmest of souls that the Yeltsin administration was in immediate, mortal danger, and only the most desperate of measures could save it. But the scenes from Ostankino – which provided a more accurate picture of the real balance of forces, and the real sources of mortal danger – were apparently not felt to be so suitable for public viewing.

Bragin was used as a convenient scapegoat for the authorities' behaviour that night; but it seems likely, in retrospect, that he was nothing more than a pawn in a game which he could barely comprehend himself. As he haplessly pointed out, in a series of embittered press interviews, it was Chernomyrdin who ordered him to go off the air. Nor was Bragin the sole possessor of the key to the airwaves. He said afterwards that a plan had been worked out with the communications ministry to make sure that the rebels, even if they broke through to the broadcasting area, could not possibly start transmitting. This would suggest that the power to stop broadcasting lay as much with the ministry as with anybody inside Ostankino.

If Bragin was a fool, he was – in Lenin's words – a useful one. He was one of the many people, all over Russia and the world, who were somehow persuaded that the battle for the television station was a finely balanced one, which might at any moment have plunged Russia into a new totalitarian takeover. Bragin says he felt abandoned and betrayed by his own masters as the terrifying fire-fight raged around him. He made frantic phone calls to his friends in the Russian government – Chernomyrdin, Shumeiko, Poltoranin – but none of them was willing to provide reinforcements. Only Yuri Luzhkov, the mayor, was of any help, finally sending 100 men.

As Bragin told one interviewer, there was something 'strange, suspicious and even treacherous' about the negligent way Ostankino was defended. But was the defence of Ostankino really so negligent? General Grachev, the defence minister, later gave the following account of the Ostankino clash:

> There were about 4,000 unarmed and 100 armed people (among the attackers) . . . They were opposed by 400 military servicemen from the interior ministry and special forces and six armoured carriers. And with the beginning of combat operations another fifteen armoured carriers and 100 militiamen had arrived . . .

He added that the defenders had managed to 'roll back' the mob within ten minutes, and there was no further danger to the building. Possibly the numbers given by Grachev are exaggerated, given that he too was under fire for failing to send regular army units to reinforce Ostankino. But with a casualty ratio of 1 to 60, it is difficult to accuse the government forces of being negligent – at least once the fighting around Ostankino had started.

There are much harder questions to answer – why was it allowed to start, and whose interest was really served by a battle that looked more unequal – even to hapless characters like Bragin who were caught in the middle of it – than it really was? Many things about the behaviour of the security forces on that dreadful weekend remain a mystery, but the following seems clear: on Saturday, 2 October, the presence of police and paramilitary forces in the centre of Moscow – who in the past few days had meted some savage beatings to unarmed demonstrators – was mysteriously reduced. This was despite the fact that a communist rally, dominated by supporters of Viktor Anpilov, was planned for Sunday afternoon, and it looked certain that the demonstrators would head for the besieged Parliament.

Sure enough, the demonstrators easily broke through the flimsy defences of the White House, and the parliamentary side suddenly began to feel that the tide was turning in their favour. Rutskoy and Hasbulatov, who were in the middle of giving a press conference, were suddenly besides themselves with the intoxication of victory, as their supporters rallied outside the building.

It seems likely, although there is no proof, that the government was using its mastery of all forms of communications to feed the parliamentarians disinformation about army units supposedly defecting to their side.

Right from the beginning of the crisis, the government's control of communications, in the broadest sense of the word, had been one of its main hidden advantages. The most powerful state body in this field was the Federal Agency for Government Communications and Information (Fapsi) which was created out of two Administrations of the old KGB and was placed, along with the Ninth Administration, under the direct control of the President after the August 1991 events. Because it had the power, through agencies like Fapsi, to monitor and sever telephone lines at will, the government side had the capacity to intercept all communication between the White House, regional politicians, army commanders and hardline political groups. This would have given the authorities the ability to play all manner of dirty tricks, including the planting of false rumours about the loyalty of various sections of the armed forces.

Disinformation of this kind is the most likely explanation for one wildly inaccurate, but historically resonant, piece of news that was relayed to the deliriously excited crowd as it demonstrated that Sunday afternoon: 'From Soviet Leningrad, the news that sailors at Kronstadt base are rallying to our side . . .'

Apart from electronics, the government was also in control of communications to and from the White House in a more literal sense; it knew, as few private citizens ever would, the layout of the intricate network of tunnels underneath the building, which were used by the defenders as a conduit to the outside world.

It is surely significant that the regime did not use its control of either physical or telephone communication to disrupt the Barkashov fighters, the Cossacks, or any of the other soldiers of fortune as they poured into the building, virtually taking it over, in the early days of the crisis. If one assumes that the government had some disinterested concern for the safety of the Muscovite public, this omission is puzzling.

It becomes easier to understand, however, when one remembers how much damage was done to the image of the parliamentary forces by the appearance in their midst of hundreds of armed extremists who were bitterly opposed to the parliamentary system. If the ultra-rightist followers of Barkashov, and the ultra-leftist devotees of Viktor Anpilov emerged rapidly as the most visible supporters of the opposition cause, part of the reason must surely be that the Yeltsin regime consciously allowed this to happen.

This was not slackness or negligence on the part of the government, which in various ways was showing itself to be quite vigilant in warding off any real threats to its position.

The internal communication system of the regular armed forces, for example, was reported to have been virtually switched off from the beginning of the crisis. Also, soldiers on the streets of Moscow who could not give a proper account of their movements were subject to arrest by Yerin's extra-vigilant policemen. Even on the Sunday afternoon when all Yeltsin's men were supposed to be surrendering, the government's forces were not as feeble or inactive as many people have suggested.

As the rebels were holding their triumphant rally outside the White House, they were fired on repeatedly from two high-rise buildings nearby – the Mir Hotel and the mayor's office – which were both strongholds of Yerin's militia. This sniping seemed to have the desired effect: it goaded Rutskoy and his supporters into storming the mayor's office – which they managed to do fairly easily – and marching off to the broadcasting centre where they were slaughtered.

Studying the many hours of film which were taken by courageous camera crews that day, there are some scenes which do look spontaneous and chaotic; the head of Moscow's Omon paramilitary forces, Vitaly Kiiko, is seen raging and cursing as his men cave in. But other shots have an almost ceremonial quality; especially the moment when several hundred young soldiers from the Dzerzhinsky Division – unarmed and in police uniform – line up to hand over their flak jackets and shields to the parliamentarians.

This dramatic act of desertion was one part of a legend about the events of 3–4 October which the authorities immediately began fostering. Another was the government forces' desperate 'race' to defend Ostankino, which is supposed, by those who believe the government really did have a close shave, to have been virtually unprotected when the rebels set off to capture it.

In fact, at least thirty Vityaz soldiers – backing up an equal number of regular policemen – had been deployed at Ostankino news centre since the beginning of the emergency on 21 September; and they had been placed in an increased state of alert over the weekend.

It is true that extra armoured personnel carriers were sent to Ostankino in a considerable hurry as the stand-off was beginning; but no APCs were needed by the government side during the early, decisive part of the battle.

A convoy of APCs overtook Makashov's supporters as they careered round Moscow's central ring-road, on the way from the White House to their deaths. The rebels were travelling in the buses and jeeps which the surrendering, or supposedly surrendering, police forces had thoughtfully left for them, complete with keys in the ignition. When the APCs sped past, the Makashov men in their intoxicated folly shouted 'our boys, our boys' – falsely believing that the vehicles belonged to a unit which had changed sides. That was how easy the rebels were to fool into overestimating their own strength, and to lure into a trap.

The sight of the armed followers of Makashov, Barkashov and other nationalist hotheads pouring on to the streets of Moscow was terrifying for ordinary people, who felt they were being left undefended against a horde of maniacs. Many people came to feel afterwards that Yerin, the interior minister, deserved some blame for allowing this situation to arise. But the President, significantly, had no complaint whatsoever against the 'remarkable man' who was responsible for the regular police, the Dzerzhinsky Division (including both Vityaz and the unarmed men who 'surrendered' to the rebels at the White House) and other sensitive units of the security forces.

Yerin was showered with praise and honours by Yeltsin, both immediately before the weekend bloodbath and immediately afterwards. Yerin, in turn, had absolutely no reproach to make against any of his men. A few days after the bloodbath, when a great deal of witch-hunting and searching for guilty – or merely neglectful – parties was going on, the interior minister made an intriguing comment: 'Not a single one of our forces broke his oath.' That can only mean that the Dzerzhinsky boys who handed over their flak jackets to the rebels with such solemnity, were doing to under orders from their commanders, who in turn were taking orders from

General Yerin. In defending his own men, Yerin was in danger of giving the game away by departing from the 'spontaneous' version of events which the world was encouraged to believe.

Whatever Yerin might say, very little of the 3 October drama makes sense if we assume what we are supposed to assume, and ascribe the whole thing to a spontaneous outburst of mayhem. Everything makes sense if we assume that the authorities, specificially Yerin and Luzhkov, foiled the parliamentarians with a stratagem no less devious than the one employed by the Cheka in 1921. In other words, it was that old Russian trick – played so effectively in the political arena the previous spring – of fooling the enemy into overestimating his strength, and thus goading him into overplaying his hand. It has rarely been used to such devastating effect.

A week after the upheaval, *Moscow News* – which is still the best-informed weekly in Russia – presented the comments of an anonymous intelligence officer, who is described as a specialist 'on the conduct of *putsches*, coups and military-political provocations' who took part in such actions on behalf of the Soviet government in Latin America and Indochina.

His observations are caustic and very much to the point. First, the 6,000 or more Omon riot police available to Luzhkov and Yerin could easily have stopped the 10,000 demonstrators, mostly unarmed, who broke through the enfeebled 'cordon' around the White House that Sunday afternoon.

The fact that the demonstration was not stopped points, in the commentator's view, to a policy decision by the mayor and the interior minister to refrain from obstructing it. On the jeeps and buses that were thoughtfully left behind for the rebel forces to commandeer, the anonymous officer had this to say: 'Motor vehicles with ignition keys "abandoned in panic" are a trick used by special forces in banana republics . . .'

As he points out, everything was done to induce a sense of euphoria in the pro-parliamentary camp, and encourage their fighters to burst out on to the streets – where they became a serious threat to ordinary citizens, but no real danger to the government's existence. The officer stated: 'Yeltsin was not bad at all at setting a trap for Rutskoy and Hasbulatov. Even though the bait they swallowed was primitive, they swallowed it hook, line and sinker.'

He does, on the other hand, acknowledge another possibility; the trap was laid not by the President, but for the President, by members of his leadership – presumably including Yerin and Luzhkov – so to as force his hand. That does not, in the long run, diminish Yeltsin's responsibility.

What exactly was the purpose of laying this trap, and allowing the Ostankino massacre to take place? One aim, presumably, was to create circumstances in which Russian citizens, and Western governments, would readily agree that there was no choice but to treat the White House with overwhelming force. Another, almost certainly, was to galvanise the regular army, which until the very last moment had shown the utmost reluctance to intervene.

In Yeltsin's own account of the events of 3 October, he protests his innocence, and his surprise at one development after another, in a way that is far from convincing. In mid-afternoon, he says, he was telephoned by Mikhail Barsukov, head of the Kremlin guard, and informed that the cordon round the White House had been broken, and the mayor's office stormed.

'My God, is it possible that things are starting now?' Yeltsin claims to have asked himself. 'They [the rebels] had done what we refused to believe possible until the last moment. They had crossed the line which the Russian people must never cross again. They had declared war, the most terrible of conflicts – civil war.'

He telephoned Grachev and Yerin and was relieved by the 'serene' tone in their voices. But there was, it seems, just a trace of emotion in the voice of the almost superhuman Yerin as he related the manner in which the police, trained to be so unflinching in the face of provocation, had been 'attacked, killed, and stripped of their uniforms . . .'

By his own account, he then received the alarming news

that Ostankino was under attack and ordered a helicopter to take him from his weekend *dacha*, where he was having an ordinary family lunch, to the Kremlin. Yeltsin's account is full of anomalies: for example, he says his helicopter landed in the Kremlin at 7.15 p.m. – by which time the battle for the Ostankino television centre was only beginning.

Right from the beginning, Yeltsin's entourage seem to have been as keenly concerned with creating the right dramatic effect as with practical measures to handle the crisis. When the helicopter landed, one of Yeltsin's security men found time to leave the Kremlin, seek out a reporter from CNN, and provide him with a videotape of the President arriving. The CNN reporter was then escorted back to the Kremlin where he was told to expect an interview with Yeltsin, which never materialised. Clearly things were not in such desperate straits as to deprive the Yeltsin team of its keen instinct for image-making.

At 8.00 p.m., Yeltsin claims, he 'observed' another alarming development: the Ostankino channel had stopped broadcasting. He soon realised that the country's fate was 'hanging by a thread' and it was no longer possible for mere 'policemen' to hold out against 'battle-hardened officers' of the parliamentary forces. Unless Yeltsin was being systematically misinformed, it is hard to imagine how he could have formed that impression: at that very time, Yerin was busily, and quite justifiably, assuring both defence minister Grachev and Prime Minister Chernomyrdin that his own Vityaz forces were in full control of the situation and had no need of reinforcement.

Reading these lines, it seems just possible that Yeltsin, too, was a victim and not a perpetrator of a grotesque trick that was played on Moscow and the world that day. But there would, in that case, be an extraordinary contrast between the naïvety which he displayed as the crisis was developing on Sunday and the effectiveness that he showed during the early hours of Monday in persuading a reluctant army to get involved.

Whether or not every detail is accurate, the story Yeltsin

tells of how he mobilised a hesitant army has a good deal more verisimilitude than his wobbly account of the previous day. At 2.30 a.m., he made the five-minute drive to the defence ministry, where the armoured cars which were blocking the main entrance graciously parted to admit his limousine. He walked into the room where the 'collegium' of defence ministry chiefs – an institution which had wavered in its attitude to the crisis over the last twelve days – was meeting, along with Chernomyrdin. The President's first enquiries about whether or not the officers might see their way to bombarding the White House were met with prevarication, and excuses that many of the soldiers in the Moscow area were needed to pick potatoes.

To Chernomyrdin's question – 'Who proposes what?' – there was a silence, broken by Yeltsin's chief bodyguard, Aleksandr Korzhakov, who ranked with Ilyushin as one of the President's two closest confidants. Korzhakov said he had drawn on his experience as one of the defenders of the White House in August 1991 to sketch out various plans for attacking it. He then summoned into the room a naval captain called Zakharov who suggested a plan of action: stun the rebels by deploying five tanks on each side of the building and firing a few well-aimed shells, then have commandos and paratroopers fight their way in.

Once the bones of the plan were laid out, the generals were happy enough to argue over the details. When it was ready, Grachev solemnly asked Yeltsin: 'Do you authorise me to use tanks in the centre of Moscow?' The President went back to the Kremlin and sent Grachev the written order he had demanded.

It seems likely, although Yeltsin does not mention it, that other things besides operational details were discussed during that tense night of negotiations. Presumably the generals extracted a price: a higher military budget, the adoption of a new military doctrine, a freer hand for the military in the republics. Moreover, the army's enthusiasm for the storming of the White House, many of whose defenders were former comrades, turned out to be far from universal, even as the assault began. General Boris Gromov, the deputy defence minister and famously popular commander of the Soviet forces during their retreat from Afghanistan, pointedly stayed out of all discussions relating to the assault.

The crack paratroop regiments – in a rerun of the August 1991 drama – were at first given ambiguous orders to 'protect' key buildings in central Moscow; several senior officers objected strongly when this turned out to mean shelling the White House.

In the end, a force of 2,000 soldiers was cobbled together from seven units, including the Taman and Kantemirov Guards, the 106th Airborne Division, which had helped to guard the White House during the last coup, and some other paratroopers who had recently been withdrawn from Lithuania. They were assisted by commandos who gained entrance to the building through the underground tunnels and then guided the fire of the tanks.

However, one élite section of the security forces, the Alpha anti-terrorist unit, was at great pains afterwards to make it known to the world that it had set its own terms for participating in the final moments of the White House drama. Alpha's officers successfully insisted that their mission must be to bring Rutskoy, Hasbulatov and their parliamentary supporters out of the building alive. They treated the defeated leaders with courtesy, and in highly dangerous conditions a path was cleared for the rebels to walk out of the building in a more or less dignified way. To the chagrin of the radicals in the Yeltsin entourage, who would have preferred to batter the White House to oblivion, the Alpha unit turned out to have an *esprit de corps*, and perhaps a sense of history, which held them back from slavishly following the orders of one faction, however powerful. Once the crisis was over, this equivocation by the Alpha unit made General Barsukov all the more determined to build up a Kremlin guard which was unflinching in its loyalty to the President.

In other sections of the armed forces, there was a good deal of barely repressed revulsion over what had taken place. Even those who held little brief for Rutskoy and Hasbulatov felt that some face-saving formula should have been found to avoid the horror of fratricide.

The army was, in fact, one of many institutions agitating for a compromise in the few days before the final clash. The fact that a compromise was very much in the air provides the political context for the final upheaval. It helps to explain why Yeltsin's hardest men so desperately needed to bring the stand-off to a confrontational head, in which all talk of meeting in the middle would be brushed aside.

During the first week of the White House drama, many things went well for the presidential side. Yeltsin's moral standing was boosted by the growing influence, within the parliamentary camp, of the extremist Barkashov, General Makashov and the armed empire loyalists. The parliamentarians had also made a terrible tactical mistake when they named rival ministers of defence; this instantly turned the existing, Yeltsin-backed holders of those jobs into implacable enemies. But as the drama moved into a second week, things looked worse for Yeltsin, as more and more influential voices suggested a compromise: fresh, simultaneous elections for Parliament and the Presidency, instead of Yeltsin's scenario of legislative elections in December and Presidential elections the following June.

The only real objection the presidential side could raise to the idea of a simultaneous ballot was the supposed danger that a 'vacuum' would arise as the results were coming in, and as a transfer from one regime to another occurred in both branches of authority. This was not a very strong argument, and there were many influential parties that it failed to convince.

The most important of these was the federation council of regional bosses. Vitaly Mukha, the governor of Russia's third city, Novosibirsk, had become an implacable opponent of Yeltsin. On 29 September he convened a meeting of local politicians from fourteen Siberian regions who threatened to proclaim a giant Eastern republic and virtually secede from Russia unless the blockade of the White House was lifted.

The following day, another influential voice, even harder for Yeltsin to ignore, weighed in: the Church.

Patriarch Alexy invited both sides in the Moscow stand-off to send representatives to the Danilovsky monastery. For one day it seemed as though the Church might be re-emerging as an independent entity in Russian politics for the first time in 300 years. There were many conservative priests inside the White House, where the symbols of Christianity were mixed in an ever more peculiar fashion with the parapher-nalia of communism. The Patriarch was expected, almost *ex officio*, to take the side of Yeltsin; but it was clear that the spiritual leader felt uncomfortable in this role, and his public comments focused on the terrible blame that would fall upon whichever party was the first to spill blood.

The Church-backed negotiations, inevitably, focused on what became known as the zero option: simultaneous elec-tions to the Presidency and Parliament. They progressed as far as an agreement on confidence-building measures: the authorities would turn on the water and electricity, while the defenders would give up their arms. The first part of the deal was carried out, but to the immense relief of the hardliners in the Yeltsin camp, the political leadership on the parliamentary side was quite incapable of 'delivering' any handover of weapons; control of the White House had long since passed from the relative moderates to the extremists.

In other quarters, however, support for a compromise remained strong. The leadership of the armed forces, in a move approved by defence minister Grachev, sent messages to both Yeltsin and Hasbulatov which urged the acceptance of simultaneous elections. Chernomyrdin is also believed to have expressed willingness to accept the zero option, in a telephone conversation with Judge Valery Zorkin, as late as the Sunday morning of 3 October.

On Tuesday, 5 October, the federation council of regional bosses was due to meet in Moscow and it looked very much as though pressure on Yeltsin to end the blockade of the White House and accept simultaneous elections would become unbearable at that point. For the strategists in the presidential camp, that sort of 'reasonable' outcome would spell disaster. It would seem clear that the crisis had been provoked by Yeltsin and resolved by the moderation of his opponents.

Oleg Rumyantsev says that in the few days before the bloody final denouement, he was authorised to work out a detailed compromise proposal by leading members of the federation council, and also by Zorkin. The compromise was to be based on the effective take-over of the country by the federation council, pending elections to both branches of government. To set the deal in motion, both President and Parliament would rescind the 'hostile' decisions they had taken since the beginning of September.

Rumyantsev says he returned to the White House on the afternoon of 3 October, shortly after the communist demonstrators had gained access to the building and created an atmosphere of euphoria. He had expected to gain access to the embattled Parliament via the underground passages, and was surprised to find that he was able to go straight to the White House virtually unimpeded.

He walked into the building, greeted Rutskoy with the triple kiss that is used by traditionalist Russians, and presented him with the document spelling out the compromise. Moments later, the rebel demonstrators came under sniper fire and Rutskoy issued his fateful appeal for a counter-attack.

If only Rutskoy had shown a bit more intelligence and self-restraint, and simply kept the situation under control until the federation council meeting had taken place, victory would have been his. But as the unnamed officer told *Moscow News*, the Vice-President gobbled up the bait – hook, line and sinker.

By the afternoon of Monday, 4 October, Yeltsin was savouring a triumph on a scale that few people could have imagined the previous week. His bitterest enemies, and about 1,000 other people, were in jail; he had closed a dozen newspapers and imposed a regime of censorship on the rest; he had sacked the Siberian governors who had acted disloyally; and best of all, he was able to cancel the dreaded federation council meeting.

He had succeeded in finding that elusive thing which every Russian leader down the centuries has searched for – the key to inspiring fear. Days earlier, there was literally nothing he could do to bring the vast and resource-rich areas of Siberia under his full authority; now the governors of those places were cowering before him in case they shared the fate of their two sacked colleagues.

The way was now clear for the holding of an election under his rules, with his appointees making up the electoral board, and with no parallel power structure, no parliamentary apparatus, to block the process. Not for the first time, Yeltsin had tactically retreated, feigned weakness, and adopted the appearance of vulnerability, in order to rise to new heights of power.

The short-term military and political victory was his, and it was massive. But even as Rutskoy and Hasbulatov were demonised and anathematised over and over again, a different, secret story was being told in the whispered exchanges of simple Russians, as had happened every time in history when a harsh leader had cracked his whip.

The conviction grew that far, far more people had died in the White House than the seventy or so the government reported. There were persistent rumours that the firemen who first entered the building (and were banned from disclosing official secrets) had seen hundreds of charred corpses – or that the building had to be cleared of corpses before the firemen were allowed to start work.

The authorities admitted that they could not tell how many weapons and dead or wounded comrades the fighters had spirited out of the White House through the vast network of underground tunnels. They might have added that the government side, too, was quite capable of using the tunnels to remove any unpleasant sights from the building.

On Tuesday, the corpses of five slain rebels still lay outside the White House, stirring memories of the Tsarist era when rebels' broken bodies were displayed in the most public of places as a way of inspiring fear. In an act of reverence that touched a profound chord, people had covered the five bodies with icons and draped them with banners depicting the Orthodox cross.

Even those citizens who were only dimly aware of what had happened in the White House heard stories of the crazed, sainted courage that the defenders had shown, ready to die and kill in the cause of old tyrants rather than accept new ones. They were, perhaps, the modern equivalent of the Old Believers – seventeenth-century protesters against liturgical reform – who locked themselves in barns and committed collective self-immolation rather than submit to the forces of a modernising Tsar.

At Ostankino, for all manner of people, a terrible ugliness was born. For many people, the most haunting image from that ghastly night at the television centre was the spectacle of sozzled old communist women, cut down by a hail of bullets as they screeched their slogans. They, at least, were granted martyrdom in the cause of the old devils, which was in many ways a better fate than eking out their final days in a stinking communal apartment that some gangster was waiting to privatise.

However, Ostankino also shattered the dreams of many young people, Russian and foreign; it marked the end of a period, begun two years earlier, when democratic Russia seemed merely to be an exciting place, a fallen gerontocracy whose senile rulers had suddenly surrendered everything to their grandchildren.

Andrei Babitsky is a diminutive Muscovite tearaway, of Tajik-Jewish parentage but raised in an orphanage. He says very amusing things in a mocking sing-song voice, and as with many people who have suffered great pain, it is hard to make him talk seriously about anything. His Oriental features bear the scars of a frightful, self-inflicted car accident. In the late 1980s, he made a name for himself as a radio reporter, specialising in the dissident world which became the pro-democracy and then the Yeltsin machine. In a sense he is one of Yeltsin's children, one of a generation of Russians whose hopes for a freer country suddenly soared with the reformist conversion of a burly party boss from Sverdlovsk.

He underwent the new Russia's baptism of fire, reporting the August 1991 coup from the heart of the White House; but as soon as he heard of the second White House siege, he sensed that it would end in tragedy. He was horrified, a few days before the end, to see the police around the White House beating demonstrators with a ferocity that he had never seen, even in 1986 or 1987, when liberal rallies were still being violently dispersed.

He was one of the few people to be standing in front of the Ostankino building when the firing began who survived. 'It was like the most furious gunfire, like a horror film,' he recalls. He helped to drag some of the wounded to safety, and when he managed to get away his arms were dripping in blood. The next day he quarrelled with his radio station, and he did not work as a reporter for many months afterwards. Somewhere in the midst of that gruesome scene, he came to a new understanding: the terrible monster of state power – which he had taunted so boldly in its days of enfeeblement – had acquired new life, and it was serving new masters.

Otto Pohl, who at the age of twenty-four had established himself as a successful photographer with the *New York Times*, was shot in the lung. He thinks he was hit by a sniper on the roof of the main broadcasting centre, opposite the besieged building. Another young American – one of the tens of thousands who had flocked to a 'Wild East' because youth had seemingly taken charge – lay beside him and comforted him.

'He kept talking to me while I was lying there, trying to keep me conscious. I saw him get up and pull other injured people away', says Pohl, relating what he remembered of the lawyer Terry Duncan. 'But then after about thirty minutes I looked up and just saw his head lying in a dark puddle.'

Rory Peck was a giant character, born into a glamorous, eccentric Anglo-Irish environment, which provided very little preparation for life in the late twentieth century but enabled him to observe reality from an unusual angle. He had hardly ever watched television when he took up a camera and became one of the most distinguished chroniclers of war of his generation.

He was gifted with talent, charm, good looks and great physical courage; but he was somehow stung by the dishonesty and pettiness of everyday life in the Western world, driven to seek out places where moral lines are drawn more sharply. In a sense, he too was a protester against the murderous expediencies of the modern world – but unlike the fascist and communist demonstrators with whom he died, his protest was not made in the name of some older version of tyranny.

His search for a starker moral world had taken him first to Afghanistan, where he taught himself the art of filming wars; and then to Moscow, where he and his wife Juliet, a kindred spirit, had set up a magical home in the woods from which they would both sally forth to gather news of the conflicts that were ravaging Russia's frontiers.

Although he played for very high stakes, he had become very skilled at finding the safest possible spots from which to film the bloodiest battles. It was not carelessness that cost him his life at Ostankino, but a compulsive sort of honesty.

Ostankino became a place of deadly danger that night for people like Andrei, Otto, Terry, and Rory because very powerful people – the people who closed down the airwaves, the people who told Bragin to keep his cameras under lock and key – had decided that neither the country, nor the world, nor posterity, should know too much about the slaughter which was being perpetrated.

Dzerzhinsky and his heirs have, after all, been quite successful in keeping their deceit out of most history books, and thus fooling future generations; only thanks to people like Dmitry Likhachov, and the brave reporters who died at Ostankino, have they been less than completely successful.

13

Zhirinovsky: From Oedipus to Geopolitics

The most flamboyant member of the ill-fated Parliament of late Imperial Russia was an extreme conservative called Vladimir Purishkevich. He was of humble origins, the grandson of a poor village priest, but precociously clever. In an extravagant metaphor based on the Duma's semi-circular shape, he once declared: 'Nobody is more right-wing than me – to the right of me there is only the wall!'

He was a maverick member of St Petersburg high society, an organiser of pogroms, an eloquent defender of the monarchy, and a party to the murder of Rasputin. Dr Walter Laqueur says of him: 'There was likely to be disturbances and scandals wherever he appeared . . . He was adept at causing commotion, but there was method behind his apparent madness. Being basically opposed to the parliamentary system, he wanted to discredit the Duma.'

A wave of fear and despondency passed through the Russian liberal world, and all the foreign sponsors of Russian democracy, in the early hours of Monday, 13 December 1993, as the election results became clear. Presented with a broad range of parties, ranging from old-time communists to market-minded reformers, almost a quarter of Russia's voters cast their ballots for a movement that despised the West and gloried in the rhetoric of militarism and imperialism.

Of the 450 seats in the lower house of the new legislature, half had been allocated to political parties on a system of proportional representation, and the other half to the winners of local contests. In the first of these battles, the Liberal Democratic party, headed by Vladimir Zhirinovsky, had surpassed all expectations – with 23 per cent of the vote, compared with just over 15 per cent for Russia's Choice, the reformist group led by Yegor Gaidar which was viewed as the presidential party and had been expected to top the poll. Zyuganov's Russian Communists came next with 12 per cent, and all other factions were reduced to single figures.

On closer inspection, it turned out that the reformers had fared much better in the constituency voting, and this ensured that the pro-Westerners of Russia's Choice, with just over ninety-six seats, would form the biggest bloc in the new legislature. But the message from the electorate was still profoundly disturbing. Any vote for the LDP was an act of faith in its boss, Zhirinovsky; the party only existed as a power base for its tub-thumping leader. The Liberal Democrats' spectacular performance meant that one Russian voter in four had expressed confidence in a man who at various times had threatened to take Alaska back from the United States; to mount a naval expedition against Japan; to secure the release of Russian prisoners in Afghanistan by bombarding Islamabad, the capital of Pakistan; and to subjugate the Baltic states by spraying them with nuclear waste.

At best, the Russian electorate was telling the world that it regarded democracy as a sick and tasteless joke, to which the appropriate response was voting for a tasteless joker. At worst, the spectacular success of Zhirinovsky marked the first step towards the seizure of total control, over the largest country on earth with a vast nuclear arsenal, by the forces of authoritarian chauvinism.

Among the diminishing number of Russians whose hopes for a democracy along more or less Western lines were still intact, there was an intense feeling of shame and embarrassment over the message their compatriots had sent to the world. It seemed as though their country, having rescued itself from the position of international villain, was energetically striving to recast itself in that role. For the Western governments and institutions which had tenderly nurtured Russia's democratic experiment as though it were a sickly child, there was a wave of anxiety and self-doubt.

Yeltsin's bombardment of the Russian Parliament, ten weeks earlier, had been defensible, at a pinch, to anyone who supposed that it was the last, painful step which had to be taken before the advent of a brave new dawn in which Russia's President, people and Parliament were as one in their commitment to reform and democracy.

It had been just about possible to stomach the ghastliness of the October bloodshed as long as the victims were deemed to be the last, stubborn obstacles to the creation of a liberal nirvana – in which all Russians would live happily and democratically ever after.

Yet now, such a short time after the serpent of totalitarian revanchism had apparently been slain, it was raising its head even higher than before. What, in that case, had all the 'slaying' been for?

In their darkest moments, the foreign guardians of Russian democracy wondered if they had unwittingly suckled a monster; and the more far-sighted among them began to see how naive they had been in imagining that the Russian 'child' had ever been their own creature, whose path to adulthood they could hope to guide.

Like the parents of many a delinquent, they feared that they had not taken sufficient care over the child's welfare. They should have fed the infant better, shown more understanding of its teething problems, acted sooner to ease the pain of adapting to a cruel world. After such a difficult start in life, the guardians earnestly concluded, how could anybody be surprised if the infant had displayed such a spectacular tantrum?

Zhirinovsky's discourse appealed directly to the lowest common denominator in the Soviet psyche, so it was assumed that the massive vote in favour of his party had been, first and foremost, an authentic scream of pain from the Russian masses. The emerging underclass, the elderly, the marginalised, the flotsam and jetsam of the cruel new Russian world had finally cried out loud that enough was enough. Western politicians who had been guiding, or trying to guide, Russia's economic policy wondered if the medicine they were administering had been too bitter for anyone to swallow. For the fourth or fifth time since the Soviet collapse, they found themselves asking in a spirit of some desperation how they could rescue Yeltsin from a humiliation that seemed ill-deserved after the heroic services he had rendered to the cause of democracy. The blessed relief which followed Yeltsin's triumph over the parliamentary rebels on 4 October had given way to a sinking feeling that this victory had been wholly or partially reversed.

These Western readings of the December 1993 ballot were at best over-simplified, at worst downright wrong. Taken as a whole, the election results were not a setback for the Russian presidency, but a success – a success, moreover, that was only made possible by the shelling of the old Parliament and the emergence of Yeltsin's men as unchallenged masters of the political scene.

For the President, the precise make-up of the revamped legislature mattered much less than the other question that was settled at the same time: the constitution. As well as choosing deputies, voters were asked to pronounce their verdict on a political system which vested far more power in the head of state than any of the proposals which had been debated and fought over so bitterly throughout the previous year. Under this new charter, the President would set the compass in both domestic and foreign affairs; he would issue decrees which Parliament could not even consider, much less rescind; choose the Prime Minister; and nominate the head of the central bank as well as key members of the judiciary. One of the most astonishing provisions laid down was that Parliament could be dismissed if it passed a vote of no confidence in the government. The procedures for impeaching the President or changing the constitution were made very difficult indeed.

If this constitution was passed, then the make-up of Parliament was a secondary issue, because its power would be firmly limited. In the awful event that the constitution was rejected, and the country slid backwards into a fresh round of chaos, then the outcome of an election to a still-born legislature would probably matter even less.

There was little doubt that Yeltsin could secure a plurality of votes for his new constitution. The October events had left him in firm control of a mighty propaganda machine, capable of exercising enormous influence over those who still had any faith at all in politics.

In the immediate aftermath of the White House battle, a strict regime of censorship was imposed. This was eased after a few days, but a banning order on the wildest of the opposition publications remained in force. Prokhanov's *Dyen* was one of the victims of this ban; it resurfaced quite rapidly under the new title of *Zavtra* (*Tomorrow*) – but never quite recovered its original verve. Vladimir Shumeiko, having apparently recovered from any damage he suffered during the summer of scandals, was now in charge of information policy, and he seemed to have dispensed entirely with liberal illusions. The purpose of the media, he stated firmly, was not to give free rein to ideas, or inform citizens on matters of public interest, but to issue clear ideological guidance. As though in response to this directive, television reporting became more stridently pro-Yeltsin than ever.

It was true that the initial wave of pro-Yeltsin euphoria which followed the White House battle had given way to a quiet revulsion amongst millions of Russians. But the people who reacted in that way tended to be alienated from the entire political process; they came to the conclusion that nothing they said or did would make any difference to the country's destiny. Among those who were still prepared to 'do their civic duty' – as voting was described in Soviet times – there was never much doubt that a majority would say 'yes' to the President's constitution.

The main challenge for Yeltsin was to establish the absolute, unquestionable legitimacy of the new order by demonstrating that more than half Russia's registered voters had taken part in the vote. To anyone who felt the atmosphere in Russia that winter, it seemed hard to imagine how Yeltsin's self-imposed target – participation by more than 50 per cent of the electorate – could possibly be met: so many people were too discouraged or marginalised to bother voting. But fulfilled it was, or at any rate so the electoral commission announced. It declared that about 55 per cent of registered voters had gone to the polls, and of these about 60 per cent had said 'yes' to the new basic law. For Yeltsin, this outcome marked the culmination of three years of struggle to establish himself as the most powerful person on the political scene. His democratic supporters might have been despairing, that December night, at the high score of Zhirinovsky, but the President himself had every reason to celebrate.

As for the make-up of the new legislature, it did not look nearly so bad for the Russian presidency as most Western observers, lamenting over the 'devastating blow' Yeltsin had suffered, appeared to think. Of course, Russia's party of power – the coalition of pro-Yeltsin forces which had emerged victorious in the October stand-off – was a broad church, ranging from former dissidents like Father Gleb Yakunin to former dissident-hunters such as Nikolai Golushko, the security minister. Within this coalition, there was a correspondingly wide variety of reactions to the new balance of political forces, from bitter dismay to quiet satisfaction. But for the toughest, most pragmatic figures inside Yeltsin's apparatus – the practitioners of old-fashioned statecraft who would just as happily have worked for Stalin or the Tsars – the election results were anything but unwelcome. In retrospect, it looks clear that the results did not reflect some sudden burst of popular discontent (which was there all the time), but were a more or less inevitable consequence of tactics that were consciously adopted by Russia's rulers in the wake of the October 1993 blood-bath.

For several weeks after shelling the White House, Yeltsin had unprecedented freedom of action – more freedom than any boss of the Kremlin had enjoyed since the Soviet power structure began to crumble under the feet of Mikhail Gorbachev. With his declared enemies in jail and almost everyone else cowering before him, he could have knocked his own supporters' heads together in almost any combination he chose. But he and his entourage decided – and from their own, machiavellian, point of view, this was the correct decision – to devote all their energies to railroading into existence a new, presidentially oriented constitution. Western commentators, and most Russian ones, still divided Russia's political parties into 'reformers' – those who, broadly speaking, favoured market economics and co-operation with the West – and opponents of reform. For the Yeltsin apparatus in late 1993, there was no such distinction: the only fault line which mattered was between supporters of the constitution – who included Gaidar and Zhirinovsky – and those who had reservations about the constitution, who ranged from Yavlinsky the reformer to Zyuganov the communist.

On 26 November, in one of his rare interventions in the election campaign, Yeltsin summoned party leaders to the Kremlin, and told them that their access to the airwaves would be restricted if they dared to attack the new political charter. 'I warn you that your free television time will be taken away if you deviate from your theme', he told them. 'Your theme is your programme. We [i.e., the presidency] will fight for the constitution, and I ask you not to touch on the constitution.'

By threatening to take away their free broadcasts, Yeltsin was, of course, hitting the contenders in the most sensitive place. Post-Soviet electioneering had come a long way from the idealistic amateurs who trod the streets of Moscow and Leningrad in the late 1980s. Voters were now being wooed through the media and the biggest single reason for Zhirinovsky's ultimate success was the way he used his television slots to deliver short, sharp messages.

Zhirinovsky also stomped up and down the country, flattering provincial towns with his knowledge of their local problems, which was always remarkably detailed and confirmed the impression that he had access to information of the highest quality. But it was through television that the LDP leader impressed himself on Russian hearts and minds.

Where Gaidar addressed the voters in long, clever words and was blunt with them about the sweat, tears and toil that lay ahead, Zhirinovsky spoke to the masses in much the same way as Yeltsin had done two years earlier. He presented himself as an ordinary, bruised, insulted, Russian man who could at once empathise with the average man's travails and transport him instantly to nirvana – away from the hellish grind of a works canteen or construction site, straight into a brave new world where Russia was once again a powerful, respected country. Zhirinovsky used his television slots to create graphic images; at one point he appeared on screen with a condom and a bottle of liquor, at another he told viewers the blood-curdling tale of an ethnic Russian who in one or other of the newly independent states had been torn apart by being tied to two horses which galloped off in opposite directions. He promised higher pensions, full employment, more opportunities for the young; there was something for all the family.

Zhirinovsky was also given plenty of time to impress these vivid images on the electorate. One of the strangest aspects of the 1993 election campaign was the privileged treatment which the LDP was accorded by the managers of state broadcasting. The rules were that each electoral bloc would have three hours' free airtime, and it could buy up to eleven more hours on a commercial basis. Russia's Choice, lavishly financed by the country's new class of bankers and investment kings, was the only party which could comfortably afford to broadcast for the maximum slot of fourteen hours. But Zhirinovsky's party also managed to obtain eleven hours of 'commercial' time, with a vague promise to pay later. This was widely hailed as proof of the LDP's *chutzpah*, its ability to pull off confidence tricks, but there was another way of looking at it – it was one of the many signs that Zhirinovsky had good friends at the top of almost every Russian hierarchy, including the media.

As Zhirinovsky's skilful use of television took effect, his rating duly rose; about a week before the election it overtook that of Gaidar and Russia's Choice; so the final pecking order was not a huge surprise to political insiders, even if the scale of the LDP's triumph was. One word from Yeltsin could have shaved five percentage points off its score, but the silence from the Kremlin was deafening. For Yeltsin's liberal supporters, this was bitterly frustrating. A curious feature of the opinion polls was the strange shift of support from the camp of Gaidar to Zhirinovsky: ostensibly a leap from one extreme to the other. However, it is possible to hazard a guess at why this happened.

The October tragedy had, among many other emotions, rekindled in Russians the ancient sentiment of deference, the idea that the Tsar knows best, even when his reasoning is opaque to ordinary people. In this atmosphere, many citizens were looking, consciously or unconsciously, for a signal from their leader as to how they should vote. When no clear signal was given, they opted at first for Russia's Choice which appeared to be the President's party because so many of his favourite, hand-picked ministers were prominent members. But in the final days of the election campaign, when Zhirinovsky seemed to be filling the television screen, millions of people – including erstwhile Gaidar supporters – switched their loyalties to the fast-talking maverick because it really seemed as if he was the person whom the powers that be wanted them to support. The vote for Zhirinovsky was not so much a protest vote as an expression, conscious or unconscious, of fealty and deference to the country's new political and ideological masters. Although the scale of Zhirinovsky's success came as a surprise to everyone, pollsters had picked up a steady rise in his rating during the final week of the campaign. The oddest trend was that many of the LDP leader's new-found admirers were defectors not from the communists or some other school of authoritarianism, but from the pro-Westerners of Russia's Choice. There is one plausible explanation for this curious migration; people were doing as they were told.

Contrary to another popular myth, Zhirinovsky's supporters were by no means concentrated among the wildest and poorest of the lumpenproletariat, who in any case rarely made it to the polls. The LDP captured the support of millions of blue- and white-collar workers, particularly in the provinces, who were by no means on the breadline but resented their country's humiliation on the world stage and perceived a threat to their own jobs from economic upheaval. The intensity of this resentment was not correlated in any simple way with economic misery. Two years earlier, when the country was in such a desperate state that highly qualified architects or surgeons seriously wondered how they could feed their families, feelings of bitterness were somehow kept under control – as though the mere business of survival was so fraught as to leave no mental space for anything else. Now that recovery was palpably under way – the average monthly wage had in hard-currency terms climbed from barely $10 to $100 over the previous two years – people once more had the spare energy to look back, with bitterness and resentment, over the pain which Russia's transformation had brought them. Zhirinovsky did a brilliant job of tapping this sentiment, which was not so much a scream of pain from the poor as a cry of wrath from people who were recovering from a period of humiliation and poverty and only now realised how angry they were.

If Yeltsin had felt any sincere interest in checking the rise of extremism in Russia, he could easily have moved to clip Zhirinovsky's wings. But Yeltsin did no such thing; during the final week of the election campaign, when Zhirinovsky's fortunes began to surge, the President maintained a public silence on all issues except the constitution.

There are unanswered questions about the extent to which Yeltsin himself was aware that the ground was being laid for Zhirinovsky's spectacular success. He must bear some responsibility for the outcome, given that his own peculiar silence on all subjects except the constitution was such an important part of the background against which the elections occurred. But did Yeltsin's advisers point out to him how well Zhirinovsky was doing, and how the President's silence might be interpreted? To judge by Yeltsin's behaviour three weeks after the election, when he claimed to have been poorly counselled, it seems that the President was not fully aware of the strategy that was unfolding; but there are, of course, times when it is expedient to feign ignorance.

When the shape of the new Parliament or Duma emerged, it was plainly a good thing for the presidency that no faction – communist, reformist or nationalist – had an outright majority; this would reduce the chances of the legislature ganging up on the President and using whatever authority it had to thwart him.

Zhirinovsky had helpfully split the anti-reform vote and channelled some of the conservative energy in directions which were relatively harmless for the President. If at some point in the future, Russia's executive authority decided to do away with the legislature altogether, it had in Zhirinovsky a person whose wild and erratic behaviour would play its part in discrediting the institution of Parliament – just as Purishkevich had done seventy years earlier.

In one sense, Zhirinovsky was a rival to Yeltsin; he had, after all, challenged Yeltsin for the presidency in June 1991 and he stated repeatedly that he intended to be Yeltsin's successor. But that did not exclude a convergence of temporary, tactical interest between the two politicians, or a considerable overlap in the élites which backed them. There was one very senior figure in Russia who saw no contradiction between conditional support for Yeltsin on one hand, and warm personal relations with Zhirinovsky on the other. That was General Pavel Grachev, the defence minister, who in April 1993, when the Liberal Democrats were holding a party congress, sent Zhirinovsky an effusive birthday greeting, with warmest wishes for 'robust health, great personal happiness and further successes in social and political activity . . .'

Like General Sterligov, Zhirinovsky was often at pains to distinguish Yeltsin himself from his liberal advisers, and to stress that there was no unbridgeable gap between the LDP and the President.

In November 1991, for example, Zhirinovsky warmly praised Yeltsin's decision to suspend regional elections and appoint provincial governors from above. He considered that a wise move – it was too bad that in other ways, the President was being 'let down' by his advisers. 'He had an alternative – joining the patriotic forces in the army and the KGB. He could rely on them, but instead he was breaking them up. And he could rely on parties which stand for Russia – with our party, for example, and certain others.'

By December 1993, Zhirinovsky had already done the presidency sterling service, as an enthusiastic supporter of the new constitution who had played a significant part in securing its approval. It would be an exaggeration to say that Zhirinovsky 'delivered' his supporters' votes for the constitution; many of them appeared to have ignored their leader's advice and voted against Yeltsin's charter. But whichever way they voted, people who might otherwise have stayed at home were drawn to the ballot-box by Zhirinovsky's rhetoric, and this would help to keep the election quorate.

He was not the only 'opposition' figure who mysteriously threw his weight behind the President in spring 1993. Another one was Dmitry Vasilyev, the leader of Pamyat and self-described fascist; but his political star was fading, and it was only because of the sympathetic publicity he received from Itar-Tass, the official news agency, that anybody knew what his views were.

Zhirinovsky, by contrast, provided the President with really useful backing. Like General Sterligov, he was the sort of opposition figure who believed in shoring up the presidency rather than squeezing or abolishing it. Zhirinovsky's stated reason for backing a strong presidency was perfectly plausible: in 1996, or even earlier, he wanted to run for that office himself. But that was tomorrow's battle – for now he and Yeltsin were on the same side.

It was true that in March 1993, Zhirinovsky, with his characteristic penchant for sexual imagery, had described Yeltsin as a failure whom the nation, like an unsatisfied woman, would soon abandon. 'The President is weak – and when a man is impotent his girlfriend goes off and finds another man', he sniggered out loud.

Nevertheless Zhirinovsky proceeded, for the remainder of

1993, to give the President every possible assistance with recovering his potency. Over a summer of tedious negotiations on Russia's future political system, he stood loyally by Yeltsin's side, and during the October events, which must surely have laid to rest any doubts about Yeltsin's prowess, Zhirinovsky rendered the President an invaluable service by saying – in his only public pronouncement on the whole bloody drama – that all decent people should stay at home.

The nation's rulers duly returned the favour – through the privileged treatment that Zhirinovsky received from state television, through the President's ear-splitting silence during the final days of the campaign, and in other ways as well.

In spring 1994, when it was far too late to make any real difference, it became clear that the whole electoral exercise of the previous December had been marred by massive fraud. A team of researchers who belonged to a liberal faction within the presidential apparatus came to the conclusion that the authorities had vastly exaggerated the turn-out, and distorted the results – with Zhirinovsky as the main beneficiary.

The electoral commission claimed that out of an electorate of 106 million – a total which had mysteriously dropped by 1 million since the previous referendum eight months earlier – some 58 million people, or well above half, had voted on that freezing Sunday in December.

In fact, as the spring 1994 study concluded, only 49 million citizens, or 46 per cent of the total, had gone to the polls, and the plebiscite was therefore inquorate. The study's chief author, Aleksandr Sobyanin, also came to the astonishing conclusion that 6 million votes had been falsely added to the score of Zhirinovsky's LDP; this suggested that his real share of the vote had been nearer 13 per cent than 23 per cent. The Sobyanin team – which was abruptly deprived of its workplace after word of its conclusions began leaking to the press – also suggested that the communists' score had been boosted artificially by 1.8 million votes, while their allies in the Agrarian and Women of Russia Parties had their scores topped up by 1.7 million and 1 million respectively. Russia's

Choice had been unfairly deprived of 2 million votes. Fraud on that scale can scarcely be attributed to the vagaries of a few corrupt or incompetent local officials; it could only have been orchestrated from above.

Senior activists in Russia's Choice said privately that they knew at least part of the story. After the October violence, Yeltsin had seized the opportunity to abolish not just Hasbulatov's Parliament but the whole nation-wide hierarchy of regional, municipal and local councils which made up the legislative arm of Russian government. One of the results of this was to leave huge holes in the country's administration: there was no effective tier of authority between the governors of Russia's eighty-eight regions and the 90,000 polling stations. Under the old system, an intermediate layer of local councils was responsible for reporting the results from all the polling stations in its area; and it was relatively easy to identify results which looked suspicious because they differed from the general pattern, or did not tally with local demography. Under the new system, regional governors could conceal the effect of fictitious ballots by adding a few dozen votes – well within the margin of human error – to each of several hundred neighbourhood polling stations.

Now it so happened that most of the regional governors were themselves candidates for election to the upper house of Parliament, or federation council. The composition of this new institution was yet another matter on which citizens were called to pronounce on 12 December, along with the fate of the constitution and the make-up of the lower house.

Many of the governors were not sufficiently popular to win a fair electoral fight, and they knew as much; they were obliged, therefore, to take full advantage of their new-found freedom of action and top up their own scores by tens of thousands of imaginary votes each. This, of course, served the President's interests too: by inflating the numbers who had gone to the polls, the regional bosses were helping to create the impression that the whole exercise had been quorate. But in order for the returns they presented to be plausible, the ambitious regional bosses had to invent votes for the lower house as well; it would have looked very odd if voting figures for the upper house had been far in excess of those for the other chamber. Right across Russia, Zhirinovsky seems to have been chosen by governors as the main beneficiary of these imaginary lower house votes – with the notable exception of the autonomous territories where non-Russian peoples, like the Muslim Bashkirs or the Buddhist Buryats, were at least nominally in charge, and the LDP's score remained low.

If this account – based on interviews with senior, respected figures within Russia's Choice – is correct, then there is a mystery as to why Zhirinovsky was singled out as the main recipient of the crooked governors' largess. One innocent explanation is that the regional bosses took a last-minute decision when they saw that early returns from the Far East showed a powerful swing in Zhirinovsky's favour. If there was a genuine surge in support for the LDP leader (and nobody doubts that there was) then he would also be the most 'plausible' recipient of extra, imaginary votes – except, perhaps, in those territories where a non-Russian minority was the dominant force. There is, however, a more disturbing possibility: that governors were instructed by some highly-placed person in Moscow to exaggerate Zhirinovsky's score, as part of a compact under which a blind eye would also be turned to the governors' own peccadilloes.

Whatever the precise reason for Zhirinovsky's generous treatment – by state television, by the President himself, and by the electoral commission – he seems, for a man who claimed to be the voice of the powerless, to have had plenty of help from the powerful. Hence the comparison with Purishkevich, whose historical significance does not lie in the fact that he was sometimes capable of mobilising large numbers of people at the very bottom of Russian society – but rather in the support he enjoyed from a small number of wealthy and influential people, and his ability to transmit ideas downwards, from the mighty to the masses, in ways that the mighty found useful. Contrary to appearances, Zhirinovsky was not, except in personal style, an outsider battering on the walls of the Kremlin; he was an insider, whose discourse – for all its apparent madness – merits as much careful study as the words of any powerful person in Russia.

On certain issues, Zhirinovsky has been remarkably consistent, at least since his presidential election campaign of spring 1991. Again and again, he has repeated that Russia should be a unitary state, avoiding the Bolsheviks' mistake of creating 'republics' for the subject nations. With similar doggedness, he has named three countries which Russia must subjugate or even dismember: Turkey, Iran and Afghanistan. Russia has no fundamental quarrel with the US, Germany, China or Japan as long as they do not obstruct her effort to subdue her southern neighbours.

Another recurring theme in Zhirinovsky's discourse is the notion that the communists made a mistake in trying to impose their ideology on peoples to whom it was alien. In terms very similar to those which had once been used by Yeltsin, Zhirinovsky railed against the Soviet regime for wasting public money on propping up regimes in Latin America and Africa, where Russia had no strategic interests. He takes care – in a way that is belied by the studied sloppiness of his prose – to stress that his project is to restore the Russian empire, and not the USSR. Zhirinovsky's Greater Russia would be divided, like the realm of the Tsar, into *gubernii* or governorships, not ethnically defined republics with the formal right to secede.

His autobiography gives a carefully filtered description of his family and upbringing in Alma-Ata, the capital of Kazakhstan. In between smutty descriptions of his first intimations of sexuality – watching girls at his kindergarten as they urinated into buckets – and loud, cacophonous groans over the poverty and loneliness of his childhood, there is a hymn of Oedipal adoration to his mother, Aleksandr Pavlovna. Yet even as he lauds her, he vents his resentment at her preoccupation with a younger lover and the rigours of work and house-keeping.

With scant regard for the sensibilities of his wife Galina – a lady whom he describes elsewhere as a legal expert who works 'in an investigative capacity for an institution I would prefer not to name', Zhirinovsky declares:

> In the course of my entire life, I never met the beloved woman I needed, but maybe one of the reasons for this was my love for my mother. I grew up without a father, and I had a stepfather who treated me badly.
>
> Everything my childish soul was capable of was directed towards my mother. I couldn't bear to think she would die or disappear one day. Probably my whole potential for love was taken up by the love of a son for his mother, including the capacity to love girls. I loved her. Very much. It was double love, triple love . . . I saw her suffering. I felt very sorry for her. Sometimes I saw her in tears, and I would ask: 'Mama, why are you crying?' And she would say: 'You will understand when you grow up, little son.'

He also introduces the reader to his grandmother, whose name – improbably suggestive of the English shires – was Fiona. The Stalinist authorities had sentenced her to a spell in the Solovetsky Island prison camp because she was a 'businesswoman' who turned her home into a makeshift café during the years of the New Economic Policy. In various interviews, but not in his autobiography, Zhirinovsky claims to have had distinguished parentage on his father's side. He said this grandfather had been a banker in America, and his father had studied at the Sorbonne. Yet everything about the paternal side of the politician's family is surrounded by mystery.

His mother was first married to a man who is not named in the autobiography: it simply states that he was a colonel who was wary of having anything to do with his in-laws because of their politically unsound past. He is said to have died of tuberculosis in 1944. Aleksandra Pavlovna married her second husband – the politician's father – a year later, only to be widowed again – this time as a result of a car accident – in 1946, when the budding politician was only a few months old.

The LDP leader names his father as Volf Andreyevich Zhirinovsky and describes him as a lawyer who worked for the administration of the railway running from Central Asia to Siberia. But the politician's own account of his antecedents does not tell the full story, according to a report filed from Alma-Ata in April 1994 by Nick Moore, a journalist with the Associated Press news agency, who had fossicked through the public records office.

Evidence gathered by Moore suggests that 'Volf Zhirinovsky' – as described in the politician's autobiography – is a synthesis of two or more people: Aleksandr Pavlovna's first husband, Colonel Andrei Zhirinovsky, who worked in the railway administration and succumbed to tuberculosis in August 1944, and a man with the Jewish name of Volf Edelstein whom Aleksandr Pavlovna married in November 1945, five months before the politician was born.

The birth certificate of the man who became famous as Vladimir Volfovich (i.e. son of Volf) Zhirinovsky describes him as Vladimir Volfovich Edelstein, with the words 'no documents for father' scribbled on the back. There is a handwritten note, dated 1964, which changes the surname to Zhirinovsky. Childhood friends say he called himself Zhirinovsky when he was at school; but the records would indicate that he only assumed that name officially when he went to Moscow, aged eighteen, to take up a place at a prestigious school of Oriental languages. Names ending in -ovsky generally originate from the western fringes of the Russian empire, and could be either Polish Catholic or Jewish, whereas the name of Edelstein is, of course, obviously Jewish. Although a spokesman for the LDP leader instantly denounced Nick Moore's report as a fabrication by the Kazakh secret services, the politician himself has given a confusing variety of signals over his Jewish origins.

He has made indignant assertions that he has 'not one drop' of Jewish blood in his veins but on one famous occasion, he let out the facetious, throw-away line: 'My mother was Russian, my father was a lawyer . . .' In the Russian context, this sounds like a witty acknowledgement that his father was indeed Jewish and had practised one of the community's favourite professions.

In the late 1980s – a period when Zhirinovsky was hopping feverishly from one political organisation to another – he co-founded a Jewish cultural organisation called Shalom, and none of his fellow activists ever doubted that he shared their ethnic origins. It also emerged, soon after his election triumph in December 1993, that ten years earlier he had gone through the elaborate procedures needed to emigrate to Israel. He told a Russian-language newspaper in Israel in 1992 that he regarded Israel as a potential ally in Russia's stand-off with Turkey and Iran. But these surprising connections did not prevent him from appealing, in his persona as a rabble-rousing politician, to the racial sentiments of traditionalist Russians.

Several details in Zhirinovsky's autobiography – the idealised mother, the abrasive encounters with a harsh woman teacher – are reminiscent of the childhood memories of another Russian populist, Boris Yeltsin. But where Yeltsin repeatedly casts himself as hero, Zhirinovsky's tale is anti-heroic. It is also laced with references to ethnic questions which hardly arose in Yeltsin's Siberian village. Among his mother's many travails, it seems, was the mere fact of being ethnic Russian in a republic controlled by Kazakhs.

'I asked mother: "Why do we have such bad living conditions? Why can't we have a separate apartment?" Mother answered: "We're not Kazakhs. It's difficult for us to get an apartment here. They give them to the Kazakhs first." ' With regard to the Jews, Zhirinovsky is less blunt, but he pointedly notes the Jewish origins of many of the teachers who mistreated him.

At the same time, Zhirinovsky is at pains to stress that his vision of Russia is not racially exclusive. He recalls fondly that more than one of his aunts married into the small racial minorities whose homelands lie within Russia, and thus accurately captures the popular Russian self-image as a nation that will coexist amiably and generously with others as long as there is no doubt about who is ultimately in charge.

Zhirinovsky's entire discourse, spoken and written, is an uncannily faithful rendition – almost a brilliant satire – of the maudlin ramblings that can be heard on the lips of millions of Soviet citizens whose characters have been disfigured by hardship, alienation and a regime that treated them like delinquent children. His burblings are carefully laced with the slyness, the bitterness, the sullen envy that characterises Soviet life at the bottom. His life story is replete with laboured descriptions of the communal lavatory in his apartment building, tales of shop-lifting and other desperate stratagems to make money.

It is a commonplace, among observers of Russia, that the urban Soviet life has warped the personality of the Soviet male more than the female. There is a vicious circle in which feckless, semi-alcoholic men, lacking any self-respect or responsibility, abandon their wives after or during their first pregnancy; so that the normal family unit is a single mother, struggling to combine work and housekeeping with the raising of one child, who is adored but perforce neglected. Zhirinovsky's story of his miserable existence as a latchkey child in a communal apartment is therefore one that millions of citizens can identify with, whether they cast themselves in the role of child or mother.

Yet half-way through the text, there is an abrupt change of subject matter, from a sentimental autobiography to a geopolitical manifesto. Zhirinovsky tries to keep up the folksy style, but the reader is conscious that this is an *intelligent* – a graduate of a prestigious seat of learning – struggling to talk like a common man, and not the reverse.

His geopolitical project is nothing less than the creation of a Russian superstate which dominates most of Asia – leaving apart China, Japan and Indochina – by dismembering Iran, Turkey and Afghanistan and consolidating Russia's friendship with India and Iraq. In a rambling argument that displays considerable knowledge of the ethnography of south Asia, Zhirinovsky suggests that Russia must either subdue its three adversaries, or be subdued by them. As any Soviet Orientalist worth his salt knows, the main reason why these countries represent a particular challenge is the overlap between their ethnic and linguistic minorities – such as the

Azeris of northern Iran, the Tajiks of northern Afghanistan, and the Kurds of eastern Turkey – and the peoples of the southern Soviet Union. Unless the Russian empire can subdue its southern neighbours, the loyalty of its own subjects will be called into question, or so the theory goes.

In return for allowing Russian hegemony in the territories on its underbelly, Zhirinovsky suggested, western Europe would be allowed freedom of action in Africa, and the United States could dominate Latin America. A Sino-Japanese condominium would prevail in South-East Asia.

There were strong racial overtones to this argument; the Russians would fight the corner of the white race in Asia, while the Americans did so in the New World – although he was pessimistic about America's chances of succeeding, and speculated gleefully that it might be disintegrating, and begging for Russian help, by the middle of next century. This might sound like demented raving to a Western reader, but it was only a slight distortion of the serious thinking that was going on in the heart of the Russian establishment: the security council, the analytical department of the KGB, and the various think-tanks attached to the Academy of Sciences.

In those august quarters, no less than in Zhirinovsky's earthy prose, there was a renewed stress on trying to secure a *de facto* division of the world into spheres of influence. This was Russia's counter-proposal in the face of the US effort to promote a new world order in which the leading Western nations, and their values, would hold sway everywhere.

The idea was that each dominant power would overlook the peccadilloes of the others – the meddling in small countries' affairs and the military operations on flimsy pretexts – on condition that its own hegemony was unchallenged.

This purist commitment to the principle of regional hegemony has some interesting implications. Zhirinovsky – unlike many other Russian nationalists – can contemplate making some concessions in Russia's territorial dispute with Japan, so long as Tokyo does not interfere with Russian interests in Central Asia. He can also imagine small adjustments of territory, or influence, in Europe. He says that part of Moldova could be ceded back to Romania and, like all Russian nationalists, he is enormously tempted by the idea of a Russo-German condominium in Europe.

The principle of 'spheres of influence' is exactly the one that Russia has been trying to establish within the Commonwealth of Independent States (CIS): international recognition of Russia as the main regulator of conflict and provider of 'peace-keeping' forces, even when the wars in question have largely been fuelled by Russia. While the Yeltsin administration was at least discreet about its practice – well-established by 1993 – of arming both sides in the conflicts on Russia's southern flank, Zhirinovsky openly advocated the sale of weapons as an instrument of state policy. Russia should as far as possible evacuate its own citizens from Transcaucasia and exercise leverage over the region's interminable wars by supplying weapons to all parties, he said.

No official or institution in Moscow was talking openly about subjugating Iran, Turkey or Afghanistan. But by 1993 Russia was an interested observer, to say the least, of the internecine strife that was reducing Kabul to ruins; and relations with Turkey were worsening daily, as Turkish officials accused Moscow of fomenting the Kurdish rebellion.

A paper presented to the Russian security council in early 1994 had uncanny echoes of the Zhirinovsky doctrine: it suggested that unimpeded access to India was of massive strategic importance to Russia, and laid out a cold-blooded formula for exploiting little known ethnic differences within Kazakhstan in order to weaken that republic and ensure an 'open road' between Moscow and New Delhi.

It is always possible that Zhirinovsky was simply an individual with a gift for divining, or even pre-empting the *Zeitgeist* that hung over the Kremlin; but there is another, more plausible explanation. He was being used by senior members of the Russian establishment to convey their thinking, in a somewhat caricatured form, to the common man.

Instead of the dry theorising of a policy paper, Zhirinovsky speaks to the Russian masses in the language they long to hear: the languages of dreams, of instant and miraculous journeys to paradise. He correctly sensed a crucial difference between the collective psychology of the Russian masses, and their former compatriots in the Baltic states, whose attitudes to almost everything were characteristically Western. As soon as they had the opportunity to do so, the Balts set about creating miniature versions of the model bourgeois state, where citizens enjoy a modest degree of prosperity by dint of moderately hard, rationally organised work and deferred gratification.

This model held no appeal for the average Russian; they would endure any hardship, suffer any agony, as long as their minds were filled with images of nirvana. Mystical forms of religion, alcohol in large quantities, and the slogans of communism were all – in their different ways – methods of trying to bring paradise nearer; and so were the speeches of Russia's best-advised politicians.

Boris Yeltsin had used exactly that principle when he was cultivating his own image as an aggrieved tribune of the people four years earlier; but his advent to power had made it all too clear that Russia's real prospects were for a steady – but not spectacular – rise from the economic abyss, in return for much harder work than the communist system had ever demanded.

One of the commonest complaints, two years into the Yeltsin administration, was that 'there is nothing to dream about . . .' In a sense, it had been easier and more compelling to dream about paradise in 1991, when the real economic situation was far more hellish.

Zhirinovsky brought new dreams. In an image that he used over and over again, he proclaimed that soon, Russian soldiers would be wearing summer uniforms and washing their boots in the Indian Ocean. The bells of Russian Orthodox churches would ring out on those sun-kissed shores, the southern fringe of an empire that would be tolerant of all traditional customs and religions – from nomadic pastoralism to Muslim polygamy – but had no room for the rational doctrines of the West.

It was just the kind of image that could sustain a Russian voter who is obliged to dig roads or lay bricks on a bleak mid-winter's day when the sun barely rises.

14
PUPILS AND TEACHERS

BORIS YELTSIN'S FACE glowed with churlish, schoolboy delight as he gazed down at the diplomats and reporters who had gathered to watch him write a page or two of history in the showy magnificence of a castle in Naples. It was plain that he had greatly enjoyed his role as the first Russian President to join the leaders of the Group of Seven capitalist countries as a participant in their annual deliberations on the state of the world, and not merely as a supplicant for aid, as Russia had been at previous meetings of the august group.

Like so many of the Western institutions that were first established, in part, as a counter-weight to the communist bloc, the club of leaders known as 'G-7' was no longer sure of its purpose. The daily, electronic flow of capital from one continent to another was by now so enormous that the Seven leaders had lost their former ability to guide the currency and credit markets of the world, even if they could agree on the desired direction. But when Yeltsin travelled to Naples in July 1994, he had none of these existential doubts; he had no particular purpose except simply to be there, and make the point that Russia, after dipping briefly below the horizon, had re-emerged as a force to be reckoned with in world affairs.

The Russian leader's presence in Naples followed a vigorous lobbying effort by Chancellor Helmut Kohl, the one Western leader of whom Yeltsin used to speak fondly, even mawkishly, as a personal friend with whom he frequently engaged in long, chatty telephone calls.

At Germany's suggestion, Russia had won the right to play a full part in all the Group of Seven's discussions on political and security issues, ranging from international terrorism to the nuclear ambitions of North Korea. Only when purely economic questions were being discussed was Russia made to wait outside the door and even then, the Russian team successfully insisted that Moscow's views be taken into account.

Small wonder that Yeltsin was beaming with pleasure. Standing uncomfortably beside him in the bright Naples sunshine, and anxiously studying his every gesture, was the man whom Yeltsin liked to address – in a way that sounded almost mocking rather than friendly – as Bill. Yeltsin always pronounced his counterpart's forename with a certain rough relish, playfully declining it as though it were a Russian noun.

Onlookers held their breath as an American woman reporter put the hardest question of the moment to Yeltsin: would Russia yield to Western pressure, and withdraw all its forces from the Baltic republic of Estonia by the agreed date of 31 August 1994, in seven weeks' time?

'No!' he bellowed, brushing aside the efforts of an aide to avoid an angry exchange. 'No, we will not.' The reason for Russia's refusal, he added, was that 'gross violations of human rights' were being perpetrated by the Estonian authorities against the ethnic Russians who had moved to the republic during the Soviet era and who now made up about 35 per cent of its resident population.

Yeltsin seemed to enjoy Clinton's discomfort as he obliterated one of the supposed basic principles governing Western policy towards the former Soviet Union: the notion that Russia must not be allowed to use its garrisons in the smaller republics as an instrument of political pressure.

In the event, Russia did meet the deadline, but only after Yeltsin had summoned Estonia's President Lennart Meri to the Kremlin and sat face to face with him for many hours, hammering out the precise conditions for withdrawal. They were very tough conditions: they included the right of indefinite residence in Estonia for a number of 'retired servicemen' who turned out, on inspection, to be able-bodied men in their thirties and forties whose fighting ability was far from spent. In fact, there was no pressing reason for Russia to keep a single serving soldier in the Baltic republics, at least during this phase of her history when consolidation still took priority over expansion. In the event of some change in geopolitical circumstances in Estonia – some carefully picked quarrel, for example, over the status of the Russian-speaking town of Narva in the north-east of the republic – Moscow could always send back in the paratroopers based in Pskov. This was an ancient Russian fortress town whose residents, partly in disgust at the Baltic states' independence, had voted solidly for Zhirinovsky the previous December.

Yeltsin, however, had not come to Naples to be seen bowing to Western pressure on Estonia or any other issue. On the contrary, his purpose was to establish once and for all the principle that no major international problem, whether it concerned Russia directly or not, could be solved without Moscow's assent. Moreover, that assent should never be taken for granted, because Russia's way of looking at the world was sharply at odds, in an unpredictable way, with everything that passed for conventional wisdom in the West.

The year had started badly for Yeltsin, and for Russia's image in the world. The signals from the Kremlin seemed to confirm the worst apprehensions of those who had seen the December 1993 election result as a body blow to reform, a bitter reversal of the hard-won triumph for 'democracy' in the battles of the autumn.

In late January, Gaidar and other pioneers of economic change were dropped from the cabinet. Foreign advisers left the country in disgust and Prime Minister Chernomyrdin dismayed Russia's Western well-wishers by declaring that 'market romanticism is over' – a remark that was interpreted, quite mistakenly as it later turned out, to indicate that a heavy-handed, Soviet approach to economic management was coming back into vogue.

The apparent abandonment of economic reform came shortly after a visit to Moscow by Clinton, who was under strict instructions from his advisers not to appear condescending. They told him the climate had changed in Russia: eager pro-Westernism was a thing of the past and people would react badly unless he made it plain that he regarded Russia as a great country which could make its own choices.

The high point of Clinton's effort to advise and communicate, without being patronising, came in a carefully pitched address to a group of young Russians which was broadcast to the whole country from the Ostankino studios. It was an attempt to convey, in trenchant but palatable form, the message of the successfully capitalist West to newly capitalist Russia. It was remarkable for what it got right, but also for what it got wrong.

Clinton began, somewhat unfortunately, by describing Ostankino, the killing field of a few months earlier, as a 'symbol of free expression, and of the brave sacrifices the Russian people have been making to build a great and free future . . .' He then proceeded to deliver a lecture on a matter that interested all Russians, including the razor-sharp, multilingual youths who sat before him, very much indeed: not material comfort for its own sake, or political and ethical values for their own sake, but greatness. 'Your nation is being called on to redefine its greatness in terms that are appropriate to the present day and the future', he told them. The information revolution had made it harder for any country to maintain state control over the economy and society: capitalist democracy was the only way.

> The greatness of nations in the twenty-first century will be defined not by whether they can dictate to millions and millions of people within and beyond their borders, but instead, by whether they can provide their citizens, without regard to race or gender, the opportunity to live up to the fullest of their ability . . .

In other words, power only came with prosperity, and 'the surest way to prosperity is the ability of people to produce and sell high-quality goods and services, both within and beyond their boundaries . . .'

Instead of fantasising about the reconquest of the Baltic states or even Alaska – this was a dig at Zhirinovsky – young Russians should seize the chance to show that 'a great power can promote patriotism without expansionism, national pride without national prejudice . . .'

The President's minders had advised him, accurately enough, of some of the reactions this lecture might arouse, and he did his best to pre-empt them.

'If I were in your place sitting listening to this speech, I might ask myself – why is this guy saying this? What is in his mind? Why is he really eager to work with us?' The answer, he suggested artfully, was that his own struggle with the 'hard choices' that lay before America gave him a certain sympathy with Russia's predicament.

Somewhat more clumsily, Clinton went on to suggest that Russian claims of American interference were faintly ridiculous:

> I am amused when I come here in the spirit of genuine partnership and respect and some people say well, the United States is trying to dictate our course. Nothing can be further from the truth. Believe me, friends, it's all we can do to deal with our own problems and we don't have time to dictate your course. But the course you take will affect us, so we want you to make the decisions that are best for you.

The last sentence was, of course, a screaming *non sequitur*; it would have been more honest, and perhaps even more popular, to say 'we want you to make the decisions that are best for us . . .'

Nevertheless in other respects the speech was well-judged, and if it had been made two years earlier, when many Russians were dazed by the fall of the Soviet Union and somewhat awe-struck by Western power, it might have had a profound effect.

As it was, the speech was much too late: the mere fact that Clinton gave it at all was an act of condescension, and if anything sounded ridiculous, it was his claim not to be interfering. The cleverest Russians, in particular the young, had long since concluded for themselves that the currency of greatness needed redefining (at least temporarily), away from military and territorial aggrandisement, in favour of economic prowess. As Clinton correctly observed, this was a painful and psychologically disorienting process for many people. However, by making himself the patron of that process, and presuming to fine-tune it, the President was merely setting himself up as a convenient scapegoat on which Russian politicians could heap all the blame for the hardship which reform was bound to bring.

Another mistake was to undermine his own credibility by advancing the patently dishonest proposition that there was no conflict of interest between an economically successful Russia and an economically successful America. Two years of capitalism had already demonstrated that the only manufactures in which Russia might have a competitive advantage – weapons, aircraft, rocket technology and nuclear technology – were the very ones in which American interests, both strategic and commercial, were deeply entrenched. President Clinton would have commanded greater respect by saying something like 'We have our interests, you have yours . . . I will not presume to tell you how you should pursue your interests, but I will make our own as clear as possible in the hope of finding an acceptable compromise'.

Clinton did one very important piece of business when he was in Moscow. With Presidents Yeltsin and Leonid Kravchuk of Ukraine, he stitched together an intricate deal under which Ukraine was induced to give up any lingering ambition to become a nuclear power in its own right. The US, in effect, agreed to bankroll the transfer of all the nuclear warheads remaining in Ukraine to Russia, where they would be dismantled and Washington would buy up the nuclear fuel.

Impressive as this agreement was, it brought to a close a period in which the US had some hope of orchestrating major developments in the former Soviet Union. For the first two years of Russia's post-Soviet existence, when the country was struggling back on to its feet, the attention it received from the US – and Washington's willingness to flatter Moscow by preserving some of the fanfare of the old superpower relationship – had been an important source of strength for Yeltsin. Russia was able to turn to its own advantage the fact that the US desperately needed an interlocutor, someone to talk to in the vast area of the globe which had been occupied by the former Soviet Union. But the stronger Russia became in its own right, the less need it had for an American crutch, and the more potential there was for a clash of interests.

Ironically, all the developments in Russia which the West had applauded most loudly – from the creation of a nationwide stock market to Yeltsin's victory over his adversaries in October 1993 – had the effect of consolidating the Russian state and enhancing its ability to resist Western pressure. By the time Yeltsin arrived in Naples, Russia's gross domestic product, expressed in dollar terms, had increased nearly threefold since mid-1992. This statistic was not an accurate picture of Russia's wildly uneven economic performance, any more than other gloomier government figures suggesting a slump in output of up to 30 per cent were accurate. However, it did mean that a given amount of dollars, whether offered by a tourist to a Muscovite taxi driver or lent to the Siberian oil industry by the World Bank, went much less far in Russia, and secured much less leverage, than it had done a few years earlier.

Western governments seemed slow to absorb this point. In early 1994, the US, and to a lesser extent other Western countries, were still addressing Russia as though it were a delinquent, unteachable child, whose main offence lay in not looking after itself properly, or in failing to prepare itself sufficiently for the moment when it was fit to mingle freely in 'civilised', adult company. In their early days, the leaders of independent Russia had played up to this myth, presenting their country as a keen, aspiring pupil in the school of capitalism and liberal democracy.

By 1994, however, this image of Russia was badly out of

date. The doltish figures who had managed the economy during the final years of the Soviet regime were steadily being winnowed out and replaced by a far more competent élite who had absorbed the techniques of capitalism – first in theory, then in practice – with extraordinary speed. The advent of a new class of highly sophisticated bankers and corporate take-over artists meant that it did not matter nearly as much as before if some of the main government posts were held by old lags or political has-beens: there was a limit to the amount of damage they could do.

As some Russians could see, it was no bad thing if the Americans persisted in treating them as though they were backward; there is often some advantage to be gained from dealing with people who persistently and insultingly underestimate one's intelligence. But this is not the sort of relationship that makes for mutual respect or warmth, and matters degenerated further when it became clear that a Russia which *did* look after its own interests, with severity and sophistication, was even more unwelcome to the Americans than one which disappointed its teachers by failing to do so.

Very shortly after Clinton completed his January 1994 visit to Moscow, having extracted a promise that reform would continue, a new administration took shape which astonished most Russia-watchers by its apparent conservatism. 'The absence from the cabinet of those known best in the West as proponents of reform is a source of real concern', said the State Department, in a tone that most Russians – whatever they thought about reform – found insufferable.

Shortly after that, in a demonstration of the fact that economic success was no longer dependent on personalities, the underlying health of the economy began to improve, and Russian-American relations started to worsen on a whole series of fronts. Contrary to what the US administration believed, Russian competence was a far greater challenge to American interests than Russian incompetence.

The upturn in the health of the economy was made possible, in large measure, by the outcome of the October 1993 battles and the endorsement of Yeltsin's constitution – both of which helped to reduce the long-term influence of the industrial lobbies which had dominated the old Parliament.

In time-honoured fashion, the winners of the October 1993 stand-off quarrelled vigorously over the spoils. These victors were a diverse bunch: Yeltsin's presidential apparatus; Golushko's political police; Yerin's regular police; Prime Minister Chernomyrdin's energy lobby; the burgeoning wealth represented by the successor to Gavriil Popov, Mayor Yuri Luzhkov, and the municipality of Moscow; and the emerging class of bankers who had become the main supporters of Gaidar and the reformers. The fact that Russia's dinosaur industries did not figure so heavily in the new cast of competing élites helped to clear the way for a rapid and badly needed run-down of what Chernomyrdin, with admirable candour, learned to describe as 'unnecessary industrial production'. Every time an old factory was closed, it helped to free resources and manpower for the sectors which were starting to boom: finance, construction, and the provision of goods and services for a population whose real income had risen by 10 per cent in the course of 1993.

There was one powerful lobby which still acted as a gratuitous drain on the country's resources: the collective farmers, who gobbled up fuel and credits, and tried to silence anyone who threatened their interests by daring to work the land efficiently. Yet if a choice had to be made, it was less expensive to buy off the 'red landlords' of the Russian countryside than to keep unwanted factories going. As one Russian reformer put it, the 'town' – the urban economy – could afford to feed the countryside.

As for the new Parliament, whose powers were strictly limited by the constitution, it horrified the world with one blazing act of defiance and then relapsed into relative quiescence and obscurity. That gesture of defiance was an amnesty for Rutskoy, Hasbulatov and the other leaders of the October 1993 rebellion. Somewhat surprisingly, one of the chief architects of this pardon was Zhirinovsky, who had virtually taken Yeltsin's side during the October events and who often remarked, quite accurately, that Rutskoy was likely to be his main rival for the hardline vote in the 1996 presidential elections. It was Zhirinovsky who stood outside Lefortovo, the old KGB prison, on the freezing day when the coup leaders stumbled out into the street. 'We've done it', he crowed, more in self-congratulation than in welcome.

Yet most of the gang seemed chastened by their defeat and incarceration. A pale Rutskoy made a gingerly return to opposition politics, but he kept repeating, like a mantra, his new-found conviction that passions must not be inflamed, and 'clashes and bloodshed' must be avoided at all costs. Hasbulatov, sensing that he had lost his one chance of supreme power in Russia, plunged into the murky politics of his native Chechnya. Far from threatening Yeltsin, the amnesty, to a certain extent, drove home the finality of his victory; the freed rebels were visibly in no condition to pose any immediate challenge to his authority. It was arguable that they posed less of a problem to the regime – and indeed to Zhirinovsky – as free but chastened men, than they would have done if they had remained in jail, covered with the glory of martyrdom.

There is no reason to think that Yeltsin himself was anything but furious about the amnesty. It did, however, provide him with the opportunity to appoint a new prosecutor-general: the impeccably loyal Alexei Ilyushenko, who had helped to formulate the presidential case, and keep the spotlight away from Yeltsin's own associates, during the scandals of the previous year. If the amnesty itself was a spectacular demonstration of the separation of executive, legislative and judicial powers, its immediate effect was to pave the way for Yeltsin to suppress the separation of powers by placing the judiciary under his thumb. Dmitry Yakubovsky, the protagonist of the 1993 witch-hunt, saw the appointment of a tame prosecutor-general as a thoroughly welcome development. 'At least in Brezhnev's time, the chief prosecutor did what he was told', he commented with approval.

Another side-effect of the amnesty was the naming of a new head of the security police, Sergei Stepashin. He was a close ally of Yeltsin's chief bodyguard, Aleksandr Korzhakov. The new appointment appeared to be part of a gradual transfer of real power away from the Lubyanka – the old KGB headquarters – to those KGB officers, like Korzhakov, who worked at the Kremlin under the direct authority of the President.

On 21 December, Yeltsin had lashed out at the 'unreformable' state security system and had given it yet another name: instead of the security ministry, the main successor to the KGB would henceforth be known as the federal counter-intelligence service. The promise of instant, radical change was belied by the fact that the security minister, the dissident-hunter Nikolai Golushko, initially remained in charge. However, the fact that the Lubyanka no longer ranked as a fully-fledged ministry was a step towards curbing its independence; and the replacement of Golushko by Stepashin was another.

Revealingly, one of Yeltsin's complaints against the 'unreformable' empire was its failure to provide him with proper advice during the election campaign – to which Golushko indignantly replied that his agency had predicted the result, within a single percentage point. Both sides of this argument may have been right. Perhaps Golushko's fault lay not so much in failing to call the election result as in failing to point out to Yeltsin the exact consequences of his silence during the final days of the campaign, and the loss of international face which Zhirinovsky's impending triumph could mean. It is even possible that Yeltsin was telling Golushko: we expected Zhirinovsky to do well, but not that well.

In any case, it is important to stress that when Yeltsin described the Lubyanka as 'unreformable' he was not making a liberal critique of its methods, but merely complaining that its loyalty to him – during the October stand-off and the months that followed – was conditional rather than total. He now set about correcting this by gathering as much as possible of the security empire under his own personal authority.

The weakness of Parliament, and the presidency's increasingly tight grip on the levers of real power, was reflected in Russia's sure-footed foreign policy. Parliament could act as a useful bogey-man, by making anti-Western noises and reminding the world that Yeltsin was under domestic pressure. But the constitution made absolutely clear that the Russian President, like that of France, was the main architect of external policy. Although the degree of interest in day-to-day policy displayed by the President himself was a mystery, and appeared to fluctuate considerably, the presidential machine – where the chief foreign policy specialist was an experienced diplomat called Dmitry Ryurikov – grew ever more skilled in the art of formulating a stance that reflected Russia's interests.

Yeltsin's appearance in Naples was the high point in a series of spectacular diplomatic successes for Russia. In the space of five weeks, Moscow managed to put a foot in the door of three of the smartest Western clubs: first Nato, then the European Union, and now the Group of Seven.

With razor-sharp instinct for the vulnerabilities of those around them, Moscow's diplomats had sensed, and turned to their own advantage, the eagerness of their Western counterparts to incorporate Russia into some neatly drawn 'architecture' in which every nation would have its proper place. Western leaders had staked their own prestige on their ability to 'handle' Russia, as though the country were a temperamental but promising adolescent who might be induced to behave if treated with enough tact and patience. It would have been extraordinary if Russia had not exploited this image for all it was worth.

At the beginning of 1994, Western leaders had formally invited all their ex-communist counterparts to participate in a low-key military co-operation programme called Partnership for Peace. It was a point of principle that all countries, from Uzbekistan to Slovenia, must enter this club on the same terms. Once they were inside the door, there could be separate negotiations with each country over how far its co-operation with the Western allies might go; but the entry form signed by each aspirant would be identical.

General Grachev, the defence minister and architect of Russia's neo-imperial policies in Georgia and Tajikistan, created a flurry of excitement when he turned up at Nato headquarters in May 1994 to announce his country's attitude to the PFP. There were audible sighs of relief from his Western counterparts when the hulking paratrooper declared, within minutes of his arrival in Brussels, that Russia was second to none in its eagerness to join the Partnership. Furthermore, he stated, it would not dream of doing anything so rude as setting any preconditions or demanding privileged entry terms. Any such behaviour would be 'inappropriate and liable to misunderstanding' said the general. He was the very soul of *bonhomie* as he received a string of Western defence ministers, most of them effete civilians with none of his combat experience, in a room at Nato headquarters which had been set aside for the Russian delegation's use. So much at ease did he appear that nobody would have been surprised if he had blurted out the standard Russian welcome: *Priezhaite po chashe* – 'come here more often'.

The following day, this thick haze of euphoria was put to formidable use. In a formal speech to his Western counterparts, the general blithely demanded a virtual redrawing of the Eurasian map. In future, he said, Nato must be subordinated to a new hierarchy of defence organisations, co-managed by Russia and the Western powers. Russia, he implied, would endorse Nato's role as principal keeper of the peace in one slice of the world – whose precise contours had yet to be negotiated – so long as the West recognised the Commonwealth of Independent States as a military, as well as political, bloc where Russian influence was paramount. Eurasia, in other words, would be divided into spheres of influence, just as a certain eccentric politician called Zhirinovsky had so recently suggested.

Grachev did not, of course, mention Zhirinovsky's name, but to drive home his point in another way, he slapped down an eight-page list of 'parameters' for the future relationship between Russia and the Western alliance. On inspection, these turned out to be an artful mixture of reasonable ideas about co-operation and wild proposals for subordinating Nato to some larger structure.

The enormity of what General Grachev was proposing did not immediately sink in; only a few days later did a few alarm bells tinkle softly in the foreign ministries of Europe. Nato did not, of course, have any intention of subjecting itself to some new Russian-designed hierarchy; but alliance bureaucrats did meekly sit down to study, and prepare detailed responses to, the general's 'parameters'. This was in contravention of their earlier promise, to themselves and the smaller nations of central Europe, that Russia would be required to join the PFP first and negotiate over details later, as every other country had done. When Andrei Kozyrev, the foreign minister, came to Brussels three weeks later to sign up formally to the Partnership, it was on terms far more favourable than any other ex-communist country had extracted. The standard-issue entry form was sweetened by a promise of consultation rights which took proper account of Russia's status as a major military power.

A couple of days later, there was another set-piece act of Russian-Western reconciliation when Yeltsin travelled to the Greek island of Corfu to sign a partnership agreement with the European Union. Western Europe's leaders briefly forgot their own petty squabbles as they contemplated the moody, impulsive visitor who sat with them late into the balmy night, proposing one toast after another and disturbing the Greek waiters by leaving his food untouched. Like his country, the visitor was exotic, unpredictable, unrefined, but impossible to ignore.

Like Nato, the EU had learned how skilful Russia could be at turning the terms of any transaction to its own advantage – even those transactions where it was ostensibly cast in the role of supplicant. Sir Leon Brittan, the British politician turned European Commissioner, had made the dreadful mistake, in an early round of talks at the Kremlin, of citing as a precedent the sort of arrangements which Brussels had made with certain small countries in Central America. 'Russia', Yeltsin rasped back, 'is not Guatemala.'

Nor was it Switzerland or Norway or Canada either, as the Eurocrats discovered in the course of many months' bargaining; it behaved like no other country they had ever dealt with. Whenever they made a concession, in the hope of eliciting some good will, Russia grabbed it and gave nothing back. In the run-up to the Russian elections of December 1993, they were instructed by their boss, Jacques Delors, to 'help Yeltsin' by giving ground. Far from showing gratitude, the President responded by abruptly banning from the Russian market the handful of West European banks which had licences to operate in Moscow. This was a concession to the fast-growing lobby of Russian banks, whose help – and contribution to the campaign funds – was far more important to the Yeltsin entourage than anything Delors could possibly offer. Like many other organisations, from Amnesty International to the International Finance Corporation, the European Union discovered that its ability to influence post-communist Russia was far less than anybody had supposed.

Quicker than most Western governments were able to comprehend, the Russian genie had transformed its international persona from that of fragile wraith, in urgent need of rescue from extinction, to that of strong-willed player on the world stage, at once indispensable and unpredictable. Not for the first time in history, the Kremlin's new masters were demonstrating that there is almost no middle ground between a dangerously weak Russia – where the government's writ hardly extends to the suburbs of Moscow – and a formidably strong one.

Once the Kremlin had remastered the technique of manipulating events as far away as Vladivostok, then it was – almost by definition – also powerful enough to make its presence felt in places far beyond Russia's border – in the Balkans, the Middle East and south Asia. Control of Russia alone was such a feat of statecraft that its effects were unlikely to stop at the legal border of Russia, or even of the former Soviet Union.

By mid-1994, the Kremlin's ability to regulate events in the Russian Far East was still not as great as it wanted; but it was gradually increasing, and there was no more talk of

Siberia declaring economic or even political independence, as there had been two years earlier.

As for the rise in Russian influence beyond the former Soviet Union, that was brought home in February 1994 when Moscow made a spectacular intervention in Bosnia's tragic war. A mortar attack on the market-place in Sarajevo, which killed over sixty people, prompted the Western powers to declare an 'exclusion zone' round the city from which all heavy weapons must be removed on pain of bombing raids by Nato. This was a threat which the Western nations had no desire to act on: it would lead to an escalating, atavistic war between Nato and the Serbs, in which the lives of thousands of Western peace-keepers would be at risk. In the very nick of time, Russia announced that it was ready to deploy several hundred paratroopers – Grachev's boys – in the Serb-held suburbs of Sarajevo. Instead of surrendering or removing their heavy weapons, the Serbs could place them under the surveillance of UN peace-keepers who happened to be Russian. It was an offer the West could not refuse, and it instantly gave Russia an influence in the affairs of the former Yugoslavia which it had not enjoyed for nearly half a century.

In economic diplomacy, Russia was acquiring a similar degree of skill. Like the treasurers of Tsarist Russia, the country's new rulers were refining the art of using their own indebtedness as a source of strength.

By the time Yeltsin arrived in Naples, Russia's governors felt they were in the happy position of having no burning need to attract capital (whether public or private) from any other country. Therefore they were relatively immune to any external pressure to repay Russia's old debts any faster than was convenient.

Thanks to the reckless profligacy of the Soviet regime in its final days, the Russian Federation was a massively indebted state, with external obligations of about $83 billion at the end of 1993, and repayments of about $28 billion due to be made in 1994. Yet Russian assets abroad probably amounted to at least $50 billion, thanks to the steady outflow into Swiss bank accounts or into property of the money that was being earned through commodity exports, the monetisation of the Communist Party and KGB assets, and crime.

The marvellous thing about this rising pool of Russian-controlled capital was its location, so to speak at exactly the right distance from the national exchequer. Because it was private capital, kept in secret foreign accounts in ostensible defiance of the authorities, the Russian administration could plausibly plead poverty to its overseas creditors, both governmental and commercial. The balance of payments had improved considerably in 1993, but official foreign exchange reserves still looked far too low to contemplate paying out $28 billion in a single year.

The Russian government could argue quite convincingly that there was only one way that it could repay its overseas debts rapidly: by allowing the public deficit to expand again. The West, having delivered so many patronising lectures on the virtues of monetary restraint, would scarcely want that.

The Western banks (mostly German) which were owed $26 billion of ex-Soviet debt complained bitterly that Russia had far more capital 'available' than it was claiming. Available in due course for investment, but not available, or so the authorities could claim, for anything so mundane as repaying old debts.

Just as the counsellors of Nicholas II had encouraged the bankers of Paris, London and Berlin to compete for Russia's custom, the new regime had demonstrated that for a country whose vast economic potential is beyond question, heavy indebtedness does not imply weakness: with skilful manipulation, it can be turned into an effective bargaining chip.

Western governments have always tried hard to present a united front to debtor nations, so as to thwart attempts to play one lender off against the other. But in Naples, where senior members of the Yeltsin entourage had separate meetings on debt with officials from Britain and Italy, the Western nations began to suspect one another of making a 'separate peace' with Russia. The fact that Russia was no longer communist took away any ideological incentive for Westerners to band together against Moscow and it might, in due course, become irresistibly tempting to compete with one another for Russian favours.

The accumulation of Russian-controlled wealth in offshore accounts was widely assumed both by foreign economists and the nationalist Russian opposition to be a sign of economic disaster. Simple souls like Aleksandr Rutskoy suggested that capital flight could be staunched by threatening Russian enterprises – or even their bankers – with dire punishments unless they brought their money home.

Yet there was no reason to be so alarmist: the bank accounts might be Swiss, but the money was unmistakably Russian. Also Russians could judge better than anyone when the moment was right to repatriate their capital. The idea of 'national' or even 'patriotic' capital was also much more acceptable to the Russian public – easier to 'sell' politically – than foreign investment. The spectacle of foreigners actually owning a significant segment of the Russian economy, as opposed to imparting know-how for a few years and then leaving, touched something deep in the national psyche, even among those who conceded that foreign employers might be more humane and efficient than domestic ones.

Moreover, Russian capitalists were better placed to legitimise themselves in the eyes of the public than foreign ones were. The 'legitimation' of private wealth – persuading the poor to accept as fair the fact that some of their compatriots are fabulously rich – will always be a harder problem in Russia than it is in the West, where respect for property and other bourgeois values have much deeper roots.

Russia's new capitalists faced the twin challenge of reconciling national opinion to the general principle of private property, and to the fact that they in particular were worthy beneficiaries of that principle, worthy stewards of Russia's fast-expanding wealth. The first task may never fully be accomplished; there are too many Russians who will always, in their heart of hearts, regard property as theft.

When it came to shoring up the reputation of specific individuals or enterprises, a good many stratagems were available to Russian capitalists which foreigners would have found hard to match. Russian capitalists could buy newspapers, television stations, journalists and politicians. If, in the early stages of wealth creation, they had relied on political friends to grant them export licences or contracts for public works, the boot was now on the other foot; the politicians were increasingly reliant on the wealth of their benefactors.

Visible on the horizon was the intriguing possibility that Russia, the most anti-bourgeois of the world's great nations, would fashion its own version of the bourgeois state.

In every sort of economy, with the exception of full-blown communism, rich individuals use their wealth to buy particular political favours for themselves. The distinguishing mark of Western political systems is the way in which the property-owning class use their collective influence to establish certain general principles about how society should be run, what sort of laws should be enforced and how they should be enforced.

They do so despite the fact that efficiency, consistency and transparency in politics and the judiciary may work to their individual disadvantage: they may lose court cases and bureaucratic battles, or fail to secure the elections of their favoured politicians. But for the property-owning class as a whole, this risk of individual loss is outweighed by the broader benefits of a well-ordered bourgeois society – stability, security and predictability.

For the new capitalist Russia, this state of affairs was some way off. Powerful economic players still preferred to settle their disputes by means of contract killers as opposed to taking their chances in court, and there was none of the consensus on property rights which underpins capitalist democracy. However, an increasing number of bankers, industrialists, and even criminals, understood the desirability of a more ordered society, with clear 'rules of the game' and procedures for enforcement. The construction of a law-based, or comparatively law-based, Russian state would not come about through Clinton's lectures on the merits of democracy. On the other hand a coalition of powerful Russian interests might yet succeed – for reasons which had nothing to do with sentiment, ethics or ideology – where Western hectoring had failed.

In its outward manifestations, its smart new suburban homes, sharp-suited youths and luxury limousines, Russia was, by mid-1994, evolving into a sort of a caricature of a capitalist state; brash and brutal but seething with creative energy. Russian capitalism promised to be many things that Russian socialism had been: a grotesque, gigantist distortion of an imported ideal, which proved to be highly effective in mobilising the country's resources.

While many of the Russian rich had made their first fortune by picking clean the bones of the communist state, their new interest now lay in the creation of a strong and well-ordered political system of the kind which made business planning possible. For the first time since Russian reforms began, industrialists, financiers, energy kings and master criminals, all with a stake in a relatively sound currency, were becoming more powerful than those economic players who leeched off a collapsing economic system.

Russians no longer needed Clinton or any other Westerner to provide them with instruction in the virtues of capitalism. The economic power which capitalism could generate was by now self-evident, and the techniques of the system could be mastered easily enough; after all, they were no more difficult than the rules of chess or the design of an atomic weapon. If Clinton had any function at all, it was to serve Russia in the role of adversary: the epitome of a West whose arrogance and hypocrisy made it necessary to embark once more on the brutal yet inspiring enterprise of becoming great. This greatness would be achieved in Russia's own stealthy, unpredictable way – the way in which Yeltsin had put his stamp on the gathering in Naples, Russian individuals had accumulated great sums of private wealth, and Russian soldiers had appeared in the suburbs of Sarajevo.

15
STALIN'S GHOST

ON 9 MAY 1995, millions of elderly Russians – the generation who would always, in their heart of hearts, be Stalin's children – were told by their masters to put aside the daily grind of their existence and rejoice, as they had rejoiced half a century earlier, over the miraculous survival of their country's greatness, in defiance of all the odds.

The message came over their television screens – screens which had insulted them, for most of the last few years, with a diet of low-grade American thrillers and advertisements for things they could never afford.

What the nation saw, on that warm May evening, was an inspiring, superbly executed Victory Day celebration: the grandest ritual display of tanks, Scud missiles and soldiers in smart, braided uniforms since the break-up of the Soviet Union; and the biggest fly-past of fighter aircraft that anybody could remember. The old practice of sending up special planes to disperse the clouds was revived, ensuring a day of balmy sunshine. It was a perfect holiday for the masses.

The passing of half a century since Nazi Germany's defeat was marked in Moscow by two separate parades. In the first, veterans with all their medals on display marched through Red Square, as Bill Clinton, John Major and about fifty other leaders looked on. The vast, cobblestoned expanse was decked out with Soviet posters, Soviet slogans and Soviet bunting. Taking pride of place was a famous, kitsch illustration of a Red Army soldier warmly greeting an American

GI. Bunched together on a separate podium, below the foreign visitors, were Georgia's Eduard Shevardnadze, President Heydar Aliyev of Azerbaijan and all the other leaders of the ex-Soviet republics. They seemed to have been cast in the role of wayward cousins who had strayed from the fold but remembered, on this important family occasion, where they ultimately belonged. This too was a comforting message.

Then a few hours later came the full-blown military parade, which took place on the broad avenue running west of Moscow, named after General Kutuzov, where a victory monument had just been completed.

Pavel Grachev, the defence minister, stood bolt upright in a long, open limousine which transported him, in stately fashion, past row after row of superbly attired soldiers. Every time the vehicle stopped, he would bellow out a message of congratulation and back from the soldiers would come a carefully rehearsed cry of 'Hurrah!' which resounded like cannon fire in a mountain pass.

Watching all this, many a Muscovite pensioner must have wondered whether all the tumult and disruption of the last few years – the collapse of the Union, the end of communism and the apparent triumph of the Western enemy – had not been just a bad dream, which was now over. Everything seemed to be slipping back into its proper place, down to the fact that Stalin was gradually regaining his position in the national pantheon. A few days earlier, Prime Minister Chernomyrdin had thrilled an audience of veterans by telling them that it would be wrong to underestimate Stalin's personal contribution to the Allied victory.

This was an astonishing break with the official discourse of the last seven or eight years, which looked on Stalin's rule as an almost unmitigated tragedy from whose physical and psychological effects the nation was only now recovering. Even Stalin's war record had been forcefully debunked by General Dmitry Volkogonov, the influential military historian and adviser to Yeltsin, who argued that the Soviet victory was achieved as much in spite of the tyrant, and his ruinous purges of the Red Army, as because of him.

Yet Chernomyrdin's statement was an accurate expression of the new *Zeitgeist*. There had been an enormous change in the national mood since the late 1980s when Gorbachev and his liberal advisers threw off their ideological shackles and denounced Stalin in almost unequivocal terms.

At that time, the communist regime – and with it the whole Soviet legacy – was disintegrating rapidly: there was a general disillusionment with crudely authoritarian, militarist ways of thinking, fuelled by the fact that the liberal societies of the West were so obviously succeeding in ways that the over-militarised Soviet Union had failed. For many young people, cynicism about the tarnished Soviet vision of greatness had led to a more general scepticism about the very notion of 'greatness' as an ideal.

By 1995, contempt for worn-out and tired versions of authoritarianism had given way to fascination with the possibility of new and more effective ones. For the young at least, Moscow was turning into a slick boom town where the atmosphere was crackling with excitement. Everyone sensed that a huge expansion in the country's economy, and a corresponding rise in Russia's standing in the world, was getting under way. It seemed unlikely that democracy would survive the process, but that did not seem to matter much: what were deputies, anyway, except a collection of easily bought hacks and time-servers? The country's new oil barons argued playfully over whether it would be ten years or fifteen before a Russian firm made a bid for Exxon. An advertising industry with annual turnover running into hundreds of millions of dollars appeared out of nowhere in the space of a year. In April 1993, a 32-year-old called Vladimir Potanin had founded a bank; it was now doing $400 million worth of foreign exchange transactions a day, and its founder was quietly confident of joining the ranks of the top 100 banks in the world. Only five years earlier, Russian society had been so stagnant that the fondest dream of any intelligent youth was to emigrate; now anybody who had the slightest connection with Russia was flocking to Moscow to cash in on the incipient bonanza. When young Russians went abroad, they were no longer jealous; they were vaguely contemptuous of the slow pace and the conventional way of thinking of those around them.

Their grandparents, the children of Stalin, did not care at all for the preoccupations of the new generation. They found the new capitalist creed as alien and repulsive as their own predecessors had found communism. But the magnificent Victory Day parade was a way of telling them, in language they understood, that Russia was once again entering a period of exhilarating expansion – the sort of expansion that would bring pain for some, untold power and privilege for others and a dramatic recovery in the country's status.

The Western visitors did not attend the second parade; it was their way of expressing a mild, wrist-slapping sort of protest against the war Russia was still waging against rebel forces in the north Caucasian enclave of Chechnya. Nobody in Moscow cared much about this Western gesture; the more important point was that Russia had by now demonstrated its ability to use as much force as it judged expedient – at least within its own territory – without forfeiting the main elements of its relationship with the rest of the world.

Even by the standards of the other conflicts taking place in the ex-communist world, the war which began in Chechnya on 11 December 1994 was unspeakably grim and brutal. Thousands of civilians were killed by waves of apparently indiscriminate aerial bombardment. Yeltsin, mysteriously laid low by a 'nose operation' on the day the conflict began, was goaded by a horrified world into issuing several public orders for the bombing to stop; but it went on unabated, reducing the city of Grozny to a fetid wasteland.

The forces which Russia hurled into the conflict were a hotch-potch of poorly co-ordinated units, who fought several furious battles with one another before realising that they were supposed to be on the same side. There were scrawny, terrified conscripts who had no idea where they were; politically reliable 'parade regiments' from the Moscow area, who were better at suppressing half-baked coups than fighting wars; and interior ministry troops who took their orders from the doggedly loyal Viktor Yerin.

In the early days of the conflict, the élite airborne units – from which General Grachev originated – were only present in small numbers; the defence minister seemed to have become so unpopular among his old comrades that they were disinclined to help him out of the mess he had created.

There are still unanswered questions about why the conflict was launched when it was, but there is no mystery about the general reason why the self-proclaimed independence of Chechnya was becoming an intolerable threat to certain powerful interests, both public and private, in Russia.

Over the past two years, the sinews of the Russian state, and its ability to regulate economic life, had gradually strengthened. Under one name or another, the former KGB had re-established control of the borders and relearned the art of regulating strategic exports, using a variety of methods which appeared to include a close and mutually beneficial relationship with the various economic players, both criminal and semi-legitimate, who engaged in that trade. In most parts of the Russian Federation, the interests of the state and the criminal world were converging in a way that was not unsatisfactory to either side, even though the balance of power was gradually shifting in the state's favour. For the first two years of Russian independence, the state had been so enfeebled that protection racketeers took over many of its roles, from the levying of 'taxes' to the settlement of disputes. But little by little, those functions were being reconcentrated in the hands of the government – in part, perhaps, because the racketeers were turning their attention to other types of business and their interests were now better served by a strong government than a weak and corrupt one.

As the interests of the Russian state and the Russian Mafia came closer to fusing, the challenge posed by the breakaway Chechen statelet – the only part of the Russian Federation where Moscow's writ did not run at all – became more acute. Before it was bombed to oblivion, Grozny airport was the one place within Russia's boundaries through which almost anything – money, guns and currency – could be exported.

Russians who defend their country's record in Chechnya will often denounce the breakaway enclave as a 'criminal state' and portray the enclave as the first government in history to have been founded and run by organised crime. Leaving aside the claim to exclusivity, which would no doubt be challenged by experts on Latin America, there is some force in this argument. However, it is important to point out that the whole of newly independent Russia was also, in many ways, a 'criminal state' where government and organised crime were so closely intertwined that the idea of the former making a concerted, all-out attack on the latter was not simply improbable; it was almost nonsensical. Nevertheless the bosses of Chechnya were uniquely immune to the efforts of the rising Russian state to co-opt them. Their unforgivable sin, in Moscow's eyes, was not that of being criminals, but of being non-Russian criminals.

The distinction which the Russian authorities drew between 'our' criminals and the 'alien' Chechens, whose close-knit social fabric and code of honour made them virtually immune to infiltration, was well illustrated by the slanted manner in which Russian journalists were briefed, from 1991 onwards, by their police sources on the turf wars that were continuously raging in Moscow between Mafia clans of various ethnic origins. The police encouraged the idea that ethnic Russian clans were steadily gaining ground, and it was plain that this was intended to be a self-fulfilling prophecy. Where the police thought they could tilt the balance in the Russian clans' favour – by releasing certain godfathers from prison, for example – they did so. The old Soviet slogan of '*nashe luche*' or 'ours is better' found a curious application in official attitudes to crime.

For all the masters of the new Russia, police chiefs, politicians and tycoons, there was an intolerable asymmetry in their relations with Dudayev, President of the self-proclaimed Chechen state. The location of an important refinery in Grozny ensured that Dudayev's state had physical control of millions of tons of oil: enough to buy the co-operation, in this or that illicit scheme, of corrupt functionaries all over Russia. So Dudayev was capable of buying his way into the Russian state, but the Russian state had no corresponding leverage over Dudayev.

The Chechen state's modest oil wealth had also helped its bosses to consolidate their *de facto* independence by purchasing arms on the Russian black market, particularly in the immediate aftermath of the Soviet collapse when a large section of the nation's arsenal was virtually privatised. In 1992, the ex-Soviet forces in Chechnya became the only garrison inside Russia that was forced to close, at least temporarily, due to a combination of circumstances that was all too familiar in the republics: hostility from the local population, a cut-off of funds from Moscow, and a manpower shortage which made it impossible to keep weapons under guard. In this situation, Russian commanders had little choice but to sell their weapons to the nationalist politicians and warlords, or else wait until they were stolen.

By the end of 1994, Moscow had gone a long way towards restoring its influence over the outer edges of the Soviet empire – places like Moldova, Georgia and Azerbaijan – by picking fights, either directly or through proxies, and winning them. From Moscow's point of view, a happy result of these wars was the destruction or neutralisation of a good deal of the armour which Russian commanders had been forced to sell or transfer to their enemies, at the low ebb of their country's power. Here again, Chechnya was the exception to the rule: a small but defiant group of nationalists remained in unchallenged control of scores of armoured cars and light aircraft.

The ferocity of the Chechen conflict, and the Chechens' early success, can be explained in part by the fact that it was a sort of civil war, with Soviet weapons on both sides and a very sophisticated understanding, among the Chechen commanders who were Soviet army veterans themselves, of the tactics and communications systems used by their Russian enemies.

Thanks to the formidable bravery of a few dozen Western and Russian newsmen, several of whom paid with their lives, the world saw how the Chechen capital of Grozny, an ugly Soviet oil town of 400,000 people, was steadily reduced to a ghostly landscape of ruined tower blocks, burnt-out tanks, and charred bodies which no one dared to collect.

Even those Russians who wanted Chechnya brought to heel – and that was almost everybody – had to agree that the price being paid was appallingly high. Hard questions were asked about why the campaign had started in such a hasty and ham-fisted manner, and the more anyone investigated, the worse things looked. The Russian authorities had been actively attempting to overthrow Dudayev since June 1994, when a so-called 'Congress of Chechen Peoples' was established at Moscow's behest and announced that it was transferring 'absolute power' to a new body known as the Interim Council. Despite the fact that it had been generously armed by Moscow with tanks, armoured cars and helicopters, the council failed to overthrow Dudayev in a carefully staged 'internal conflict' which began in September. Dudayev triumphantly announced that he had captured senior officers of the FSK – the main successor agency of the KGB – who freely admitted the role of both Yeltsin and the Lubyanka in mounting covert operations.

Russian soldiers from the Kantemirov and Taman Divisions – élite units whose loyalty was crucial to Yeltsin's success in the stand-offs of August 1991 and October 1993 – were among the 'opposition' forces who were taken prisoner by Dudayev. They were paraded before the Russian media and described how the FSK had recruited them. It looked as though one of the main reasons why full-scale war against Dudayev was launched in early December was to cover the traces of the bungled covert operation and prevent further embarrassing revelations.

As for the untidy mixture of troops that was thrown into battle, that appeared to be the result of feverish competition for funding and influence between various parts of the security forces: Grachev's regular armed forces; Yerin's interior ministry; the FSK headed by Sergei Stepashin; and the fast-expanding security empire which was building up within the presidential entourage. The most visible figure within this world was General Aleksandr Korzhakov, Yeltsin's chief bodyguard, but the shadowy General Mikhail Barsukov may have been even more powerful.

The determination of the presidential apparatus to put a stop to embarrassing news from Chechnya had apparently been one of the factors behind an extraordinary incident which had taken place in Moscow a week before the onslaught began. It was an incident which made it all too plain that even in a capitalist Russia, property rights were still subject to the vagaries of political power.

The main offices of the publishing, banking and property empire known as the Most group were surrounded by armed soldiers from the presidential security service, who beat up the business empire's bodyguards and warned its owner, Vladimir Gusinsky, that his days in the sun were over. Gusinsky, a flamboyant former theatre director who had become one of Russia's most powerful men, was forced to go into temporary exile in England, one of several Western countries in which he owned property.

Often cited as an example of a new symbiosis between political and financial power, Gusinsky made no secret of the fact that he had a close relationship with the mayor of Moscow, Yuri Luzhkov. Gusinsky was both a creator and a beneficiary of Moscow's construction boom, and as chief banker to the city hall, he could claim, without much exaggeration, that the wages of every policeman, fireman and street-cleaner in the city passed through his hands. Like all the other bankers who were forging a relationship with one or other of Russia's political masters, Gusinsky could provide his patron with a skill in the handling of money which the antiquated state bureaucracy could not possibly match. Luzhkov could offer his banker friend a degree of political protection, a 'friend at court' without whom no Russian neo-capitalist could function.

However, Luzhkov's protection was not enough, it seemed.

On 10 December, over a sumptuous lunch at the Savoy Hotel in London, Gusinsky held forth on the real reasons why Yeltsin's security men had obliged him to go into exile. They had been enraged, he believed, by the frank reporting of his newspaper *Sevodnya* and his television channel NTV on the bungled efforts of the FSK to overthrow the rebel Chechen regime. Gusinsky was adamant that his own forced departure from Russia was a very bad omen: it would further untie the hands of the clique of Yeltsin advisers who were determined to settle the Chechen question by force. 'The party of war is attacking', he proclaimed. Some of his listeners wondered if he was exaggerating, but the following day, tanks rolled into Grozny and the nightmare began.

The first, appalling weeks of the Chechen war prompted a wave of 'pessimism' among virtually all Western observers of Russia, even those – like Germany's Chancellor Helmut Kohl and Strobe Talbott, the staunchly Russophile adviser to President Clinton – who were most determined to be 'optimistic' about the country's prospects.

Whatever view one took, the words 'optimism' and 'pessimism' continued to be used in almost all Western discourse on Russia. The persistence of this false distinction reflected a woolly way of thinking which underestimated Russia's ability to discern and pursue its own interests, and refused even to consider the possibility that those interests might diverge rather sharply from the rest of the world. Either one was an optimist, believing that Russia would be 'sensible' and look after its own interests, which were assumed for some reason to coincide with those of everybody else; or one was a pessimist and feared that Russia would fail its exams and mismanage its affairs, to the detriment of itself and the rest of the world.

This naïve way of thinking was in part a legacy of Mikhail Gorbachev, whose talk of 'all-human values' had convinced the world that there was no real divergence of interest between Russia and the West. This view had long since been abandoned in Russia, but Westerners still held on to it, through a mixture of complacency and fear. It was conceded, of course, that there might be degrees of optimism or pessimism, but the answer to the Russian riddle was still assumed to lie somewhere along a straight line which ran between those two poles. And in December 1994, Western governments and opinion-makers sharply revised their forecasts in favour of 'pessimism' about the future.

Russia, they feared, might be forfeiting its only chance to become a rational, well-administered state of a Western kind which kept the use of force to a minimum and solved its problems through negotiation wherever possible. Instead of seizing that opportunity, it was squandering the first fruits of its hard-won economic success on a cruel, counter-productive war which would bankrupt the exchequer, weaken democratic institutions and undermine, rather than consolidate, the integrity of the Russian Federation.

The 'pessimists' – who believed that mistaken military adventures and every other sort of misbehaviour were likely to go hand in hand – were confirmed in their gloom by some dramatic developments in economic life which coincided with the start of the Chechen war.

The biggest cause for alarm was the sudden appearance, in November 1994, of an obscure geologist named Vladimir Polevanov as minister for privatisation. Polevanov banned foreign advisers from his ministry and suggested the renationalisation of the oil and aluminium industries. He appeared to be acting in open defiance of his notional boss, the deputy Prime Minister, and hero of economic reform, Anatoly Chubais.

Chubais had so far proved to be an extraordinary survivor. He was the most enduring product of the Leningrad spring. He had learned his free-market economics, along with the political theories of Hayek and Popper, as a lecturer in that city and then put those theories into practice by overseeing the privatisation of no less than 16,000 large and medium-sized enterprises in the space of just eighteen months. Yet the advent of Polevanov, who seemed to have protectors in Yeltsin's immediate entourage, threatened to undo all Chubais' achievements. If Polevanov's view prevailed, billions of dollars in potential foreign capital would be driven away from the Russian market and the chance of strong, sustainable growth for years to come would be missed.

The war in Chechnya, the Polevanov phenomenon and the campaign against Gusinsky all seemed to point to one single, pessimistic conclusion: the vested interests of certain individuals and institutions were prevailing over Russia's broader strategic interest, which lay in an open economy, an open media and an open society. The Chechen conflict, for example, was believed to be in the interest of the former KGB, and this was certainly one of the factors involved. Any development which increased the objective likelihood of terrorism in Moscow, and the risk of attempts on the President's life, could only strengthen the case of both the Lubyanka and the Kremlin security services for extra funding, and for a more secretive style of government.

The holders of this 'pessimistic' view generally qualified their conclusion by pointing to a few reassuring signs. Crumbs of comfort were still to be found in the boldness with which the media, and a large part of the political spectrum, voiced their objections to the conflict. Yegor Gaidar and most of his fellow members of Russia's Choice, the main reformist party, denounced the war unequivocally as a humanitarian outrage and a deadly threat to democracy. Sergei Kovalyov, an astonishingly courageous dissident of the old Sakharov school, drew the world's attention to the agony of Grozny by staying in the city as Russian aircraft unleashed their destructive power; so did Sergei Yushenkov, the champion of reform who had started life as an army lecturer in Marxism. The horrors of the war and the protests of liberal politicians were well reported by the Russian media. All this suggested that the civil society which had struggled into existence in Moscow and Leningrad in the late 1980s, and provided one of the most important motors of political change, was not yet dead. The forces of darkness might have taken the upper hand, but they did not have the field to themselves: there was still a chance that the authors of the war – beginning with General Grachev – would be called to account and forced to pay the political price for their disastrous decisions.

This view was reinforced by the fact that Yeltsin's rating in the opinion polls, already languishing at an all-time low of around 14 per cent in late 1994, had declined by several more percentage points as the full horror of the Chechen fighting came home. Perhaps Yeltsin – who had proved to be such a shrewd judge of public opinion during his rise to power – would eventually respond to the popular mood and bring a dose of reason to his country's policies, both military and economic.

Conventional Western wisdom was correct in saying that the Chechen war was cruel – staggeringly cruel – and in its early stages, very incompetently conducted. But everything else about the Western view, the view which might be described as 'deep but qualified pessimism', was wrong.

Whatever narrow sectional interests were also served, the subjugation of Dudayev did conform to Russia's broadest strategic interests. Indeed, the stakes for Russia were so high that from her point of view, it was well worth putting up with a few mild words of rebuke, and even a few mild measures of retaliation, from the West. Chechnya's importance lay in its position as a sort of nodal point in the network of pipelines which, in Russia's view, ought to be chosen as the main route westwards for the oil that would soon be flowing, in huge quantities, from the Caspian Sea. Russia was already very unhappy about the position which Western oil companies had established in the Caspian by signing contracts with the newly independent governments of Azerbaijan and Kazakhstan. She was unhappier still about the fact that the US government had thrown its weight behind the efforts of the Ankara government to ensure that the key pipelines passed through Turkish, rather than Russian, territory. If Russia had its way, most of the Caspian oil would be exported from the Black Sea port of Novorossisk, after passing through the heart of Chechnya.

These were the long-term stakes in Chechnya; in the short term Russia would recoup the costs of the war by once more taking control of the Grozny refinery, and recapturing the modest quantities of oil which were produced in Chechnya itself. Western countries were right to say the Chechen war was brutal, but they were wrong to call it an economic mistake. Westerners were, to put it mildly, somewhat carried away by their own liberal rhetoric when they suggested that humanity and economic expediency always pointed in the same direction. The new governors of Russia were less sentimental: they had learned with astonishing speed how to swim in what Karl Marx, in a famous description of capitalism, had once described as 'the icy waters of egotistical calculation'. Something they were becoming particularly good at calculating was the precise dosage of liberal capitalism which the country needed and could absorb.

The ice-cold economic logic of the Chechen war was laid out by no less enlightened a figure than Anatoly Chubais, who had always been seen as one of the main sources of Western 'optimism' about Russia. At the World Economic Forum in the Swiss mountain resort of Davos – an annual gathering of the business and political élite of the world – Chubais provided a revealing insight into official attitudes to the war.

'It may surprise you to hear me say this, but the Chechnya affair is not just expense for Russia . . . but also a kind of revenue', he said. 'In 1994, Chechnya produced 2 million tons of oil.'

The suppression of Dudayev, whatever the cost in human misery, was in Russia's strategic interest, and therefore it was pursued. From mid-January onwards, the level of military competence increased as marines, paratroopers and special forces poured into Grozny from all over Russia and established a sort of control over the city, although there was still a lot of sniping at night. Much of the city was in ruins, but the oil refinery was easy to start up again.

The antics of Polevanov, by contrast, were not in Russia's strategic interest, and they stopped. He was dismissed from office on 24 January and little more was heard of him. It was simply far too early a stage in Russia's capitalist development for the country to allow itself the luxury of petulant xenophobia or renationalising assets which the state was not remotely capable of managing.

Just as the sums at stake in the Caspian oil bonanza ran into many billions of dollars, so did the foreign investment which Chubais hoped to draw into Russia's emerging equity market. The prospect of a sustained economic boom was real enough to concentrate minds very hard, both among the new class of Russian bankers, and the growing community of Western yuppies who sensed that Russia offered more opportunities for 'mastery of the universe' – the dream of the American bond trader in the 1980s – than any of the tired old nations of the West. A very powerful coalition of interests stood in the way of mavericks like Polevanov. Just as Stalin's regime had turned its fury on the foreign advisers and 'bourgeois specialists' who laid the foundations of the Soviet Union's industrial revolution, capitalist Russia might one day turn furiously on its benefactors. But it was much too early for that.

Prime Minister Chernomyrdin, ever the shrewd, stolid pragmatist, personified the mentality which accepted the expediency of waging the Chechen war but saw no reason, at this point, to alienate the West gratuitously. As a captain of energy, whose old company Gazprom controlled more than one-third of the world's known reserves of gas, he understood the logic of the conflict as well as anyone. On the other hand he also saw that enterprises like Gazprom could only take their place among the world's really powerful institutions if they accepted – on carefully calibrated terms – a dose of Western capital and expertise. The same applied to the Russian economy as a whole.

While never questioning the conflict itself, he made it known to the media that he had used his influence in the security council – a secretive policy-making body whose power had grown steadily over the last three years – to press for a relatively mild approach to the conduct of the war: negotiating local truces wherever possible and allowing the Chechens to surrender without too much dishonour.

Chernomyrdin was nowhere to be seen in the early days of the war, but he regained influence in January as an advocate of economic reason, and the man best placed to convince the world that a certain, qualified 'optimism' about Russia was still justified.

On 10 March, the Prime Minister had secured the promise of an enormous credit, worth $6.4 billion, from the International Monetary Fund. This was the second biggest loan in the IMF's history, and by far the biggest single injection of foreign capital which post-Soviet Russia had managed to obtain. In order to secure the loan, the Russian government promised to liberalise foreign trade, scrap tax privileges and cut inflation from a peak of 18 per cent in January to a monthly rate of 1 per cent by the end of the year. These were ambitious targets, and past practice suggested that they would probably not be met. Yet a growing proportion of the most influential people in Russia realised that it was in the country's interest to come as close to the goal as possible: not to satisfy the whims of foreigners, but to pursue Russia's own interests. Once the Holy Grail of economic stabilisation had been achieved, a period of surging economic growth was almost inevitable, as the rationalising power of a sophisticated capital market went to work on the country's underused resources. Prospects for this had never looked better.

Yeltsin emerged from a period of relative seclusion to meet a small group of journalists at the Kremlin on 16 March. He had lost none of his earthy charisma, nor his ability to command attention by alternating unpredictably from whimsical generosity and charm to furious anger. Two things made his face darken with rage: one was the mention of the Chechen leader Dudayev, and the other was the suggestion, widespread in the liberal press, that members of the presidential guard might be interfering with the economy or obstructing reform.

'All the important decisions are taken by the President', he declared, in a gravelly tone with a terrifying edge of anger that only softened gradually. 'The presidential guard protects the President from terrorism, and they don't poke their noses into the economy, because they understand nothing about it.'

On the procedures for taking economic decisions, Yeltsin had this to say: 'Every Tuesday, Chernomyrdin and I meet at my office and we decide the fundamental questions of reform. After that, nobody, neither the Prime Minister nor the deputy Prime Minister nor anybody in the presidential apparatus can change those decisions.' As for the nature of those decisions, there should be no doubt: 'I decided to pursue a stricter financial policy this year, and we will pursue it.'

Nevertheless the President's commitment to the sort of economic policy that Westerners approved did not imply any let-up in his campaign against Dudayev's forces.

> I have no intention of meeting Dudayev because he is a bandit who ought to be tried for having annihilated so many of his own people . . . He has assembled the criminal world around him and collected money all over the world so that he can organise a rebellion against Russia.

The other message was that he would take it very badly indeed if Clinton did not come to the Victory Day celebrations. 'Clinton is somewhat concerned by the planning of the event, he does not want there to be a military parade . . . I think that we will comply with those conditions.'

In the depths of mid-winter despair, when the war began, people had drawn the conclusion that one of two things would happen: either Yeltsin would be forced to change course in Chechnya, or he would face a plunge in his fortunes, both on the domestic and the international front. In fact, neither of these things happened. The President was pursuing the war, maintaining his international standing in the areas that mattered, and was under no particular threat domestically. He was no longer popular, but very few people were prepared to demonstrate against him. He was in control of an increasingly sophisticated propaganda machine, and the reporting of Russian television on the Chechen conflict had already become a great deal more 'loyal' to the regime.

The Chechen war seemed at first to have triggered a wave

of pacifist, anti-military sentiment. The nation was horrified by the reports of mothers who travelled thousands of miles to Chechnya to search for their missing conscript sons, and sometimes found that they were better treated by the Chechens as prisoners of war, than by their own commanders.

The longer-term effect, however, was the opposite: in the most unlikely quarters a new consensus emerged on the need for a stronger conventional army. It was very much a sign of the time when a prominent liberal journalist, Mikhail Leontiev – a warm, amusing bohemian who had written with brilliant wit on the vagaries of the Russian economy – underwent a dramatic conversion to the cause of military excellence, as a result of several visits to the Chechen war front. He became enraged by military incompetence, in the same way that economic incompetence had once infuriated him; and correspondingly he showed great respect for those commanders who had proved brave and effective on the battlefield. He published a long and sympathetic interview with General Vladislav Achalov, the paratroop commander who had played a prominent role on the losing, hardline side in the stand-offs of both August 1991 and October 1993.

General Grachev seemed quite untroubled by the protests of human rights campaigners like Sergei Kovalyov – whom he publicly described as a 'sleazebag' – over the humanitarian consequences of the war. On the other hand, he did feel pressure to reorganise and strengthen the armed forces, and this was soon reflected in the increased influence of the General Staff, the 'brains' of the Russian military whose job it was to co-ordinate the services and plans for war, whether domestic or international. The growing consensus on the need for a strong army was reflected in a remarkable decision by the Duma, at a closed-door meeting, to tighten the terms of conscription. There are not many parliaments in the world who would do that in a year when legislative elections are due.

Russia's Choice, the Gaidar party, found itself pushed to the side-lines of political life when it opposed the war. Andrei Kozyrev, the foreign minister who had a keen sense of how the political climate was moving, resigned from Gaidar's movement and became an unqualified apologist for the Chechen engagement. To bolster his case, he scoured American history to find instances – of which the Civil War was only the most obvious – when US Presidents had used force to defend their country's territorial integrity. Zhirinovsky's LDP did sterling service for General Grachev in blocking motions of censure and ensuring that nobody in the government was held to account by Parliament for the conduct of the Chechen war.

Perhaps the hardest blow for Russia's Choice was the withdrawal of support from its biggest financial backer, the thirty-year-old head of a $1.5 billion financial empire called Oleg Boyko. Boyko and a group of fellow members of the financial élite declared themselves to be unequivocal supporters of the President, and more ominously they said they were against the holding of early elections, on grounds that the ballot-box could only throw up a worse government than the existing one. Democracy had been all very well for the five years when it served to weed out the most scurrilous and incompetent members of the old communist élite. Now that the nation's destiny rested mainly in the hands of a new financial élite, bristling with talent and arrogance, there seemed less need to bother with the niceties of democratic procedure.

By mid-summer 1995, the prognosis for democracy was darkening, as the forecast for the economy improved. The Yeltsin entourage, backed by a formidable secret service which was rumoured to be dabbling in the occult as well as spying on one another furiously, seemed to be searching for a way round the challenge of the parliamentary elections due in December and the presidential elections in June 1996. One theory held that Yeltsin would use Zhirinovsky as a bogeyman: having created an artificial choice between 'me or the communists' in 1993, he would now engineer a situation where the choice lay between 'me or the ultra-rightists' – in other words, Yeltsin or Zhirinovsky.

In St Petersburg, which had relapsed into provincial obscurity while Moscow grew wealthier and more self-confident, Mayor Sobchak observed the prospect of increased influence for Zhirinovsky with the cultured disdain of that city's intelligentsia. 'If the country goes Zhirinovsky's way, I will do everything I can to declare my city independent', he stated. Some of the ideas born in Leningrad five years earlier had been transferred to the headier atmosphere of the Russian capital. The economic theories of Chubais were preparing the way for Russia's investment boom, while the works of Lev Gumilyov had won another sort of respectability. Mr Sergei Shakhrai – a young deputy Prime Minister whose legal expertise had helped to lay the foundations for the new Russian state – was sponsoring the publication of the nationalist historian's complete works: the theories of the super-ethnos had arrived in the corridors of the Kremlin.

As for Nevzorov, he used his seat in the Duma to denounce the 'treachery' of the early, hard-hitting television footage from Chechnya, and ensure that Russian broadcasters took a more patriotic line in their coverage of the conflict. In mid-1995, Gusinsky was allowed back to Russia – but not before his own television station had considerably moderated its criticism of the conduct of the Chechen war.

St Petersburg's Bishop Ioann continued, in his sermons, to warn against the temptation of liberal democracy and other pernicious Western influences, and so powerful was the public consensus in favour of a more authoritarian form of governance – the sort which could fight wars properly, for example – that the deeply conservative cleric found admirers in the most unlikely quarters. Prominent members of the city's Jewish community said they agreed heartily with Ioann's calls for a strong Russia, even if they could not quite concur with everything else he said.

In Moscow, work had started on a spectacular demonstration of Russia's renewed faith in herself: the rebuilding of the Cathedral of Christ the Saviour, which had been dynamited in 1933 – an act which Russian nationalists ascribed not to Stalin, who was in his own way one of them, but to his Jewish henchman Lazar Kaganovich.

If anyone had doubts about where the new Russian steamroller was leading, they were mostly repressed. Russian power had never been gentle before, and there was little enough reason to suppose it would be gentle now – to its own citizens, or anybody else. Nevertheless the process of economic, diplomatic and military reconstruction was so fascinating to behold that it somehow harnessed the talents of everyone who came anywhere near it, even those who sensed that they could be among its first victims.

Five years earlier, the main worry of intelligent Russians had been the fear – well expressed by Solzhenitsyn – of being 'buried under the rubble' of a collapsing Soviet state. Now the process of reconstruction had begun and the fall-out from that process might prove to be even more dangerous. It already appeared that the last vestiges of the democratic procedure could be one of the first things to go. This, however, was not a danger that many Russians cared to see.

Bibliography and Sources

There are a handful of essential books which become constant companions for any journalist writing about modern Russia. These include the authoritative works of Harvard University's Professor Richard Pipes, *The Russian Revolution* (Knopf, New York, 1991), and *Russia Under the Old Regime* (Scribner's, New York, 1974). Also two outstanding biographies of Stalin: *Stalin, A Political Biography* (Penguin, London, 1990) by Isaac Deutscher and *Stalin, Breaker of Nations* (Weidenfeld, London, 1993) by Robert Conquest. Geoffrey Hosking's *History of the Soviet Union* (Fontana, London, 1985) became another indispensable tool, and in a different way I was much helped by *Nicholas II: Emperor of All the Russias* (John Murray, London, 1993) by Dominic Lieven. *Soviet Disunion* by Nahaylo and Swoboda (Hamish Hamilton, London, 1990) is an encyclopaedia of policy towards the republics. Among books written by colleagues, I have been awe-struck and inspired by David Remnick's *Lenin's Tomb* (Random House, New York, 1993) and greatly helped by *The Second Russian Revolution* (BBC Books, London, 1991) by Angus Roxburgh, as well as *Melting Snow* (Appletree Press, Belfast, 1991) by Conor O'Clery.

The publications of the Radio Free Europe/Radio Liberty Research Institute have been of invaluable help with every part of this book, as have conversations with several of the staff there, such as Vera Tolz, Julia Wishnevsky and Victor Yasmann. Reporters and commentators for that radio station have at various times been extremely generous with their time and knowledge – among them Mark Deich, Dmitry Volchek, Mark Smirnov, Andrei Babitsky and Viktor Rizunkov. At the time of writing the staff of RFE/RL have just moved, in somewhat reduced numbers, from Munich to Prague and it can only be hoped that this remarkable repository of Sovietological and post-Sovietological expertise can be preserved.

Section by section, here is some information about my sources:

Chapters 1–2

I visited Leningrad in July 1990, and had the first of several long talks with the original and engaging Professor Gleb Lebedev. I went back in June 1991, when a referendum showed a small majority in favour of reverting to the historic name. For an insight into Leningrad's conservative camp, I spent a morning on the hustings with Yevgeny Krasnitsky, the communist dock-worker who was the chief opponent of the name change. I went back to the city – by that time St Petersburg – in November 1991 for the visit of Grand Duke Vladimir Kirillovich, and again in April 1992 for his funeral. In January 1994, I was privileged to have a long talk with Academician Dmitry Likhachov, during which he signed my copy of the English-language collection of his works – *Reflections on Russia* (Westview Press, Boulder, Colorado, 1991). Mayor Sobchak's book *Khozhdenie vo Vlast* (Novosti, Moscow, 1991) was an important source, as was Peter Duncan's chapter on Leningrad in *The Road to Post-Communism* (Pinter Publishers, London, 1992). Mayor Sobchak spells out his disillusionment with Yeltsin's policies in an interview with the daily *Komsomolskaya Pravda* published on 3 March 1992. A good starting point for understanding Lev Gumilyov's theories of Russian history is *Ot Rusi K Rossii* (Ekopros, Moscow, 1992). For the psycho-history of Nevzorov, I have drawn on the excellent account written by Andrew Meier in the June/July 1991 issue of *Moscow Magazine*.

Chapters 3–4

In the course of 1992, the foreign press corps in Moscow saw a good deal of Yegor Gaidar, and even more of his adviser Alexei Ulukayev. Jeffrey Sachs, the American guru of post-communist economics, was less frequent in his public appearances but equally provocative. Anders Aslund, a formidable Swedish analyst of the Russian economy, explains the failure of the late Soviet regime in *Gorbachev's Struggle for Economic Reform* (Pinter Publishers, London, 1989). He writes of the first glimmerings of success –

along with some distinguished co-authors – in *Economic Transformation in Russia* (Pinter Publishers, London, 1994). I met Vladimir Mau, another associate of Gaidar, in Vancouver in September 1994 and he guided me to the quarterly *Review of Russian Economy* which is prepared by the Institute of the Economy in Transition and published (in Russian) by the University of East Anglia. Professor Richard Layard of the London School of Economics, and the publications of his Centre for Economic Performance, are also indispensable sources for anyone who is dabbling in the Russian economy, especially a rank amateur. Gennady Burbulis laid out his theories about the world's debt to Russia at a lunch for foreign correspondents shortly after the August 1991 coup, organised by Jonathan Steele of the *Guardian*.

Chapters 5–6

I was a witness to the removal of the Dzerzhinsky statue on 22 August 1991. Yelena Bonner's views on the difficult prospects for a law-based state were published in *Izvestia* on 29 August 1991. During the months that followed, the KGB chairman Vadim Bakatin was unusually communicative to the (Russian) press for a holder of that office. Among the many press accounts of his attempts to reform the Lubyanka, *Trud* published an article headlined 'Farewell, KGB' on 25 October, 1991 and *Pravda* on the same day reported Bakatin's statements that 'Dissidents are no longer followed'. Bakatin gave a full account of his time in office in his book *Izbavlenie ot KGB*, or *Getting Rid of the KGB* (Progress, Moscow, 1992). In 1992, the security ministry continued to be talkative, though in a different spirit.

Along with many colleagues in the foreign press, I attended press conferences at the Lubyanka in July and August 1992, when senior officers made clear their fury over the leakage of documents about KGB co-operation with the Church, and stressed their agency's vital role in regulating exports. Interfax news agency reported on 14 July 1992 that the security ministry was referring to the prosecutor's office the case of Father Gleb Yakunin and Lev Ponomaryev, the two parliamentarians who leaked KGB documents. In March 1992, I had an hour-long interview with Leonid Shebarshin, the former intelligence chief, which to my embarrassment was held over by my employers, *The Times*, until the material had ceased – in newspaper terms – to be topical.

Tatyana Samolis, the spokeswoman of the foreign intelligence service, gave briefings on 9 September 1992 and 28 October 1992 on her agency's activities. During the first of these she was accompanied by Sergei Stephashin, then chairman of the parliamentary committee on security. The growing indifference of the Russian press to the rehabilitation of purge victims was highlighted in an interview with senior security officers in *Vechernaya Moskva* on 25 September 1992.

For an understanding of the political consequences of Eastern Orthodoxy, I have spoken to representatives of many tendencies within the Church, whose views differed so widely they would not all recognise one another as fellow members of the same Christian family. While still working for *The Times*, I covered the April 1992 conference of bishops which led to the 'defrocking' of Metropolitan Filaret. The research facilities of the Keston Institute in Oxford were invaluable, as was the advice of its director Canon Michael Bourdeaux. Among English converts to Orthodoxy, Bishop Kallistos Ware and the late Dr Philip Sherrard have influenced me profoundly, and not just in the areas treated in this book.

In January 1993, thanks to the help of some dear friends, I met Metropolitan Vitaly, the head of the Synod of the Russian Orthodox Church-in-Exile who explained to me the chasm which existed between his organisation and the Moscow Patriarchate. I have read trenchant critiques of the Patriarchate's record by Father Viktor Potapov of Washington, DC, and an articulate defence of that organisation by Professor Dmitry Popielowsky of the University of Western Ontario. In July 1993, I had a long talk with Father Gleb Yakunin, his friend and fellow dissident Mrs Zoya Krakhmalnikova, and his adversary Father Kirill Sakharov. Father Vsevolod Cheplin helped to explain the Patriarchate's point of view. It cannot be stressed too strongly that this is a book about politics, culture and political culture: not about theology, which is too profound a subject to be treated in a book of this kind.

Chapters 7–9

From the start of my stay in Russia, I had a fascination with the discourse, organisational problems and squabbles of tiny political parties, and spent more time on this subject than it objectively justified. For an understanding of the pro-Yeltsin coalition known as Democratic Russia, I am grateful to Arkady Murashov and his wife Olga; also Vladimir Boxer, Mikhail Sneyder, Ilya Zaslavsky and Mikhail Gokhman, all of whom I met while working for *The Times*. I attended the Democratic Russia conference in November 1991 when the movement split. I also attended the Congress of Patriotic Forces organised by Viktor Aksyuchits in February 1992, and the founding conference in October 1992 of the National Salvation Front. As a mine of information on Russia's embryonic political parties, I cannot recommend too strongly a makeshift data bank and information service called Panorama, which is located on the top floor of a tower block in southern Moscow; or its leading expert on parties of every hue, Vladimir Pribilovsky. His *Dictionary of Political Parties and Organisations in Russia* was republished by the Centre for Strategic and International Studies in Washington in 1992. *The Troubled Birth of Russian Democracy: Parties, Personalities and Programs* by Sergei Markov and Michael McFaul (Hoover Press, Stanford, 1993) is also extremely useful. For a better understanding of opposition politics, I interviewed Viktor Aksyuchits, Vladimir Isakov and Aleksandr Prokhanov in July 1993. For insights into the roots of modern nationalism and national-Bolshevism, Stephen Carter's *Russian Nationalism: Yesterday, Today, Tomorrow* is indispensable (Pinter Publishers, London, 1990). So, too is *Black Hundred: The Rise of the Extreme Right in Russia* (HarperCollins, New York, 1993) by Walter Laqueur. Valentin Rasputin's *Farewell to Matyora* was published in English in 1991 by Northwestern University Press by arrangement with Macmillan Inc.

On the ultra-right, Aleksandr Barkashov introduced himself to mainstream Russian newspaper readers, and explained his quarrel with Pamyat's Dmitry Vasilyev, in an interview in *Komsomolskaya Pravda* on 29 November 1991. The respectability of General Sterligov's Sobor – compared with the 'unwashed hair' of other ultranationalist groups – was noted with approval by Andrei Zhukov in *Rossiskaya Gazeta*, on 25 August 1993.

The quotations from the weekly newspaper *Dyen* come mostly from the first half of 1993. For Aleksandr Dugin and his interest in Alain de Benoist, see no. 19, page 4; for Anatoly Lukyanov's interest in Lev Gumilyov, see no. 8, page 5; for the revival of pro-Axis Russian *émigrés* of the pre-war period, see the extract from Anastas Vonsiatsky in no. 15, page 8. For the writings of Bishop Ioann, see no. 7, page 5; for the revival of geopolitics, see Anatoly Glivakovsky's article in no. 12, page 3; for praise of Stalin, see no.

25, page 2; for commentary on the Easter 1993 killings at the Optina monastery, see no. 16, page 1, and no. 22, page 5.

Chapters 10–12

I spent the first two weeks of April 1993 in Moscow, monitoring the political crisis and the campaign for the 25 April referendum. I followed Yeltsin on the campaign trail, and watched him 'work the crowds' after opening Moscow's new international telephone exchange. I spent an hour with Vice-President Rutskoy, acting as interpreter during an interview conducted by the German television station ARD. I also had a long conversation with Galina Starovoitova, Yeltsin's former adviser on ethnic affairs. My insights into the 'summer of scandals' which followed were enhanced by a meeting in March 1994 with Dmitry Yakubovsky, which turned into a stimulating sort of sparring match on subjects ranging from Russian attitudes to law to the record of Mikhail Gorbachev.

I should make it plain that I was not in Moscow myself during the battles of 3–4 October, although I had been staying there – and observing the growing tension in the city – during the previous week, at the home of my friend Rory Peck, who was killed at the Ostankino television station on 3 October. I have discussed the 3–4 October events in considerable detail with about twenty eyewitnesses and although many questions remain open, I find the 'conspiracy theory' advanced by *Moscow News* (no. 42, 15 October 1993) and by my colleague Jonathan Steele in the *Guardian* on 13 November 1993, stretches credulity much less than the authorities' version of events. The peculiar behaviour of the Ostankino management on the night of 3 October is well documented in the Russian press: see *Nezavisimaya Gazeta*, 9 October; *Literaturnaya Gazeta* no. 40; *Izvestia* 13 October, and *Kuranty*, 15 October.

The Economist editorial quoted in Chapter 10 was published on 13 March 1993.

Chapter 13

Working as a correspondent in Moscow between 1990 and 1992, I frequently had the opportunity to observe Zhirinovsky holding forth at street rallies, and appearing as a gate-crasher in the corridors of the Russian Parliament. I skimmed some of the lesser-known parts of the Russian press to assemble a picture of Zhirinovsky's arrival on the national scene in 1990–91. I discovered a plethora of interviews he had given to little-known publications: these ranged from his views on health care in *Meditsinskaya Gazeta*, 1 November 1991, to his self-description as an atheist in *Literaturnaya Rossiya*, 7 July 1991, and his hymn of praise to the state security services in *Sibirskaya Gazeta*, no. 21, 1991. Zhirinovsky's philosophy of national-socialism [*sic*] was elaborated on in considerable detail in *Izvestia* on 28 August 1993. The richest source of material on Zhirinovsky's doctrine and psychological quirks is his 140-page campaign autobiography *Posledni Brosok Na Iug* (*Last Leap to the South*) published in Moscow by his Liberal Democratic Party in 1993. The Moscow Jewish community's memories of Zhirinovsky were reported by Associated Press on 16 December 1993. Reports of massive electoral fraud in the December 1993 elections began to surface in the Russian press in April and May 1994. They were well summarised by my colleague Tony Barber in the *Independent*, 9 April 1994, and laid out in more detail by John Lloyd in the *Financial Times*, 6 May 1994.

AP reported from Kazakhstan on 4 April 1994 that Zhirinovsky's original name according to his birth certificate had been Edelstein: the same day it carried a strong denial of this assertion from his aides.

Chapters 14–15

For the final two chapters, which deal with the revival of Russian self-confidence on the international stage, I have drawn heavily and shamelessly on my experience of observing Russian foreign policy in action in my capacity, since April 1994, as a diplomatic reporter for the *Financial Times*. For better or worse, life has given me more opportunity to observe Russian policy at a somewhat rarefied level, and rather less chance to experience the travails of ordinary Muscovite life, than I enjoyed when the early part of the book was being researched.

As part of a team of *Financial Times* journalists, I helped to cover Boris Yeltsin's appearance at the Group of Seven summit in Naples in July 1994, and the appearance at Nato headquarters in Brussels of General Pavel Grachev on 24 May 1994. I also covered the Nato foreign ministers' meeting in Istanbul on 10 June 1994, where Russia's tough stand over the final communiqué was described as 'disgraceful' by senior Western diplomats – the very same diplomats who on 23 June 1994 warmly welcomed Andrei Kozyrev, the Russian foreign minister, to Brussels as a new member of Partnership for Peace, the military co-operation programme. The chapter's references to Estonia are coloured by a visit I paid to that republic in January 1994, during which I helped to interview President Lennart Meri – who memorably described the US-Russian summit then in progress as a 'masked ball' – and also the foreign minister, Juri Luik, who was the first person I recall mentioning the truism that Russia 'is always stronger and weaker than it looks'.

Vladimir Lukin, the chairman of the foreign affairs committee of the Duma, gave me some valuable insights into the mood and substance of Russia's external policy during a long conversation in March 1994. His sons, Aleksandr and Pavel, are scholars and sparring partners whose company and hospitality I have greatly enjoyed.

The VE-Day celebrations in Moscow on 9 May 1995 had the feel of a giant landmark in Russia's revival, and in the nation's rediscovery of pride in Soviet traditions. At the beginning of the book, I referred to public events in Mayor Sobchak's Leningrad which fed the illusion that the Soviet era had hardly happened at all: it had simply been a brief, irrelevant interlude in the pageant of Russian history. Now, in 1995, a new illusion was in the making – the idea that the Soviet period had never ended, and the first grinding years of capitalism had simply been a bad dream. Two months before attending the festivities, I had been a member of a small group of journalists – one from each of seven countries – who were invited to Moscow and allowed, on 16 March, to put questions to President Yeltsin. He made plain at that time the vast importance he attached to the Victory Day celebrations, and how personally he would take it if President Clinton stayed away.

I have not visited the Chechen conflict zone, and I stand in humble, admiring awe of those colleagues and friends who did so during the first ghastly weeks of the war, including Anatol Lieven, John Lloyd, Steve Levine, Andrew Higgins and David Hearst. It would have been absurd for me to comment in much detail on the course of the war; and only time will tell whether speculation about its main cause – the need to secure pipeline routes – is asking the right question.

INDEX